The WI Diamond Jubilee

Bee Nilson, a graduate in Home Science at Otago University, New Zealand, has worked in England for the last forty years. During the war she was responsible for the cookery material used in government publicity and advertising, serving as head of the experimental kitchens at the Ministry of Food.

Her first major cookery book was published in 1952 and since then she has written fifteen other books on cookery, nutrition and dietetics. Her interest in modern aspects of cooking is reflected in her books on deep freezing, herb cookery, blender cooking, cooking with yogurt, and fondue and flambé cookery. She tests all the recipes included in her books in the kitchen of her North London home. Bee Nilson is also a keen amateur gardener.

The WI Diamond Jubilee Cookbook

edited by Bee Nilson
illustrated by Delia Delderfield

Pan Books
in association with William Heinemann

First published 1975 by William Heinemann Ltd
This edition published 1977 by Pan Books Ltd,
Cavaye Place, London SW10 9PG,
in association with William Heinemann Ltd
© A. R. Nilson and National Federation of
Women's Institutes 1975
ISBN 0 330 25201 1
Printed and bound in Great Britain by
Cox & Wyman Ltd, London, Reading and Fakenham

Contents

Introduction

The recipes in this book have been chosen from thirty-five cookery books compiled by members of the National Federation of Women's Institutes.

In making the choice I was not looking for the 'best' recipes – a subjective and impertinent exercise anyway. Rather I wanted a selection which reflected the great variety of tastes, both traditional and modern, among members of the Women's Institutes.

Everyone knows that country women are good cooks but not everyone knows that through these books Women's Institute members have been preserving traditional recipes, not as museum pieces but as practical recipes for modern cooks. Naturally I have included many of these.

For the rest of the book I have chosen recipes for a variety of reasons. Many have been used for their clear instructions with quantities carefully prescribed when this is important, so that the user will have a reasonable chance of success. Some very interesting recipes were obviously written for experienced cooks and with these I have taken the liberty of adding a 'Note for beginners'. In some others I have inserted information on temperatures and cooking times I used when testing them. I hope the owners of the recipes will not mind.

Some recipes I tried because the names intrigued me – Sly Cakes, King George First's Christmas Pudding, Buttery Dick, Guernsey Bean Jar, Oozie-woozie Tart, Australian Jack, Stone Cream, Cawl Mamgu, Fat Rascals, Lord Welby's Sauce, to mention but a few.

I was also guided by the preference for certain types of foods as shown by the large number of similar recipes. For example, the undoubted preference for soup as a first course; the importance of pork and bacon recipes and the interesting recipes for using cheaper cuts of other meats; the importance of yeast cookery; the delicious home-made biscuits and cookies; and in the cake section the preference for fruit cakes, gingerbreads and cakes using pastry.

I found some interesting regional differences of opinion on the best way of cooking certain foods and have included a number of these, for example, on how to cook salmon; on cooking vegetables; on stewing rhubarb; and on making a fruit salad.

To help the reader identify the origin of each recipe they are all labelled with the name of the county from whose book I took the recipe. They are the old county names because the books were published before the formation of new boundaries.

The whole collection is unique among cookery books and brings to a wider public the good cooking of the country women of England, Wales and the Island of Guernsey. I am honoured and privileged to have been asked to make this selection.

Bee Nilson, London 1975

1 Weights, measures & temperatures

Quantities in the recipes are in both ounces, pounds or pints and the metric grammes, kilogrammes or litres.

16 ounces (oz) = 1 pound (lb)
20 fluid ounces (fl oz) = 1 pint
1,000 grammes (g) = 1 kilogramme (kg) = approximately 2 lb 3 oz
1,000 millilitres (ml) = 1 litre (l) = approximately 1¾ pints

Cake tin sizes are given in both inches and the metric centimetres or millimetres.
250 millimetres (mm) = 2.5 centimetres (cm) = approximately 1 inch

When a definite size of mould or pie-dish is recommended in a recipe, this is given in volume measures of pints with the metric equivalent in millilitres or litres.

Temperatures are in both Centigrade (°C) and Fahrenheit (°F) followed by the equivalent number on a gas cooker.

When translating ounces, pounds and pints into their metric equivalents certain compromises have to be made in order to produce quantities which can be weighed on domestic scales or measured with spoons and jugs. To take one example: an ounce equals 28.35 grammes but this is an impossible quantity to weigh on domestic scales. These usually do not weigh less than 5 grammes; so we have the choice of counting an ounce as either 25 grammes or 30 grammes. In most of these recipes an ounce has been taken as 25 grammes.

In the same way larger quantities have to be adjusted to give metric quantities which are multiples of 5 grammes. In doing this it is important to keep the same balance of ingredients as in the original recipe which is why sometimes you may, for example, find 4 ounces translated as 100 grammes and sometimes as 125 grammes; or 8 ounces as 200 grammes or 225 grammes. Which of the two alternatives is the better choice depends on the quantities of other ingredients in the recipe.

To complete the metric conversion, spoon measures have been given as millilitres. The British Standards Institution's recommended spoon measures include 20, 15, 10, 5 and $2\frac{1}{2}$ millilitres; but are not given specific names. In translating these recipes a level tablespoon has been taken as 15 millilitres (the same as a medicinal tablespoon or an average table tablespoon). A level dessertspoon has been taken as 10 millilitres and a level teaspoon as 5 millilitres.

In the original recipes spoon measures may be level, rounded or heaped and this has been taken into account in giving the millilitre equivalents.

In general the metric version is a trifle smaller than the original recipe but this is not usually enough to significantly alter sizes of tins required or recommended cooking times.

The original recipes from which this book has been compiled were tested by members of the Women's Institutes; with the exception of the preserve recipes, they have all been tested again using the metric quantities.

2 First courses

Soups

Garnishes and accompaniments for soups

This list has been compiled from information in books from
Cumberland, Durham and Yorkshire.

Almonds shredded, roast.
Apple diced raw.
Bacon chopped, grilled or fried.
Butter balls to thicken and add richness to purées. They are made
from equal quantities of flour and butter blended together and
made into small balls about the size of a marble, dropped into the
boiling soup one at a time, before serving.
Cheese grated. Use dry cheese and grate it finely. Serve it separately
or sprinkle on the soup before serving. As an alternative garnish,
mix it with chopped parsley or watercress.
Cheese straws.
Chives chopped.
Cornflakes crushed.

Cream seasoned, whipped.

Croûtons. Toasted bread cut into small dice; or cut small dice and either bake until crisp and brown or fry them.

Cucumber sliced.

Dumplings small ones, plain or with herbs, in broth.

Egg chopped hardboiled.

Frankfurter sausages sliced.

Herbs chopped green – added at last minute.

Leeks chopped, fried.

Lemon sliced.

Mushroom shreds. This garnish is suitable for thick soups. Cut mushrooms and stalks across into shreds and fry lightly.

Olives chopped.

Onion raw grated.

Onion rings. Cut an onion into thin rings, soak in milk and fry in a little fat until brown and crisp. Add to soup just before serving.

Orange grated rind or slivers of rind.

Pasta. Specially suitable for minestrone or any thin clear soup. Break in small lengths and add to the soup, allowing 20–30 minutes for macaroni to cook, less time for small shapes.

Potato crisps crushed.

Potato rings. Cream 500 g mashed potatoes (1 lb), with 25 g margarine (1 oz), 15 ml (1 tablespoon) milk and 1 egg. Pipe on to a greased tin and cook for 5–10 minutes in a hot oven, or until crisp.

Radishes sliced.

Artichoke soup

Put the artichokes, celery, potato and ham into an enamel, aluminium, or stainless steel saucepan. Cover with the water and boil until cooked. Put all through a hair or nylon sieve, add the milk and butter, thicken with flour, bring to boiling point and add seasoning – serve. Serves 4–5.

Somerset

500 g (1 lb) Jerusalem artichokes
1 stick celery
1 potato
25 g (1 oz) lean ham or rinds of
   bacon

800 ml (1½ pints) of water
300 ml (½ pint) milk
25 g (1 oz) butter
20 ml (1 dessertspoon) flour
salt, pepper and nutmeg to taste

Wash and peel the artichokes and cut them up before cooking.
Slice the celery. If the artichokes are prepared some time before
cooking, cover them with cold water to which a tablespoon of vinegar
has been added – this keeps them white. Allow about $\frac{1}{2}$ hour for
cooking the vegetables. This may be done in advance and the soup
completed just before serving.

Cawl mamgu
Granny's broth

Cover meat with cold water in pan. Add salt and pepper. Bring to
boil, skim. Add swede, carrots, white of leeks. Simmer 2–2$\frac{1}{2}$ hours.
   Add potatoes, simmer another 30 minutes. When potatoes almost
cooked, thicken with flour and a little water. Lastly add green of
leeks and parsley (chopped) and simmer further 10 minutes. Serve
in basins while hot. Serves 8.
Pembrokeshire

1 kg (2 lb) best end of neck (Welsh
   lamb)
salt and pepper
1 small swede, sliced
250 g (8 oz) carrots, cut in half

2 large leeks
500 g (1 lb) potatoes, cut in
   quarters
15 g ($\frac{1}{2}$ oz) flour
25 g (1 oz) parsley

Celery cream purée

Wash celery and cut into 5-cm (2-inch) pieces. Prepare onion and
chop. Place vegetables in pan with stock, bouquet garni and
seasoning. Simmer gently after bringing to boiling point. Pass
through a sieve.
   Melt the butter in the stewpan, add flour and cook together. Add
the milk gradually and the purée and stir until boiling. Boil for 5
minutes, cool slightly, add cream and serve. Serves 6.
Cumberland

about 500 g, 1 or 2 heads of celery
   according to size
1 small onion
600 ml (1 pint) white stock
bouquet garni

seasoning
40 g (1$\frac{1}{2}$ oz) butter
40 g (1$\frac{1}{2}$ oz) flour
600 ml (1 pint) milk
150 ml ($\frac{1}{4}$ pint) cream

Note for beginners

Start making the soup at least 1 hour before serving time. The celery will take about 45 minutes to soften sufficiently for sieving.

Cheese soup

Gently fry onion in butter until tender but not brown. Stir in milk and water. When nearly boiling stir in eggs, cheese and seasoning. Heat gently but do not boil.

Garnish
Cut small rings or crescents from bread and fry in hot butter until golden brown, drain.
   Ladle soup into bowls, add 3–4 rings of bread and serve at once.
Serves 6.
Cumberland

1 medium onion (finely chopped)	salt and pepper
25 g (1 oz) butter	
600 ml (1 pint) water	*Garnish*
600 ml (1 pint) milk	4 slices thin white bread
2 eggs (lightly beaten)	50 g (2 oz) butter
200 g (8 oz) grated Cheddar cheese	

Cock-a-leekie soup

Stone prunes, remove the green from the leeks, wash the white stems and shred. Put prunes and shredded leeks into the chicken stock, add salt and pepper to taste. Bring to the boil and simmer for ¾ hour.
Serves 6.
Surrey

12 prunes steeped overnight in warm water	2¼ l (4 pints) chicken stock
8 or 10 leeks	salt and pepper

Conger soup

Clean and wash fish, cover with cold water, add seasoning, thyme, parsley, bay leaf, chopped onion. Simmer 2 hours. Strain.
   To fish stock add the peas, carrot, dough balls and boil 30 minutes.

Then, about 15 minutes before serving, add milk and marigold petals. Taste for seasoning. Serves 8–10.

Guernsey

1 conger head and good tail piece or a piece of conger
1 sprig thyme
parsley
bay leaf
chopped onion
300 ml shelled (1 lb shelled) green peas

1 finely diced carrot
marble-sized dough balls (2 per person), small dumplings
600 ml (1 pint) milk
2 flower heads of soucis (marigold petals)
seasoning

Curried apple soup
Cold

Sizzle the chopped shallots in the butter until transparent. Add the curry powder and stock. Stir well and bring to the boil. Make the arrowroot into a smooth cream with water and stir into the soup. Simmer for 5 minutes. Take off the heat, cool for a few minutes and then put it in the liquidizer with one apple peeled, cored and diced, the egg yolks and the cream. Put to cool.

Peel and core the second apple, dice it, and cover with lemon juice to stop it going brown. Stir into the soup just before you serve it. Check for seasoning. Serves 4 (at a pinch).

Hampshire

2 shallots, chopped
25 g (2 tablespoons) butter
600 ml (1 pint) stock
15 ml (1 level tablespoon) curry powder
30 ml (1 tablespoon) arrowroot

2 apples, pippins are best
2 egg yolks
150 ml ($\frac{1}{4}$ pint) single cream
15 ml (1 tablespoon) lemon juice
salt and pepper

Iced cucumber soup

Cut the cucumber into small cubes. Keep an inch or two back. Chop up the onion and simmer it in the stock. Add the cucumber and about 10 mint leaves, simmer again until the cucumber is soft.

Purée this in the blender, or use a small mouli-legume, and return to the saucepan. Mix the cornflour to a smooth paste with the cream and a tablespoon of the soup. Stir it into the soup and bring to the boil while stirring. Taste it and season with salt. Take it off the heat and when cold put it in a basin or jug in the refrigerator. It will take several hours to chill completely unless you turn your refrigerator to the coldest position. Garnish it with very small sticks of cucumber.

Lettuce soup can be made in the same way, and this is a good use of a glut lettuce. Garnish with a little pinch of finely chiffoned lettuce leaf. Serves 4–6.

Hampshire

500 g (2) washed but unpeeled cucumbers
1 small onion
900 ml (1½ pints) stock (a white Oxo cube or two serves the purpose well)

10 mint leaves
20 ml (1 dessertspoon) cornflour
75 ml (½ gill) single cream
salt

Mushroom soup
Cold

Melt butter, add flour, cook without colouring, add stock gradually and boil. Wash mushrooms and press through a fine wire sieve. Add to soup along with cream, milk and seasoning. Simmer 3 minutes, pour into bowl, whisking frequently until quite cold. Serves 6.

Westmorland

30 g (1 oz) butter, good weight
30 g (1 oz) flour, good weight
900 ml (1½ pints) chicken stock, bouillon cubes are good
175 g (6 oz) light-coloured mushrooms

150 ml (¼ pint) milk
150 ml (¼ pint) cream or 300 ml (½ pint) single cream
salt and pepper

Note for beginners

The mushrooms can be processed in the electric blender, with the milk.

Mushroom soup
Hot

Wash and peel mushrooms, including stalks, chop mushrooms and onion and cook gently in the butter for 10 minutes.

Stir in flour and mix well, add stock and bay leaf. Stir until boiling. Add milk, simmer 15 minutes.

Rub through a sieve, re-heat and season to taste. Serve very hot.
Especially good if 2 or 3 tablespoons cream added after removed from heat. Serves 4–6.

Westmorland

200 g (8 oz) mushrooms
1 onion
50 g (2 oz) butter
40 g (1½ oz) flour
600 ml (1 pint) stock

1 bay leaf
600 ml (1 pint) milk
30–45 ml (2 or 3 tablespoons)
  cream (optional)
salt and pepper

Onion soup

Melt butter in pan. Add sliced onion and cook gently for 15 minutes without burning.

Remove crusts from bread and add bread, milk and water to pan. Add the bouquet garni and seasoning. Boil for 5 minutes, then simmer for approximately 40 minutes. Sieve, return to rinsed pan and re-heat.

Serve sprinkled with grated cheese and a little parsley. Serves 4.

Cumberland

25 g (1 oz) butter
500 g (1 lb) onions
2 slices stale bread
600 ml (1 pint) milk
300 ml (½ pint) water

seasoning
bouquet garni
grated cheese
chopped parsley

Parsnip soup

Clean and slice vegetables, fry in butter or dripping for 5–10 minutes, then add stock. Simmer until vegetables are tender, about 30 minutes. Rub through a sieve and return purée to pan. Add milk and seasoning to taste. Re-heat to just under boiling point.

If wished, juice of 1 small lemon can be added to lessen sweetness. Serves 6.

Westmorland

4 parsnips
1 onion
2 sticks celery
butter or dripping

1¼ l (2 pints) stock
600 ml (1 pint) milk
salt and pepper
juice of 1 small lemon, optional

Pea soup

Soak peas overnight. Rinse and strain. Cut onion up roughly. Put peas into saucepan. Add ham bone and onion and water. Simmer gently until peas are soft. Remove the bone. Sieve if necessary. Stir in a nut of butter and season to taste. Serves 4–6.
Hampshire

Variation
Herbs may be added if liked. Mint, fresh or dried, may be sprinkled over before serving. Lentils may be used in place of dried peas (no need to soak). Split peas may be used.

300 ml (½ pint) dried peas
1 onion
1 ham bone or hock end with
  more bone than meat

1½ l (2½ pints) water
nut of butter
seasoning

Note for beginners

The cooking time for dried peas averages about 2 hours, lentils and split peas about 1 hour. Do not skimp the cooking time as the ham bone needs time to flavour the soup. Bits of meat left on the bone can be diced and added to the soup.

Purée of Brussels sprouts

Boil sprouts till tender, keep them very green, pass through hair sieve. Then put into a saucepan with the boiling stock and cream. Season with pepper and salt. Get it quite hot but do not allow it to boil or the colour will be spoilt. Serve with snippets of toast. Serves 8.
Northamptonshire and Soke of Peterborough

500 g (1 lb) sprouts
1¾ l (3 pints) boiling white stock
150 ml (1 gill) thick cream

pepper and salt
snippets of toast

Note for beginners

Instead of passing the cooked sprouts through a hair sieve they may be processed in the electric blender with a little of the stock.

Sorrel soup

Melt butter and add finely chopped onion. Cook over low heat for a few minutes. Add washed and chopped sorrel leaves and thinly cut potatoes. Cook all together in the butter for 5 minutes, stirring all the time. Cover with water or stock, add seasoning and simmer until tender. Sieve if preferred, and if too thick add more stock, or if water has been used, a little milk. Serve with chopped watercress. Serves 4.
Yorkshire

25 g (1 oz) butter
1 large onion
1 good handful of sorrel leaves
  (to be found in the fields in late
  spring or early summer)

3 large potatoes
water or stock
seasoning
watercress

Note for beginners

It is advisable to strip the leafy part of the sorrel from the stalks and centre ribs and discard these.

Tomato and carrot soup

Cut up vegetables and brown lightly in butter or margarine, add stock, and cook until vegetables are tender, approximately ½ hour. Sieve or put through a blender. Then thicken with the flour mixed with milk and boil for 3 or 4 minutes. Season to taste. Very delicious. Serves 4.
Shropshire

4 large tomatoes
1 large carrot
1 onion
25 g (1 oz) butter or margarine

600 ml (1 pint) stock or water
300 ml (½ pint) milk
25 g (1 oz) flour
salt and pepper

Tripe soup

Cut tripe into small pieces and put it into stock; add onions and potatoes, cook slowly together for about 1 hour, then thicken with the butter well rubbed into the flour. Add the milk, some chopped parsley and pepper and salt to taste just before serving. Serves 8.
Northumberland

1 kg (2 lb) fresh tripe
2¼ l (2 quarts) white stock
2 onions, minced
2 potatoes, sliced
25 g (1 oz) butter

25 g (1 oz) flour
100 ml (small teacup) milk
salt and pepper
chopped parsley

Turkey corn soup

Place sweet corn, finely chopped onion, sliced red pepper, bay leaf
and stock into pan with seasoning. Bring to the boil and simmer
gently 15–20 minutes, then sieve. Return to pan and add the cornflour
blended with a little of the milk. Add remaining milk. Boil 3 or 4
minutes. Adjust seasoning. Garnish and serve. Serves 3–4.
Surrey

1 tin creamed sweet corn (283 g)
1 onion
½ red pepper
1 bay leaf
600 ml (1 pint) turkey stock
salt and pepper
20 ml (2 tablespoons) cornflour

150 ml (¼ pint) milk

Garnish
chopped chives, parsley and rings
  of red pepper. Sprinkle with
  paprika.

Starters

Cucumber cocktail

Mix all ingredients together, except fruit and vegetables, to make a dressing. Marinade the melon, cucumber and pears in the dressing for at least ½ hour.

Remove and drain, place in individual dishes. Serve chilled, topped with watercress clusters.

This looks marvellous in tall-stemmed hock glasses. Serves 8.
Cumberland

1 clove garlic, finely chopped	black pepper
juice of 1 lemon	brown sugar
75 ml (5 tablespoons) salad oil	½ honeydew melon, diced
5 ml (1 teaspoon) salt	½ cucumber, diced
10 ml (1 dessertspoon) made	2 pears, diced
mustard	½ bunch watercress

Devon trout and mushroom pâté

Clean the trout but do not remove the heads.

Put a knob of butter into the slit stomachs, wrap in greaseproof paper and steam for ½ hour.

While the fish is cooking, chop the mushrooms (including stalks) very small and fry in butter.

When fish is ready, carefully remove all bones, skin and heads, but retain any liquid, melted butter, etc, from the paper.

Mash the meat with a fork, add the liquid and the fried mushrooms together with any butter left in the pan, add a dash of anchovy sauce and pepper and salt.

Melt remaining butter and mix.

Beat the mixture with a fork until smooth and creamy, then place in pots (empty meat paste pots are ideal), packing the pâté down well. Fill nearly to the top, then seal with a small amount of melted butter.

Put in a cool place, preferably a fridge, to set.

When cold cover as jam. (Makes about 400 g or 12 oz.)
Devon

This pâté can also be made with salmon or peal (sea trout). It is delicious eaten on hot toast, or in sandwiches, or makes an unusual hors d'oeuvre.

700 g (1½ lb) fresh-caught trout
   (either one large fish or several
   small)
100 g (4 oz) farm butter

50 g (2 oz) field mushrooms
salt and pepper
dash of anchovy sauce

Fish cocktails

Shake well and serve over any cooked flaked fish or shellfish.
Cheshire

100 ml (6 tablespoons) tomato
   ketchup
40 ml (1½ tablespoons) wine
   vinegar
2½ ml (½ teaspoon) Worcestershire
   sauce

30 ml (2 tablespoons) wine
juice of half lemon
cayenne and salt to taste

Fruit cocktails

Serve the fruit cocktails in glasses using:

1 Cubed apples, pears and peaches garnished with cherries.
2 Grapefruit sections or halved grapefruit garnished with a cherry.
3 Avocado pear and pineapple.
4 Fresh strawberries, grapes and orange slices.
5 Watermelon cut into balls.

Dress with either of the following dressings:

(a) 100 g (4 oz) sugar, 75 ml (⅛ pint) sherry, 30 ml (2 tablespoons)
lemon juice.
(b) Mix together lemon and orange juice and sweeten with sugar.

Chill and serve over fruit and sprinkle with chopped nuts.
Cheshire

Grapefruit cocktail

Squeeze the grapefruit – add the syrup. Add orange and lemon juice.
Cover and chill well.
   Strain and add sherry just before serving. Serve in small glasses
(never overfill). Serves 4–6.
Cumberland

1 grapefruit
15 ml (1 tablespoon) stock syrup
½ orange

1 lemon
15 ml (1 tablespoon) sherry

Stock Syrup
100 g (4 oz) sugar
150 ml (¼ pint) water
Boil 3 minutes. Use as required.

Ham and pineapple cocktail

Cut the ham and pineapple in fine shreds. Mix together the cream, ketchup and lemon juice. Mix together the ham, pineapple and dressing.

Arrange a little shredded lettuce in the base of individual glasses. Spoon mixture on top. Garnish with paprika. Serves 4.

Cumberland

150 g (6 oz) cooked ham (lean)
1 slice pineapple
30 ml (2 tablespoons) cream,
  whipped
10 ml (1 dessertspoon) tomato
  ketchup

juice of ½ lemon
shredded lettuce
paprika to garnish

Note: Prawns may be used instead of ham.

Liver pâté

Chop the liver, onion and garlic. Melt the butter in a pan. Add the onion, garlic, liver and tomato purée. Cook gently, stirring often, until tender. Season. When cool, put all through a sieve or the fine plate of a mincer twice. Put into small pots and cover with melted butter. Serves 4.

Hampshire

250 g (8 oz) pig's liver
1 small onion
sliver of garlic, if liked
75 g (3 oz) butter

10 ml (1 dessertspoon) tomato
  purée
seasoning

Variations

Herbs to taste may be added or a little red wine used to assist in cooking.

Note for beginners

The mixture is suitable for pulping in an electric blender. Do this while the mixture is still warm.

Prawn cocktail

Shell the prawns. Mix all ingredients together, chill and serve on a lettuce leaf with chopped lettuce for decoration. Serves 4.

Northumberland

500–600 ml (1 pint) shrimps or prawns
30 ml (2 tablespoons) thick mayonnaise
45 ml (3 tablespoons) double cream, whipped
15 ml (1 tablespoon) tomato ketchup or purée
15 ml (1 tablespoon) Worcestershire sauce
15 ml (1 tablespoon) lemon juice
5 ml (1 teaspoon) finely chopped onion
5 ml (1 teaspoon) finely chopped celery or 2½ ml (½ teaspoon) celery salt
salt to taste
lettuce

Shropshire pâté

Put all ingredients in pan (except spices and sherry or brandy). With enough water to cover, simmer for 35–40 minutes, allow to cool in juices, remove herbs, then put all in a liquidizer with a little of the stock. Blend finely, add nutmeg, mace, pepper, salt and sherry or brandy to taste. Put in a crock and seal with melted butter. This freezes very well. Serves 8.

Shropshire

250 g (8 oz) chicken livers
onion or shallot
250 g (8 oz) streaky bacon
bouquet garni
spices, (nutmeg, mace)
pepper
sherry or brandy (optional)

Skipper pâté

Mash skippers with juices from can until fairly smooth.

Blend in remaining ingredients, mix well.

Turn into small serving dish, cover with foil lid, chill in refrigerator until required.

Serve with warm toast and unsalted butter as a starter or snack. Srves 4.

Deerbyshire

106 g (3¾ oz) John West Skippers in oil
85 g (3 oz) packet Philadelphia cream cheese spread

juice of ½ lemon
few drops tabasco
freshly ground black pepper

Note for beginners

This recipe can be made with any full-fat soft cheese.

Taramasalata

This is a smoked cod's roe pâté. Serve in little pots. Individual porcelain soufflé cases are a very useful buy.

Skin the cod's roe and mash it and all the other ingredients with a fork. Pile it casually but tidily into the little dishes and garnish with a small sprig of watercress and a twist of lemon. Serve with dry toast. About 2 tablespoonsful each will be enough. Serves 6.

Hampshire

175 g (8 oz) smoked cod's roe (can be bought at most big fish shops)
125 g (4 oz) cream cheese
30 ml (1 tablespoon) chopped chives

15 ml (1 tablespoon) lemon juice
sprigs of watercress
twists of lemon
dry toast

3 Fish

Baked fish

Wash and drain the fish but do not dry it.

Melt sufficient fat in a pie-dish to well cover the bottom. When hot dip the fish into the hot fat so that each piece is coated on both sides. Lay the fish back in the dish with the halved tomatoes at the sides, add pepper and salt and a little sugar on the tomatoes.

Place the bacon rashers on the top and bake in a moderate oven, 190°C (375°F), Gas 5, for about 20–30 minutes or until the fish is cooked through and the bacon crisp.

This is very good served with Chinese Sweet-sour sauce. Serves 4.
Devon

as many fillets as required
a little fat or dripping
3 or 4 rashers of streaky bacon

2 or 3 tomatoes
pepper and salt and a little sugar

Baked fish with mushrooms and bacon

If the fish is cooked whole, clean well and stuff with mushrooms sprinkled with lemon juice.

If fillets are used place mushrooms round them. In either case place the fish and mushrooms in a greased baking dish, season well and cover with strips of streaky bacon.

Bake without a lid in a moderate oven, 180°C (350°F), Gas 4, for 20–30 minutes, according to the size of the fish.

Oxfordshire

whole bream, hake or fresh haddock or use fillets	lemon juice
	salt and pepper
mushrooms	streaky bacon

Barbecue fish steaks

Heat the oil or margarine in a heavy frying pan. Brown fish quickly on both sides – lower heat. Remove the fish from pan and place on a fireproof serving dish. Chop onion. De-seed pepper and chop finely with parsley and mushrooms. Fry gently until soft. Add tomatoes, tomato ketchup and mustard. Season well and pour over the fish. Bake in a moderate oven 20–30 minutes at 190°C (375°F), Gas 5.

If fresh tomatoes are used add 10 ml (2 teaspoons) water.

Cumberland

45 ml (3 tablespoons) oil or margarine	2–3 mushrooms
	1 small tin or 225 g ($\frac{1}{2}$ lb) tomatoes
4 steaks of cod, haddock or any firm white fish	30 ml (2 tablespoons) tomato ketchup
1 small onion	5 ml ($\frac{1}{2}$ teaspoon) dry mustard
1 small green papper	salt and pepper
parsley	

Fish and egg mornay

Put the fish and halved eggs in a fireproof dish. Mix chopped parsley with cheese sauce, and pour over eggs and fish. Sprinkle grated cheese over the top, and put into the oven to heat thoroughly until it is crispy brown on top, 200°C (400°F), Gas 6, for about 20 minutes. Serves 4.

Gloucestershire

225 g (8 oz) cold cooked white fish	300 ml ($\frac{1}{2}$ pint) thick cheese sauce
2 hardboiled eggs	grated cheese
chopped parsley	

Fish dish

Place fillets in greased fireproof dish. Mix sauce ingredients smoothly. Spread sauce over fish. Slice onion thinly and lay on top. Add halved tomatoes. Cover with greased paper, bake ½ hour or less, according to thickness of fish, in moderate oven, 190°C (375°F), Gas 5. Serves 4.

Cambridgeshire

500 g (1 lb) fillet of cod or other white fish
1 onion
a few small tomatoes

Sauce
10 ml (1 teaspoon) curry powder
2½ ml (¼ teaspoon) dry mustard

10 ml (2 teaspoons) salad oil or dripping
10 ml (2 teaspoons) vinegar
10 ml (2 teaspoons) tomato sauce
5 ml (1 teaspoon) mushroom ketchup
salt

Fish envelope

Roll pastry into a 20-cm (8-inch) square. Trim edges if necessary. Flake fish, mix with sauce, egg, parsley and seasonings and place on centre of pastry. Moisten edges of pastry and fold into an envelope shape. Seal edges well and flute. Brush with milk. Decorate with leaves from pastry trimmings. Bake in a hot oven, 220°C (425°F), Gas 7, for ¾ hour reducing heat after first 10 minutes to 180°C (350°F), Gas 4. Serves 4.

Durham

250 g (8 oz) flaky pastry
250 g (8 oz) cooked white fish
30 ml (2 tablespoons) thick white sauce or top of bottle of milk
1 hardboiled egg

10 ml (1 teaspoon) chopped parsley
10 ml (1 teaspoon) chopped gherkins or capers
salt and pepper

Fish pie

Wash fish and put in greased dish, pour over 150 ml (¼ pint) milk and cook in moderate oven, 180°C (350°F), Gas 4, for 20 minutes. Strain off liquid and make up to 300 ml (½ pint) with rest of milk.

Melt margarine in pan, blend in flour, add milk gradually and cook until sauce is smooth. Stir in cheese, chutney and sultanas, and season to taste.

Flake fish in dish, pour over sauce mixture, sprinkle top with breadcrumbs and return to oven to cook for 10 minutes. Serves 4.
Northumberland

500 g (1 lb) cod fillet	30 ml (1 tablespoon) chutney
300 ml (½ pint) milk	50 g (2 oz) sultanas
15 g (½ oz) margarine	salt and pepper
15 g (½ oz) flour	30 ml (1 tablespoon) breadcrumbs
75 g (3 oz) grated cheese	

Fish soufflé
Steamed or baked

Melt butter in pan, add flour, cook for a minute or two, stirring; draw aside and add milk, stir till it boils. Remove from heat, then add fish and seasonings, 1 whole egg and 1 yolk. Rub through wire sieve, stir in cream and lemon juice. Beat white stiff and fold in. Pour into greased 600-ml (1-pint) mould and steam very gently till firm from 1 to 1¼ hours. Turn out and coat with sauce and decorate to taste.

If baked, serve in dish in which it is cooked. Cook at 190°C (375°F), Gas 5, for about 30 minutes. Serves 3.
Cheshire

25 g (1 oz) butter	pepper and salt
25 g (1 oz) flour or 20 g (¾ oz) if baked	2 eggs
150 ml (1 gill) milk	30 ml (2 tablespoons) cream
225 g (8 oz) cooked white fish, flaked	juice of ½ lemon
	sauce for coating

Fish with capers

Brown the onions in a frying pan in hot fat, add the fish cut into 5-cm (2-inch) lengths, season, add sour milk or cream, lemon juice and rind, a little chopped parsley and the capers. Mix well and simmer gently until the fish is tender, 5–10 minutes. Serves 4.
Oxfordshire

3 or 4 onions (small)	juice of 1 small lemon
fat for frying	5 ml (1 teaspoon) grated lemon rind
700 g (1½ lb) any white fish	
salt and pepper	chopped parsley
100 ml (6 tablespoons) sour milk or cream	40 ml (2 or 3 tablespoons) capers

Pickled fish
Delicious hot or cold

Flour the cut fish and fry in fat. Remove from pan. Fry onions, add curry powder, salt and sugar; mix well, stir in vinegar. Cook for a few minutes and pour over fish.

The flavour of this dish is improved with keeping and may be served 48 hours after making.

Northamptonshire and Soke of Peterborough

500 g (1 lb) white fish
15 ml (1 teaspoon) cornflour or
  flour
fat for frying
2 or 3 sliced onions

10 ml (½ tablespoon) curry powder
salt
10 ml (½ tablespoon) sugar
150 ml (¼ pint) malt vinegar

Devilled grilled cod

Place the prepared fish in a greased ovenproof dish and grill quickly for 2–3 minutes on one side.

Cream the softened margarine and chutney, curry powder, salt and pepper and mustard together, adding the anchovy essence if liked.

Turn the fish over and spread the uncooked side with the devilled mixture. Return to the grill. Reduce the heat slightly and cook for a further 10–12 minutes until the coating is browned and the fish is cooked through. Serve at once.

Cod fillets can be used instead of cutlets. Allow 500–750 g (1–1½ pounds) fish and cut into four portions before cooking.

Derbyshire

4 cutlets of steaks of cod about
  2½ cm (1 inch) thick
25 g (1 oz) margarine
5 ml (1 level teaspoon) chutney
5 ml (1 level teaspoon) curry
  powder

salt and pepper
5 ml (1 level teaspoon) dry
  mustard
5 ml (1 teaspoon) anchovy essence
  (optional)

Oven-fried cod cutlets or fillets

Fish cooked in this way looks and tastes like fried fish, but uses very little fat, and causes no smell in the kitchen.

Season fish and dip in milk, and then coat with brown crumbs. Lay

on well-greased tin, dot with fat and cover with greased paper.
Cook 15–20 minutes, according to thickness of fish, in a moderate
oven, 190°C (375°F), Gas 5. This method can be used for any white
fish.
Gloucestershire

fish cutlets or fillets	brown breadcrumbs
seasoning	fat
milk	

Cheese and crab ramekins

Chop eggs coarsely. Add crab meat, butter and eggs to the sauce.
Heat gently. Do not allow to boil.

Transfer to buttered ramekin dishes or individual fireproof
buttered dishes. Sprinkle tops with cheese. Brown under a hot grill.

Garnish with watercress. Serve with hot buttered toast. Serves 3–4.
Derbyshire

3 hardboiled eggs	25 g (1 oz) grated cheese
100 g (4 oz) cooked crab meat	watercress
25 g (1 oz) butter	4 slices hot buttered toast
150 ml (¼ pint) cheese coating sauce	

To boil a crab

Have a large pan of boiling water and a handful of salt, and plunge
the crab into it. Let it boil quickly for about 20 minutes. It is better
to lay the crab on its feet while boiling.
Cornwall

Stewed eels

Cut eels into pieces and wash well. Place in pan with enough water
to cover and simmer for about 20 minutes. Strain the water from
them and add them to a white or parsley sauce. Put into a casserole
and cook in the oven for 1 hour at 190°C (375°F), Gas 5. Serve in the
casserole.
Isle of Ely

Talmousse of Finnan haddock

Make pastry and cut into two rounds. Put a little of the filling in
centre, wet edges of circle and pinch up over the filling (as for a

Cornish pasty). Bake in a hot oven, 220°C (425°F), Gas 7, for 15 minutes. Garnish with parsley. Serves 1.
Yorkshire

Pastry	*Filling*
50 g (2 oz) flour	100 g (4 oz) shredded cooked
25 g (1 oz) margarine	Finnan haddock
25 g (1 oz) grated cheese	15 ml (1 tablespoon) white sauce
seasoning	to moisten
water to mix	30 ml (1 tablespoon) cheese
	pepper to season
	beaten egg to bind
	parsley to garnish

A new way for fresh herrings

Clean and thoroughly dry the fish – they must be dry. Sprinkle a little cooking salt in a heavy frying pan and, when extremely hot, put the herrings in and cook until a crisp golden brown each side.

In another pan, fry some sliced onions in a little butter. Lay herrings in a shallow dish and smother in the rich brown onion rings.
Herefordshire

fresh herrings	onions
cooking salt	butter for frying

Baked herrings Normande

Split and bone herrings. Wash, dry and lay flat. Chop the onion very finely, dice apple and mix all together with herbs. Season the inside of herrings with salt and black pepper, and sprinkle on the onion mixture. Roll up head to tail. Melt butter and brush inside of fireproof dish with it, put in herrings and the rest of the butter with vinegar. Bake in a slow oven for 45–50 minutes at 160°C (325°F), Gas 3.
Durham

4 herrings	salt and freshly ground black
1 onion	pepper
1 large apple	25 g (1 oz) butter
20 ml (1 dessertspoon) chopped	30 ml (2 tablespoons) vinegar
herbs, parsley, chives, thyme	

Margareta herrings

Clean, wash and fillet herrings. Place a butter knob on each fillet and roll, skin out. Pack into casserole and sprinkle with salt.

Mix mustard, tomato purée and cream and spread over the top.
Bake, 200°C (400°F), Gas 6, for about 30 minutes.
Serve with mashed potatoes.
Pembrokeshire

4 large herrings
50 g (2 oz) butter
salt
60 ml (4 tablespoons) French
  mustard

60 ml (4 tablespoons) tomato
  purée
60 ml (4 tablespoons) cream

Limpets

Carefully wash the sand off the limpets, put on the fire in a pan of cold water, and boil until they slip out of their shells. Serve cold with vinegar and pepper.
Cornwall

Marinated mackerel

Clean and prepare the mackerel and arrange in a pie-dish, chop the onion and parsley and sprinkle over the fish. Add other ingredients with salt to taste. Pour over sufficient vinegar to cover well and bake in a moderate oven, 180°C (350°F), Gas 4, for 40 or 50 minutes.

When cooked put fish carefully on a dish and strain vinegar over them. Leave until cold and serve.
Cornwall

4 or more mackerel
1 onion
1 sprig parsley
2 chopped bay leaves
6 cloves

blade of mace
10 peppercorns
salt
vinegar

Roast mackerel

Roast the mackerel with fennel; after they are cooked open them and take out the bone; then make a good sauce with butter, parsley and gooseberries, all seasoned; soak your mackerel a very little with your sauce, then serve them hot.

mackerel	chopped parsley
sprigs of fennel	gooseberry purée
butter	salt and pepper

Note for beginners
Put fennel sprigs inside the mackerel, and on top as well for good
flavour. Roast at 190°C (375°F), Gas 5, for 20–30 minutes, depending
on size (no fat required).

To make gooseberry sauce for 4, use not less than 225 g (8 oz)
green gooseberries or 150 ml (¼ pint) purée; add butter, parsley and
seasoning to taste.
Cornwall

Casseroled ormers

Roll ormers in flour, fry till brown. Place in casserole with slice of
bacon, small sprig of parsley, salt to taste. Pour over thick gravy.
Bake in slow oven for 4 hours, the longer the better.

Note: The ormer is a species of univalve mollusc abundant in
Guernsey.
Guernsey

ormers	small sprig parsley
flour	salt
fat for frying	thick gravy
slice of bacon	

Savoury plaice

Skin plaice and roll each fillet skin-side inside. Put on a greased
plate and steam for 20 minutes. Place in a greased fireproof dish.

Fry mushrooms and place at ends of dish.

Make the cheese sauce by melting the margarine in a pan, adding
the flour and cooking for a minute or so. Gradually add the milk and
stir till it thickens. Add the grated cheese and pepper and salt to
taste. Pour this sauce over the fish and mushrooms. Slice the
tomatoes and fry. Lay them gently at both ends of the dish, sprinkle
with sugar. Sprinkle a few breadcrumbs over the whole, brown
under a grill and garnish with parsley.
Yorkshire

4 fillets plaice
100 g (4 oz) mushrooms
little butter for frying
300 ml (½ pint) cheese sauce
100 g (4 oz) tomatoes
sugar
breadcrumbs
parsley to garnish

Cheese sauce
25 g (1 oz) margarine
25 g (1 oz) flour
300 ml (½ pint) milk
50 g (2 oz) grated cheese
pepper and salt

Quick method of boiling salmon

Wrap salmon in piece of muslin and place in a pan of boiling water
with a close-fitting lid and keep at a full rolling boil for 5 minutes.
Remove from heat and leave in liquor till cold.
Cheshire

Salmon

Wipe fish all over with oil and sprinkle with salt and pepper. Wrap
in foil. Place in saucepan with cold water to cover. Bring slowly to
the boil and simmer for 5 minutes. Leave in water to cool.
Devon

any size from whole fish to steak
for one

oil or melted butter
salt and pepper

Tweed salmon

The cooking of Tweed salmon is peculiar to the Tweed Valley.
Take a whole fresh salmon and weigh it. Cut it down the back and
lay it open on a board. Clean the fish, saving roe and liver. Cut the
fish across from side to side in strips 2½ cm (1 inch) wide. The fish is
placed on the tray taken from the fish kettle, being careful to keep
the fish skin-side up and in the shape of the fish. The tray is now
lowered into the fish kettle, which should have been filled with
enough well-salted boiling water to cover the fish. Bring to the boil.
Boil rapidly allowing 1 minute for every ½ kg (1 pound) of fish.
Remove tray from pan and drain.

Salmon should be served cold with a little of the water (called
Dover) in which it has been cooked.
Northumberland

Salmon cream

Dissolve gelatine in hot water. Mash salmon well, removing skin and bones. Mix with mayonnaise and season well. Fold in stiffly whipped cream and dissolved gelatine. Pour into a wetted 15-cm (6-inch) cake tin and allow to set. Turn out on to a bed of lettuce and garnish with overlapping pieces of cucumber. Serves 6.

Durham

15 g ($\frac{1}{2}$ oz) gelatine
45 ml (3 tablespoons) hot water
226-g (8-oz) tin salmon
150 ml ($\frac{1}{4}$ pint) mayonnaise

salt and pepper
300 ml ($\frac{1}{2}$ pint) double cream
cucumber and lettuce to garnish

Trout with almonds

Wash trout and wipe dry. Mix flour, salt and pepper and coat fish.

Put 75 g (3 oz) butter and the oil into a pan and fry trout until golden and cooked through – approximately 5 minutes on each side. Remove to serving dish and keep warm.

Add remainder of butter to pan and fry the almonds gently until golden. Pour hot butter and almonds over fish. Garnish with lemon and parsley.

Cumberland

4 trout
60 ml (4 level tablespoons) flour
2$\frac{1}{2}$ ml ($\frac{1}{2}$ level teaspoon) salt
shake of cayenne pepper
100 g (4 oz) butter

10 ml (2 teaspoons) corn oil
75 g (3 oz) blanched almonds
lemon wedges
parsley

Trout with mint

Trim tail and fins and remove eyes – wash. Sprinkle inside with seasoning, place sprig of mint inside fish. Arrange in an ovenproof dish – dot with butter and pour over the lemon juice.

Cover with kitchen foil – cook at 190°C (375°F), Gas 5, for 20–30 minutes.

Garnish with lemon butterflies and mint.

Cumberland

3 frozen or fresh trout
salt and pepper
3 sprigs fresh mint or 1 teaspoon
  dried mint

50 g (2 oz) butter
juice of 1 lemon
$\frac{1}{2}$ lemon thinly sliced
sprigs of mint to garnish

4 Meat

Beef recipes

Beef with green vegetables

Cut the beef in small pieces and coat well with the cornflour. Slice
the shallots and most of the cucumber thinly (do not peel). Remove
all seeds from the pepper and cut in thin strips.

Sauté the meat, vegetables and almonds in the oil for 10 minutes
or until the meat is well browned. Put in a casserole, add the stock to
the frying pan, simmer gently for 1 minute then pour over the meat,
etc, in the casserole. Stir in the soy sauce, cover and cook at 180°C
(350°F), Gas 4, for 1½ hours until meat is tender.

Garnish with the fresh cucumber.

Serves 2.

Cumberland

250 g (8 oz) casserole steak
20 ml (2 teaspoons) cornflour
4 shallots
½ cucumber
1 small green pepper
25 g (1 oz) blanched almonds, halved

30 ml (2 tablespoons) or 25 g (1 oz) margarine
150 ml (¼ pint) stock
10 ml (1 dessertspoon) soy sauce
salt

Beefsteak pudding

Cut steak into thin strips, and roll in seasoned flour. Line a well-greased basin, 900-ml (1½-pint) size, with ⅔ of the pastry. Put in steak and kidney cut in small pieces. Season each layer. Half fill basin with water. Cover with lid of pastry. Cover with two thicknesses of greased paper. Steam for 3 hours.

Alternatively, the meat can be stewed for 1½ hours and then made into pudding, steaming 1½–2 hours. Reserve some of the gravy to serve with the pudding. Serves 4.

Yorkshire

500 g (1 lb) stewing steak
100 g (4 oz) kidney
flour

salt and pepper
8 oz suet crust pastry (225 g flour)

Braised brisket

Melt fat in thick saucepan and brown joint lightly on both sides. Remove meat and put in onions and carrots (cut if large), and brown these lightly. Any other root vegetables can be added if liked. Season with salt and pepper and replace meat, putting the bone down the side. Add bouquet garni if liked. Cover the top with small slices of potato and season well. Add 300 ml (½ pint) of water, cover pan tightly and bring to simmering point. Let it braise slowly, simmering all the time for 2½–3 hours. If necessary, add more water as cooking proceeds.

25 g (1 tablespoon) dripping
1½–2 kg (3–4 lb) middle cut of brisket
onion to taste
6 or 8 carrots

other root vegetables (optional)
salt and pepper
bouquet garni
few potatoes
300–600 ml (½–1 pint) water

Note for beginners

Cooking can be done on top of or in the oven at about 160–180°C

(325–350°F), Gas 3–4. When the meat is cooked, lift it out and keep hot. Lift the vegetables out with a strainer or perforated spoon and serve them with the meat. Remove surplus fat from the top of the gravy and serve it with the meat.
Yorkshire

Danish circles

Cook rice and strain, add to minced beef, breadcrumbs and finely chopped onion, season and bind with beaten egg. Make into four rounds flattened to about 2½ cm (1 inch) in depth. Wrap round each with streaky bacon and secure with cocktail sticks.

Bake in dripping, 190°C (375°F), Gas 5, for 20 minutes, turn when half cooked. Serve with mashed potatoes or potato nests. Serves 4.
Denbighshire

25 g (1 oz) rice
100 g (4 oz) minced beef
30 ml (1 tablespoon) fresh
 breadcrumbs
1 small onion

salt and pepper
1 small egg
4 rashers streaky bacon
cocktail sticks
25 g (1 oz) dripping

Potato nests

Creamed potatoes piped into neat shapes. Fill with cooked peas.
Denbighshire

Galantine

Put the beef and bacon through a mincer, add breadcrumbs, seasoning and a dash of any thick sauce. Mix in the well-beaten egg and milk.

Place in a greased 850-ml (1½-pint) basin, cover with greaseproof paper and steam for 3 hours. Press, but leave in basin until quite cold.

Turn out and serve slices with any green salad or the following dressing:

30 ml (2 tablespoons) vinegar
10 ml (2 teaspoons) sugar
1 small onion
1 small lettuce

Place vinegar in small bowl, add sugar and stir till dissolved. Chop
the onion and lettuce finely and add to the vinegar. Serves 6–8.
Herefordshire

450 g (1 lb) stewing steak – fresh
   and lean
225 g (8 oz) bacon – collar is
   suitable
1 thick slice of bread (50 g) rubbed
   into breadcrumbs

salt and pepper
2 eggs or 1 egg and 45–60 ml (3 or
   4 tablespoons) milk
a little thick sauce (optional)

Savoury meat squares

Mix all together except dripping and breadcrumbs. Pack in
well-greased tin. Sprinkle top with breadcrumbs and cover with
pats of dripping. Bake in a slow oven for 1½–2 hours, 160°C (325°F),
Gas 3.
   Cut into squares. Serves 4–6.
Denbighshire

200 g (8 oz) minced beef
200 g (8 oz) grated raw potato
150 g (6 oz) grated raw carrot
100 g (4 oz) minced onion
125 ml (¼ pint) water

5 ml (1 teaspoon) Marmite
pinch mixed herbs
salt and pepper
75 g (3 oz) white breadcrumbs
25 g (1 oz) dripping

Spiced beef

Place beef in baking tin. Stick half the cloves into it and put the rest
in the tin with the peppercorns and the mace. Almost fill tin with
water and enough salt to make it rather briny.
   Cover with another baking tin. Put in a fairly slow oven until it
boils, then keep to moderate heat till done.
   A nice economical joint to be eaten cold.
Somerset

brisket of beef
16–20 cloves
8–10 peppercorns

small piece of mace
water
salt

Note for beginners

This can be cooked in a casserole instead of a baking tin, adding about 4 cm (1½ inches) water. Do the main cooking at about 160°C (325°F), Gas 3, first bringing the water to the boil at a higher temperature or on the hotplate. Use the same times as for boiling beef: for a piece weighing 1–1½ kg (2–3 lb) allow 2–3 hours; for 2–2½ kg (4–5 lb) allow 3–4 hours.

   The stock will be spicy and salty but is good mixed with unsalted stock or water for a soup or sauce.

Somerset

Steak and kidney pie

Cut up steak and kidney and roll in seasoned flour. Place in a pan or casserole with cold water barely to cover and stew gently for 1½–2 hours. Allow meat to cool. Put it in a 600-ml (1-pint) pie-dish or a 20-cm (8-inch) pie plate. Wet the edges of the pie-dish and put strips of pastry on. Wet the lined edges slightly and cover with the crust taking care to cut crust larger than the dish. Make hole in the middle and flake edges, and brush over with egg or milk. Bake in a hot oven, 220°C (425°F), Gas 7, for about 30 minutes. Serves 4–5.

Yorkshire

450 g (1 lb) stewing steak	salt and pepper
100 g (4 oz) kidney	using 200 g flour (8 oz) flaky
flour	pastry

Lamb and Mutton

A new way with lamb breasts

Arrange onion, carrots and bouquet in a large flat baking dish. On top lay a breast of lamb cut in two. Add seasoning and stock or water. Cover and cook in a very slow oven for 3 hours, 120°C (250°F), Gas ½.

   Remove meat and when cool cut out bones. Cut meat on the slant into strips about 2½ cm (1 inch) wide. Coat with beaten egg and breadcrumbs. Leave on a wire rack for coating to set. Then put in a grill pan, sprinkle with melted margarine and grill gently on both sides until outside is crisp. Serve with lemon or tartare sauce. Serves 6–8 depending on size of breast.

Oxfordshire

1 large sliced onion
2 sliced carrots
bouquet of herbs
1 breast of lamb
seasoning

300 ml ($\frac{1}{2}$ pint) stock or water
egg
fine breadcrumbs
melted margarine
lemon or tartare sauce

Note for beginners

The preliminary cooking can be done the day before, at the same time as some other dish needing long, slow cooking. What many butchers call a breast of lamb is in fact a half breast so ask for a whole one if you want it to serve 6–8.

Fresh meat curry

Slice onions and heat butter and oil. Cook but do not brown. Keep lid on pan and cook gently for 15 minutes.

Add curry powder and when well mixed with onion add cut-up apple and cook until tender. Add stock and all other ingredients except meat and cook gently for 20 minutes.

Add the fresh cut-up meat and cook for 1$\frac{1}{2}$ hours. Serves 3–4.
Durham

2 onions
50 g (2 oz) butter
15 ml (1 tablespoon) oil
30 ml (2 level tablespoons) curry
  powder
2 cooking apples
600 ml (1 pint) stock

60 ml (2 tablespoons) chutney
juice of 1 lemon
25 g (1 oz) sultanas
5 ml (1 teaspoon) salt
1 bay leaf
500 g (1 lb) lamb

Side dishes
100–150 g (4–6 oz) cooked rice
mango chutney
coconut

lemon wedges
sliced banana
sliced tomato

Grilled lamb cutlets with mint butter

Pound the mint in a mortar, add the butter and pound to a smooth ointment; season with salt (very little if salt butter is being used), ground black pepper, a squeeze of lemon juice. This quantity will make enough for eight cutlets.

To grill the cutlets

Score the meat lightly on both sides and coat it with the butter. Leave for an hour.

Grill the cutlets, first on each side close to the grill, then turn them over twice again, cooking farther away from the flame. They will take about 10 minutes altogether.

At the same time, if there is room, grill some half tomatoes and serve with some of the butter poured over them.

Berkshire

8 lamb cutlets	salt
100 ml (2 large tablespoons) fresh mint leaves	ground black pepper
50 g (2 oz) butter	a squeeze of lemon juice

Mock bacon roll

Skin and bone breast, trim rashers and lay neatly on, putting lean part of rasher to fat of lamb. Roll and tie securely. Cook slowly in a little salted water until tender. Leave to cool before taking it from the saucepan, cut into rings, arrange it suitably on dish, dressing it attractively with snippets of salad for table. (Economical with decided flavour of bacon.) Serves 4.

Oxfordshire

1 unchopped breast of lamb
2 or 3 rashers bacon, bacon pieces
  or end of ham

Note for beginners

Tie the roll at about 2½-cm (1-inch) intervals using a fine white string. Cooking time for an average breast will be about 1½ hours.

Do not allow it to cool completely before taking it from the pan, about half an hour is long enough. It is dangerous to leave meat in a warm stock. When the roll is completely cold, store it in cold larder or refrigerator.

Squab pie

As taught by the Phoenicians when they mined tin in Cornwall.

Pie-dish, brown earthenware preferred.

Put layers of mutton, about 8 cm (3 inches) square, over bottom of pie-dish. Put layer of apple 2½ cm (1 inch) thick, sprinkle sugar. Put layer of onions 1 cm (½ inch), only one layer, salt. Put layer of currants, 1 cm (½ inch), sprinkle spice or layer of apples. Then put layer of mutton as at first. Finish with layer of apples. Pour on small quantity of stock. Boil uncovered (except a dish on top) 1½ hours on slow fire.

Make light, thin pastry, put on and bake 1 hour in oven.
Cornwall

Ingredients according to size of pie:	sugar (brown, sprinkled thinly)
mutton chops, all fat removed, bones boiled separately for stock	spice, very little
	salt
apples, chopped fine	stock
onions, chopped fine	pastry
currants	

Note for beginners

Cook the filling in advance and allow it to become cold before covering with pastry. It may be cooked in a slow oven as for a casserole, covering the top with another pie-dish or a loose lid of foil. Before covering with pastry, make sure the filling is piled up enough to support the pastry; or use a pie funnel. Bake at 220°C (425°F), Gas 7.

Bacon, ham, pork

Bacon and pineapple

Simmer the gammon in water for ¾ hour. Lift and remove skin. Lay in a shallow baking dish and sprinkle with the sugar and lay pineapple (rings or bars), 1 or 2 per person on top. Brown lightly under grill.

Cover with foil and place in oven, 140°C (275°F), Gas 1, for about ¾ hour.
Devon

gammon or similar rasher cut 2½ cm (1 inch) thick	15 ml (1 tablespoon) demerara sugar
	pineapple rings or bars

Baked forehock with apple rings

Soak forehock 3–4 hours and rinse well. Simmer for 1½ hours.
Allow to cool a little, but remove skin while still hot. Place in baking
tin. Heat syrup, butter and stock till blended and pour over bacon.
Bake in a moderate oven 1 hour, basting often until the fat is golden
brown. Core, but don't peel, apples, and cut into slices 6 mm (¼ inch)
thick. Place on top of bacon, brush over with syrup from tin and
sprinkle with brown sugar. Return to oven 10–15 minutes until
apples are soft and lightly browned.

Garnish with Duchesse potatoes and serve with peas and green
salad.
Isle of Ely

1 whole and boned forehock	30 ml (2 tablespoons) bacon stock
60 ml (4 tablespoons) golden syrup	3 medium-sized apples
25 g (1 oz) butter	30 ml (1 tablespoon) brown sugar

Note for beginners

A forehock of bacon weighs about 2 kg (4 lb) before boning. A
gammon hock is about the same size but is more expensive. A
suitable temperature for the baking would be 180°C (350°F), Gas 4.

Ham and pineapple

Slightly grill the ham, then place slice of pineapple on each slice of
ham. Place in shallow fireproof dish and pour in the cider. Cover
with lid or foil and cook in slow to moderate oven, 180°C (350°F),
Gas 4, for ¾ hour.
Denbighshire

4 thick slices raw ham	about 150 ml (¼ pint) cider
4 slices pineapple	

Somerset dinner

Take a piece of streaky bacon or ham, place in cold water, bring
steadily to the boil, gently simmer until cooked, then take out on
dish.

Then cook any cabbage or sprouting in the water the meat has been
cooked in – also broad beans are nice cooked in the same way.

Serve with dry boiled potatoes.

This should take about 2 hours according to size of bacon or ham.
Somerset

a piece of streaky bacon or ham   dry boiled potatoes
cabbage or sprouting or broad
  beans

Stuffed bacon

Divide the sausage meat into three and spread rasher with it to
within 2½ cm (1 inch) of the end. Roll up and put the rolls in a baking
tin. Bake in moderate oven for 20 minutes.
Yorkshire

3 back rashers of bacon   100 g (4 oz) sausage meat

Note for beginners

These are very good indeed but I prefer them cooked for longer than
20 minutes; for my taste 30 minutes at 200°C (400°F), Gas 6, was
about right, cooking them until the fatty ends look crisp.
   Allow one or two per person.

Various methods of cooking hams and boiling joints

In casserole
Place washed and soaked joint into casserole. Add a bay leaf, some
black peppercorns, and 6 berries of allspice, and 3 cloves. Pour
water on to about two-thirds depth of joint. Cover closely and cook
in fairly hot oven, 190°C (375°F), Gas 5, about 30 minutes per ½ kg
(pound).

To bake in foil
Soak gammon or ham for 24 hours, changing water two or three
times. Drain well and scrape to remove any 'bloom'. Have ready a
sheet of foil large enough to envelop joint completely. Put joint on
to foil and add 6 berries of allspice, 4 cloves, 6 peppercorns and 2
bay leaves. Wrap up neatly, making a double fold at top, and turning
ends up to retain juices. Cook in moderate oven, 190°C (375°F),
Gas 5. Cooking times: 20 minutes per ½ kg (pound) for large joints:
20 minutes per ½ kg (pound) plus 20 minutes for smaller joints.

Place wrapped joint in meat tin and put in centre of oven. When cooked remove foil, skin joint and cover with brown crumbs.

Note! The liquor from the joint should be strained into a basin. Use the fat for frying and add the jelly underneath to the water for cooking greens. This is especially delicious with sprouts.

To glaze a boiled joint
After removing skin, score fat with a sharp knife.
  Make a syrup from 30 ml (2 tablespoons) golden syrup, 60 ml (4 tablespoons) brown sugar, 60 ml (2 tablespoons) flour.
  Brush over well, stick a clove at each line. Bake in moderate oven, 190°C (375°F), Gas 5, for 30–40 minutes.

To cook with black treacle and beer
Wash ham well. Rub with treacle. Soak overnight. Drain and rub again with treacle. Place in water in pan. Add beer and vegetables. Simmer about 20 minutes to the ½ kg (pound) plus 20 minutes.

one ham or piece of bacon
450 g (1 lb) black treacle
1 small bottle dark beer

225 g (8 oz) carrots
225 g (8 oz) onions

To cook with pineapple
Put bacon – shoulder is very good – into pan, and bring to boil. Drain. Put into casserole. Pour over ¼ tin pineapple juice (125 ml). Cover closely and cook in slow oven, about 120°C (250°F), Gas ½, for 3 hours. May need basting.
Hampshire

Casserole
Cheap and tasty

Peel and slice apple and onion and place in bottom of casserole. Put meat on top. Dissolve stock cube in hot water and pour in casserole. Season and bake at 180°C (350°F), Gas 4, for 2 hours. Serves 4–6.
Durham

1 apple
1 onion
¾–1 kg (1½–2 lb) belly of pork

1 beef stock cube
150 ml (¼ pint) hot water
salt and pepper

Cheese and pork casserole

Season the pork and fry until well browned on both sides. Grate a little bed of cheese into the bottom of a tin into which the pork will fit. Lay the pork on this, then the onion and apple finely chopped. Season with a little salt and pepper. Cover with a thick layer of cheese.

Cover with foil and cook in a moderate oven for 40–45 minutes, 190–200°C (375–400°F), Gas 5 or 6.

Remove the foil and cook for a further 10 minutes.

Derbyshire

1 pork chop or a slice of shoulder pork per person	25 g (1 oz) cheese per piece of pork
salt and pepper	1 small onion per slice of pork
fat or oil for frying	1 large cooking apple

Continental pork casserole

Cut the meat from the bone and remove any fat before cutting the meat into 2½-cm (1-inch) pieces. Toss the pork in seasoned flour until it is well coated.

Heat the oil and butter in a pan, and fry the meat until it is light golden brown. Add the sliced onions and continue frying for a further 2–3 minutes.

Meanwhile cut the pepper in half, remove the core and seeds and cut the flesh into strips. Add the pepper strips, consommé, parsley and stock to the pork and, stirring all the time, bring them back to the boil for 2 minutes. Transfer the ingredients to a 1½-l (3-pint) casserole and cook it covered for about 1½ hours at 160°C (325°F), Gas 3. Ten minutes before the cooking time is completed, quarter and core the apple, cut in small pieces and stir into the casserole. Serves 4–6.

Derbyshire

700 g (1½ lb) spare rib of pork	284 g (10 oz) tin consommé soup
25 g (1 oz) seasoned flour	250 ml (½ pint) chicken stock
30 ml (2 tablespoons) cooking oil	15 ml (1 level tablespoon) chopped parsley
15 g (½ oz) butter	1 red-skinned apple
2 medium onions, thinly sliced	
1 green pepper	

Pork chops in savoury sauce

Trim the fat off the chops and plunge them into boiling salted water for 5 minutes. Remove and drain.

Prepare the sauce. Melt butter in a fairly large pan. Draw aside and add the flour. Mix well, cook slightly, then add the tomato purée together with the water. Add all other ingredients with the exception of the mustard and vinegar. Bring slowly to simmering point. Put the chops or cutlets into the pan and cover with greaseproof paper and the lid. Cook over gentle heat or in the oven for 20–25 minutes.

Just before serving, stir in the French mustard and vinegar. Arrange the chops slightly overlapping in a serving dish and garnish with a few onions or gherkins. Serve very hot.

Berkshire

using 4 pork chops or cutlets
Savoury sauce made with:
25 g (1 oz) butter or margarine
25 g (1 oz) flour
30 ml (2 tablespoons) concentrated tomato purée
400 ml (¾ pint) water
60 ml (2 tablespoons) chopped gherkins
60 ml (2 tablespoons) cocktail onions
30 ml (1 tablespoon) chopped capers
salt and pepper
15 ml (1 tablespoon) French mustard
5 ml (1 teaspoon) tarragon vinegar
a few onions or gherkins to garnish

Note for beginners

The cooking time given above is for small cutlets or thin chops, larger and thicker ones will need 45 minutes' cooking or even longer. The pork will come to no harm while cooking gently in the sauce and it is better to overcook than undercook.

Pork crisps

Bone the pork and cut it into fairly thin slices with a sharp knife.

Beat the egg and put on a plate.

Mix together the breadcrumbs, lemon rind, salt and mustard.

Dip the pork slices into the egg then coat with the breadcrumb mixture. Put the slices into a roasting tin, and bake in the oven at 200°C (400°F), Gas 6, for the first 15 minutes, then reduce to 180°C (350°F), Gas 4, for approximately 45 minutes until crisp. Serves 3–4.
Derbyshire

500 g (1 lb) belly of pork
1 large egg
100 g (4 oz) browned breadcrumbs
grated rind of 1 lemon

salt
15 ml (1 level tablespoon) dry
  mustard

Pork ribs – Chinese style

Heat all sauce ingredients in saucepan. Put pork ribs into casserole, pour sauce over. Cover with lid and bake in slow oven, 150°C (300°F), Gas 2, for 3 hours. Serve with rice.

The sauce is enough for 4–6 portions.

Isle of Ely

pork ribs (according to number of
  people)

Sauce
10 ml (1 dessertspoon) honey
60 ml (4 tablespoons) vinegar

1 medium chopped onion
30 ml (2 tablespoons)
  Worcestershire sauce
5 ml (1 teaspoon) salt
5 ml (1 teaspoon) dry mustard
5 ml (1 teaspoon) paprika pepper

Pork that really crackles

Score pork finely, rub in 3 parts salt to 1 part pepper and slow roast at 180°C (350°F), Gas 4, allowing 25 minutes per ½ kg (pound).

Step up heat to 220°C (425°F), Gas 7. Baste well; roast for 15 minutes. Baste again and roast for a further 15 minutes.

Cambridgeshire

Traditional brawn

Ask your butcher to salt the half head and trotters for you. Soak for 2 hours or so, according to degree of saltiness liked. Put into large pan with the spices and fresh cold water to cover. Bring up to boil, and then simmer until all meat will fall off bones, about 4 hours. Cool until able to handle.

Remove meat from bones, and cut into pieces, but do not mince. Wet a deep pie-dish or other suitable dish. Ornament bottom and sides with slices of hardboiled egg. Put in meat pieces.

Boil liquor again to reduce by a third or half. Skim and strain sufficient of the liquor from pan. Cover meat with this. Leave overnight. Turn out to serve.

Note: Some butchers salt meat more than others. If in doubt, do not add spices at first, but simmer for 30 minutes and then throw that water away and reboil, adding spices. Continue to cook as above. Extra trotters improve stiffness of jelly and are usually easily obtained.

Variations
1 Add onion and root vegetables instead of spices, and serve top of head separately with these while hot.
2 Some recipes add 250 g (½ lb) shin of beef, or other stewing beef.
Hampshire

½ pig's head	spices – bay leaf (or 2 small ones),
2 pig's trotters	peppercorns, whole allspice, a
	few cloves
	hardboiled eggs

Veal

Goulash
An Austrian recipe

Fry the finely chopped onions in the butter to a golden brown – add the paprika – stir well. Put in the meat cut in cubes and seasoned. Let it stew a little, then add the stock a little at a time until the meat is tender. This should only be simmered and therefore takes several hours (about 3). The sauce by then should be nice and thick.

Pie veal is by far and away the best meat to use for this, although one can use stewing steak. Serves 4.
Berkshire

5 medium-sized onions	1 kg (2 lb) pie veal or stewing steak
150 g (6 oz) butter	seasoning
20–40 ml (4 teaspoons) paprika	a little stock

Veau chasseur

Chop the meat into convenient-sized pieces, discarding fat and gristle. Dip each piece into seasoned flour. Put 40 g (1½ oz) butter and the oil into a thick sauté pan. When it is hot, add the veal and turn quickly until it is brown on all sides. Remove from the pan – add a little more butter if needed. Then brown the finely chopped onion.

Stir in the flour and tomato purée. Mix well – add the wine and stock, together with the bouquet garni, seasoning and crushed clove of garlic. Bring it to simmering point.

Return the veal to the pan. Cover with greaseproof paper and the lid. Place on a very low heat or in a moderate oven, 190°C (375°F), Gas 5, for 1 hour. At the end of that time, add the mushrooms cut in slices. Cook for a further 10 minutes. Serve in a hot dish. Sprinkle lightly with finely chopped parsley. Arrange fried croûtons round the sides and serve at once. Serves 3–4.

Berkshire

500–750 g (1–1½ lb) stewing veal
seasoned flour
40–50 g (1½–2 oz) butter
15 ml (1 tablespoon) oil
1 small onion
10 ml (1 teaspoon) flour
10 ml (1 teaspoon) tomato purée
  (concentrated)
150 ml (1 gill) white wine or dry
  cider

300 ml (½ pint) stock
bouquet garni
salt and pepper
1 clove garlic
100 g (4 oz) mushrooms

To finish
Fried croûtons
Finely chopped parsley

Veal escalopes with cucumber sauce

Have veal beaten thinly, dip in seasoned flour. Heat all but 15 g (½ oz) of butter in frying pan, add meat and fry for about 8 minutes, browning both sides. Remove and keep hot.

Add peeled and chopped cucumber (de-seeded) to hot butter with seasoning. Fry gently until tender. Stir in cream and one rounded teaspoonful of seasoned flour creamed with remaining butter. Stir over low heat until sauce thickens. Replace veal in sauce and allow to heat through. Check seasoning, sprinkle chopped parsley. A delicious special occasion dish. Serves 4.

Cambridgeshire

4 veal escalopes
salt and black pepper
50 g (2 oz) butter
1 small cucumber

150 ml (¼ pint) single cream
10 ml (1 rounded teaspoon)
  seasoned flour
chopped parsley

Various

Bobotee

This is a variation of the Indian curry dish.

Soak the bread in half the milk. Fry the onion gently in butter or margarine till cooked, stir in the curry powder, sugar, salt and pepper. Mix meat and bread together and add to onion. Put in a greased pie-dish and pour over the beaten egg with remainder of milk. Lastly add lemon juice. Bake in a moderate oven, 190°C (375°F), Gas 5, about 20 minutes. Serve with boiled rice.
Westmorland

1 slice white bread (25 g)
170 ml (1 teacup) milk
1 small onion, chopped
25 g (1 oz) butter or margarine
10 ml (1 teaspoon) curry powder
10 ml (1 teaspoon) sugar

salt and pepper
225 g (8 oz) cold meat, minced
1 egg
10 ml (1 dessertspoon) lemon juice
  or vinegar

Curry with cold meat

Melt butter or dripping from the cooked meat. When smoking hot add onion and flour mixed with the curry powder. Cook slowly for a minute or two, stirring constantly.

Peel and chop apple or tomato, add to pan with stock, and salt to taste. Stir till sauce comes to the boil, lower heat and cover. Simmer gently for 30 minutes, stirring occasionally. Cool.

Add meat. Stand for 30 minutes, then re-heat. Stir in cream and chutney. When almost boiling, add lemon juice. Arrange on hot dish. Serve with boiled rice. Serves 3-4.
Cumberland

50 g (2 oz) butter or dripping
1 chopped onion
15 g (½ oz) flour
15 g (½ oz) curry powder
1 apple or tomato
250 ml (½ pint) stock

salt to taste
200 g (8 oz) cooked meat
75 ml (⅓ pint) cream or top of milk
25 g (1 oz) chutney
5 ml (1 teaspoon) lemon juice

53

Start making the sauce well in advance so that it can be cooled before
the meat is added. When re-heating the curry it is wise to boil it for a
few minutes before serving. If the meat is cut in fairly small cubes
this will ensure that it heats through quickly and thoroughly.

Liver casserole

Chop liver, bacon, onions and carrots and roll all in flour. Fry lightly
in butter. Add water to cover and bring to boil, add seasoning. Turn
into casserole and cook slowly for $1\frac{1}{2}$ hours, 180°C (350°F), Gas 4.

Two lamb's kidneys may be added to liver for extra richness.
Serves 4.
Pembrokeshire

250 g (8 oz) lamb's liver	50 g (2 oz) butter
3 rashers bacon	water
3 medium onions	salt and pepper
2 carrots	2 lamb's kidneys (optional)
flour	

Oxtail shape

Wash and joint the oxtail, put in pan or stew jar with the onion
stuck with cloves and cover with water. Simmer gently for 3 hours.
Remove the onion, take all the meat from the bones and cut into
pieces. Strain the liquor and return meat and liquor to pan. Season
with salt and pepper and bring to the boil. Halve the two hardboiled
eggs and place them cut sides to bottom of a mould. Put in meat
mixture and leave overnight to set.

1 oxtail	salt and pepper
1 small onion	2 hardboiled eggs
4 cloves	

Savoury sausage casserole

Peel and chop the onion and mix it with the sausage meat and herbs,
and plenty of salt and pepper. Divide the mixture into 16 pieces,
roll each piece into a ball and toss them in the seasoned flour.

Melt the lard in a frying pan, add the meat balls and fry them quickly to brown all over. Transfer them to a plate.

Stir the curry powder and the rest of the flour into the fat in the pan and cook for a few seconds, then remove the pan from the heat and gradually stir in the stock. Return the pan to the heat and stirring all the time bring the sauce to the boil for 2 minutes to thicken.

Peel the carrots and cut them into small sticks and wipe and roughly chop the mushrooms; stir them both into the sauce with the meat balls.

Cover the pan with a lid or a piece of kitchen foil and simmer the casserole on a low heat for about $\frac{1}{2}$ hour until the meat balls are cooked. Serve the casserole with rice. Serves 4.
Derbyshire

1 large onion (175 g)	25 g (1 oz) lard
500 g (1 lb) pork sausage meat	10 ml (1 level dessertspoon) curry
pinch of mixed herbs	powder
salt and pepper	400 ml ($\frac{3}{4}$ pint) stock
15 ml (1 level tablespoon) plain	100 g (4 oz) carrots
flour seasoned with salt and	100 g (4 oz) mushrooms
pepper	rice

Stewed tripe and onions

Wash the tripe in cold water, drain and cut into small pieces. Peel and slice the onions. Put tripe and onions into a pan, cover with the milk. Simmer for 1 hour. Strain the tripe into a hot dish, keeping the milk. Rinse out the pan and melt the butter in the pan, stir in the flour, keep stirring until it turns yellow. Add the milk and stir until it boils. Boil gently for 5 minutes, adding salt and pepper to taste. Add the tripe and re-heat. Serve sprinkled with chopped parsley. Serves 4.
Yorkshire

500 g (1 lb) dressed tripe	25 g (1 oz) flour
4 onions	salt and pepper
600 ml (1 pint) milk	chopped parsley
25 g (1 oz) butter	

5 Poultry & Game

Poultry

How to joint a chicken

1 Place chicken on chopping board and with sharp knife cut through
and along length of breastbone. Use poultry scissors if preferred.
2 Open bird out, then cut through along length of backbone. If
liked, backbone can be removed entirely by cutting along close to
either side. Tap back of knife sharply with heavy weight to cut
through bony sections. Bird is now in two halves.
3 Lay halves of chicken skin side up on board and divide each in
half again by cutting diagonally across between wing and thigh. Bird
is now in four quarters, two wing and breast joints, two thigh and
drumstick joints. Joints are neater if leg shanks and wing tips are
removed.
4 To make six joints divide each thigh and drumstick portion in half
by cutting through at ball and socket joint.
Surrey

Chicken and ham pancakes

Sieve together salt and flour. Add egg then gradually add half the milk, beating well into a smooth batter. Stir in remaining milk and oil.

Put a little oil into the frying pan and heat. Pour off surplus oil. Pour about 2 tablespoons batter into frying pan and tilt so that the batter covers the base thinly. Cook until underside is golden. Toss or turn pancake and fry other side. Turn out of pan and keep hot. Repeat with remaining batter to give 8 pancakes.

Filling
Melt butter in pan, add flour and cook for a minute. Remove from heat and gradually stir in milk. Return to heat and bring to boil, stir until it thickens. Add chopped ham and chicken and season well. Divide filling between pancakes and roll up. Serve garnished with grilled tomato slices and parsley sprigs. Serves 4.
Yorkshire

100 g (4 oz) plain flour	*Filling*
pinch of salt	40 g (1½ oz) butter
1 egg	40 g (1½ oz) flour
250 ml (½ pint) milk	400 ml (¾ pint) milk
15 ml (1 tablespoon) oil	175 g (6 oz) cooked ham
oil for frying	175 g (6 oz) cooked chicken
	salt and pepper
	tomato slices
	parsley sprigs

Chicken and ham roll

Mince chicken and ham together. Add chopped pineapple and cream cheese and blend well together. Season to taste.

Roll out pastry in oblong approximately 15 × 30 cm (6 × 12 inches). Place mixture on pastry in a sausage shape, roll up and seal edges. Brush top with beaten egg and slash about 2½ cm (1 inch) apart.

Bake at 230°C (650°F), Gas 8, for 20–25 minutes. Can be served either hot or cold. Very good for picnics or buffet snacks. Serves 4.
Cumberland

100 g (4 oz) cooked chicken	75 g (3 oz) cream cheese
50 g (2 oz) cooked ham	salt and pepper
75 g (3 oz) chopped pineapple chunks	125 g (4 oz) puff pastry
	little beaten egg for glazing

Chicken in brandy
A luxury dish

Season chicken with salt and pepper. Cook in the butter in a heavy
pan, over moderate heat for 30 minutes, until brown and tender.
Add the sliced mushrooms and cook for another 5 minutes. Pour in
the warmed brandy and set alight. Remove the chicken and
mushrooms, and keep hot. Blend flour in the pan, stirring in the
tomato sauce, cream, and seasoning, if necessary. Simmer for 10
minutes and pour over the chicken.

Allow approximately 1 hour total cooking time. Serves 4.
Northumberland

1 young chicken, jointed	20 ml or more (1 tablespoon) brandy
salt and pepper	15 ml (1 tablespoon) flour
100 g (4 oz) butter	15 ml (1½ teaspoons) tomato sauce
200 g (8 oz) sliced mushrooms	400 ml (¾ pint) cream

Chicken pilaf

Melt butter in omelette pan and add rice. Cook 3 minutes. Add
tomatoes, chicken and enough stock to moisten. Cook 5 minutes
and season lightly with salt and cayenne. Add more butter if
desired. Serves 3–4.
Cheshire

40 g (3 tablespoons) butter	75 g (½ cup) diced cooked chicken
250 g (2 cups) hot cooked rice	veal or chicken stock, highly
75 g (½ cup) fresh or canned	seasoned
tomatoes, cut up	salt and cayenne

Note for beginners

About 125 g (1 cup) of raw rice will give double the quantity when
boiled.

Herbs can be used for flavouring the stock, for example, bay leaf,
rosemary or tarragon, or add fresh chopped herbs to the cooked
dish.

It is also very good made with other left-over poultry and the
appropriate stock.

Chicken roasted in wine with oranges
A simple dish with the luxury flavour

Stuff the chicken with one whole orange. Cut the other orange and
rub over the skin of the chicken. Spread a little honey over the
chicken and roast. Fifteen minutes before end of cooking time pour
the wine over the bird.

The oranges give the chicken an unusual flavour, and the honey
gives a sweet and crisp flavour to the skin.
Surrey

1 chicken	honey
2 oranges	150 ml (¼ pint) white wine

Chicken with almonds

Cut almonds into strips.

Fry onions and mushrooms in butter in a saucepan until pale gold.
Add cornflour. Cook 1 minute. Gradually blend in milk. Cook,
stirring until sauce comes to the boil. Add chicken (in bite-sized
pieces), ginger and grated nutmeg. Heat gently 5–7 minutes.

Beat yogurt and egg yolks well together. Add to chicken mixture.
Cook very slowly, without boiling, until thickened. Season to taste.
Pour into warmed serving dish. Scatter almonds over the top.
Serves 4.
Cumberland

25 g (1 oz) blanched and toasted almonds	200–300 g (½–¾ lb) cooked chicken
1 small chopped onion	1 ml (¼ level teaspoon) ground ginger
50 g (2 oz) sliced mushrooms and stalks	1 ml (¼ level teaspoon) grated nutmeg
25 g (1 oz) butter	140 ml (5 oz) carton natural yogurt
10 ml (1 level dessertspoon) cornflour	2 egg yolks
150 ml (¼ pint) milk	salt and pepper

Cock-a-leekie

Wash the leeks and cut into pieces 2½ cm (1 inch) long. Put into pot
with trussed fowl and stock; add seasoning. Simmer gently for 4

hours. Skim occasionally; half an hour before serving, add prunes.

When ready to serve, take out fowl and cut into pieces. Place in a tureen and pour the broth over it.

Berkshire

3 large leeks	seasoning
1 fowl	8 prunes
stock	

Crunchy crisp baked chicken

Pre-heat oven to 180°C (350°F), Gas 4.

Mix flour, salt and curry powder. Crush the potato crisps with a rolling pin. Coat the chicken joints with the seasoned flour. Dip the joints in the milk, and coat thickly and evenly with potato crisp crumbs. Arrange skin-side up on a baking sheet. Bake for 40–45 minutes.

Serve hot or cold with green salad and sauté or fried potatoes. Serves 4.

Surrey

This tasty crisp chicken is excellent cold for picnics.

60 ml (2 rounded tablespoons) flour	2 packets potato crisps (50–60 g)
10 ml (1 rounded teaspoon) salt	4 chicken quarters
2½ ml (¼ rounded teaspoon) curry powder	a little creamy milk

English farmhouse chicken

Fry the shredded bacon lightly. Lift it out and keep it hot. Add the margarine or chicken fat to the frying pan – fry the jointed chicken until lightly browned and keep it hot.

Half stew the shredded vegetables in the fat with the seasoning and a little sugar. Mix in the bacon and turn all into a casserole dish. Lay the chicken on top. Cover the dish and complete the cooking in the oven at 180°C (350°F), Gas 4, for about an hour. Just before serving sprinkle on the chicken stock.

Allow about 1½ hours' total cooking time.

Berkshire

2 bacon rashers
25–50 g (1–2 oz) margarine or
  chicken fat
a jointed chicken – to serve 4–6
  people
75 g (3 oz) shredded carrot

75 g (3 oz) shredded turnip
50 g (2 oz) celery heart, sliced
½ onion, sliced
salt, pepper and a little sugar
60–75 ml (4 or 5 tablespoons) hot
  chicken stock

Fried chicken with white wine sauce

Wash, dry and season chicken.

Melt butter in pan, add chicken and fry lightly. Cover pan with a
lid, lower heat and fry very gently until chicken is cooked (about
40–45 minutes).

Remove chicken from pan, place on serving dish and keep warm.
Put shallot or onion in pan. Cover with lid and fry gently until
cooked (about 5 minutes).

Drain off surplus fat, add white wine and boil rapidly for 1 minute.
Add stock and tomato, simmer for 5–10 minutes.

Correct seasoning and pour over chicken. Sprinkle with chopped
parsley and garnish with lightly fried mushrooms.

Isle of Ely

4 chicken joints
50 g (2 oz) butter
25 g (1 oz) chopped onion or
  shallot
75 ml (⅛ pint) cheap white wine
300 ml (½ pint) stock (can be made
  with chicken cube)

tomato with skin and pips
  removed
salt and pepper
chopped parsley
100 g (4 oz) button mushrooms
fat for frying

Hindle Wakes fowl

Rub the outside of the fowl with a cut lemon. Put the lemon inside
the bird, place in a casserole, half cover with a mixture of cider and
water. Put on lid and simmer very slowly for at least 8 hours in a
cool oven, 100°C (200°F), Gas LOW.

Berkshire

1 old boiling fowl
1 lemon

cider and water mixed

How to take years off an old hen

Put a trussed old hen into a small pan full of cold water with 150 ml (a teacupful) of vinegar. The pan should be sufficiently deep to enable the cold water and vinegar to cover the hen. Soak overnight.

The next day wash the hen under the cold tap to remove all trace of vinegar, and dry thoroughly.

Roast in the ordinary way. The vinegar makes the flesh white and tender, and it will taste like a roast chicken.
Leicestershire and Rutland

Poulet sauté Normand

Fry chicken joints in oil until golden brown – about 10 minutes. Add apple juice and water and cook for $\frac{1}{2}$ hour. Remove chicken, add cream and seasoning to liquid. Pour over chicken and decorate with stuffed olives. Serves 4.
Durham

1 small chicken, jointed	20 ml (2 dessertspoons) cream
30 ml (2 tablespoons) corn oil	salt and pepper
200 ml (1 cup) apple juice	stuffed olives
400 ml (2 cups) water	

Note for beginners

Should there be rather too much liquid left when the chicken is cooked, after removing it, boil the liquid rapidly to reduce it before adding seasoning and cream. If you cook the chicken in a pan with a lid, add only half the amount of water.

Roast chicken and accompaniments

Cooking time: 18–20 minutes per 450 g (pound), plus 20 minutes. Prepare the bird and stuff with sausage forcemeat or a simple herb forcemeat. Lay one or two fat rashers of bacon over breast and place the bird on a trivet in a roasting tin containing some dripping. Cook in a hot oven $1\frac{1}{2}$–2 hours, 230°C (450°F), Gas 8, for 15–20 minutes then reduce the heat to 190°C (375°F), Gas 5. Remove the bacon 15 minutes before cooking is completed to allow the breast to brown.

The breast may be frothed (i.e. dredged with flour and basted) when the bacon has been taken off.

Sausage forcemeat
Melt the dripping, chop the onion finely and mix with the sausage meat. Lightly sauté the sausage meat and onion in the dripping for a few minutes to give a good flavour, mix in the other ingredients and use as required.

Bread sauce
Peel the onion and stick the cloves into it, place in a saucepan with the milk, salt and peppercorns, bring almost to boiling point and leave in a warm place for about 20 minutes in order to extract the flavour from the onion. Remove the peppercorns and add the butter and breadcrumbs. Mix well and allow to infuse for about 15 minutes, then remove the onion.

If preferred the onion may be removed before adding the breadcrumbs, but a better flavour is obtained by allowing the flavour of the onion to penetrate the breadcrumbs by infusing them together.
Surrey

2 kg (4 lb) chicken

Sausage forcemeat
25 g (1 oz) dripping
1 large onion
450 g (1 lb) pork sausage meat
125 ml (4 tablespoons)
  breadcrumbs
5 ml (½ teaspoon) mixed herbs
10 ml (1 teaspoon) chopped parsley
seasoning

Bread sauce
1 medium-sized onion
2 cloves
425 ml (¾ pint) milk
salt
a few peppercorns
20 g (¾ oz) butter
75 g (3 oz) breadcrumbs

Accompaniments
chipolatas
bacon rolls
roast potatoes
gravy

Spring chicken with mushrooms

Cut chicken into joints and fry in butter until brown. Season and add chopped onion, mushrooms and ham. Cover with milk and

simmer slowly for 25 minutes. Remove chicken and thicken milk
with a little cornflour and serve poured over the chicken. Serves 4.
Yorkshire

1 small chicken	50 g (2 oz) mushrooms
25 g (1 oz) butter	50 g (2 oz) chopped ham
seasoning	milk to cover
1 small onion	little cornflour

To use up cooked chicken legs

Make cuts in the legs, marinate in the liquid for at least 1 hour,
spooning it into the cuts. Grill and pour any remaining liquid over
before serving.
Berkshire

Mix together:	15 ml (1 tablespoon) vinegar
30 ml (2 tablespoons)	30 ml (2 tablespoons) melted butter
Worcestershire sauce	20 ml (2 teaspoons) dry mustard

Devil mixture for legs of poultry, etc

Mix all this together, score legs and insert mixture. It is better
prepared early and allowed to soak into the meat. Grill until brown
and heated through.
Berkshire

Equal quantities of:	*Twice as much:*
dry mustard	salad oil
chutney	*and*
anchovy sauce	a pinch of cayenne

Braised duck

Joint the duck. Prepare vegetables and cut up roughly. Heat butter
in a large pan and lightly brown vegetables and bacon. Add grated
orange rind, herbs and seasoning, and put in enough stock to barely
cover vegetables. Put in duck joints, cover with greaseproof paper
and a tightly fitting lid. Cook gently for about 45 minutes.

Remove lid, pour in wine and cook uncovered in oven for about
35 minutes. Arrange joints on a heated serving dish.

Strain liquid and make a gravy allowing 40 g (a heaped tablespoon) of flour to 500 ml (1 pint) of liquid. Add orange juice. Strain gravy over duck and garnish with orange rings, croûtons of bread and parsley.

Shropshire

1 duck	seasoning
1 large onion	stock
2 medium carrots	150 ml (1 gill) red wine
50 g (2 oz) mushrooms	flour
1 rasher bacon, roughly chopped	croûtons of bread
50 g (2 oz) butter	parsley
1 orange	orange rings
bouquet garni	

Note for beginners

To allow plenty of time for dishing up and thickening the gravy begin cooking the braised duck about 2 hours before serving time. After the preliminary frying, cooking can be in the oven at about 180°C (350°F), Gas 4.

To avoid having the dish too fatty, trim some surplus fat from the joints before cooking; or even remove skin and fat entirely.

The quantities in this recipe are enough for a 2-kg (4-lb) duck which will serve 5–6, depending on its condition.

Roast duckling with stuffed apples

Stuff duckling with sage and onion stuffing, cook in hot oven according to size, 200°C (400°F), Gas 6, allowing 15–20 minutes per ½ kg (pound).

Twenty-five minutes before serving add as many cooking apples as required, cored and stuffed with very well seasoned sausage meat. Serve at table with cooked apples round duck.

Pembrokeshire

duckling	cooking apples
sage and onion stuffing	sausage meat, well seasoned

Roast turkey
The traditional way

Both crop and body can be stuffed, the crop with sage and onion stuffing, the body with pork sausage meat.

When crop is stuffed draw the flap back and skewer or sew in position to hold stuffing neatly. Spread a little seasoned, softened butter over the turkey then place in roasting tin, cover with aluminium foil.

Get the oven really hot before putting in the bird, then set oven at 160°C (325°F), Gas 3. Baste every ½ hour, at the same time turning bird from side to side.

Leave off covering for the last 30 minutes. Serve with giblet gravy, bread sauce, cranberry jelly, roast potatoes, Brussels sprouts.

Note: If the bird is stuffed with sausage meat, weigh the whole bird as extra cooking time is needed.
Surrey

Guide to roasting time

2¾ to 3½ kg (6 to 8 lb)	2½ to 3 hours approx
4 to 5½ kg (9 to 12 lb)	3½ to 4½ hours approx
5¾ to 7¼ kg (13 to 16 lb)	4½ to 5 hours approx
7¾ to 9 kg (17 to 20 lb)	6 to 6¼ hours approx

Turkey salad

Prepare the peppers and shred finely. Mix all the ingredients well together except for the cucumber which is used for decoration. (The sweet corn may be fresh, tinned or frozen.)
Surrey

red and green pepper
200 g (8 oz) cooked Patna rice
25 0g (8 oz) cooked diced turkey
20 g (1 oz) walnuts, chopped
52 g (1 oz) sultanas

sweet corn
French dressing
seasoning
cucumber

Game

To prepare game for roasting

Game birds should be hung by the neck in a cool, airy place to develop flavour and to ensure the flesh being tender. To prevent them becoming too 'high', examine occasionally. For most people, the bird is sufficiently mature when tail or breast feathers can be easily plucked.

Pluck and draw the bird as for chicken, but do not draw any sinews and leave on the feet (remove the claws). Wipe inside the bird with a clean damp cloth and insert a piece of rump steak or butter to keep the bird moist. Cut off the wings at the first joint and truss as for roast chicken. Cover the breast with strips of fat bacon in order to prevent the flesh of a game bird drying up and losing flavour.

Cooking
Young birds should be roasted, older birds should be braised or cooked in a casserole. The length of time for cooking will depend on time of hanging and age of bird.
Gloucestershire

Fried or browned crumbs to serve with game

Heat the butter without discolouring. Add the breadcrumbs and stir over a moderate heat until brown, being careful to have them all of a uniform shade. Season and use.

Crumbs can also be done in the oven.
Gloucestershire

50 g (2 oz) breadcrumbs   25 g (1 oz) butter

Roast grouse
Season: 12 August to 15 December

Prepare the grouse, wipe well, season with salt and pepper and wrap in thin slices of fat pork or bacon. Roast in a very hot oven 230°C (450°F), Gas 8, for 10–15 minutes.

Remove the birds and skim off all the fat from the pan juices. Add butter and stock. Reduce this sauce very quickly, stirring and scraping the pan. Place each bird on a piece of buttered toast. Serve with bread sauce and redcurrant jelly.
Cumberland

grouse   75 ml (⅛ pint) stock per bird
salt and pepper   buttered toast
thin slices fat pork or bacon   bread sauce
15 g (½ oz) butter per bird   redcurrant jelly

Roast guinea fowl
Season: February to August

Draw and truss the guinea fowl. Cover the breast with fat bacon
and place some inside. Roast for ¾–1 hour at 190°C (375°F), Gas 5.
Serve with watercress, gravy and salad.
Cumberland

guinea fowl	watercress
fat bacon	orange or pineapple salad
gravy	

Roast partridge
Season: 1 September to 1 February

Draw and truss the bird. Cover the breast with bacon. Roast for
30–45 minutes at 220°C (425°F), Gas 7. Serve with gravy, game
chips, fried crumbs and green salad.
Cumberland

partridge	game chips
fat bacon	fried crumbs
butter for basting	green salad
gravy	

Pheasant in madeira

Pluck and draw the pheasant and place in a pan with the bacon,
ham, onion, celery, parsley, carrot, butter and seasonings. Cook
together slowly until the pheasant begins to brown then add the
madeira and stock. Cover and allow the bird to finish cooking for
about 45 minutes.

   Place the bird on a hot dish, strain the fat from the sauce, sieve it
and pour over the bird. Send to the table garnished with the
croûtons of fried bread.

   Serves 2–4, depending on size of bird.
Yorkshire

1 pheasant	½ onion (cut small)
4 slices fat bacon (cut small)	1 stick celery (chopped fine)
2 slices ham (cut small)	10 ml (1 teaspoon) chopped parsley

1 carrot, diced   125 ml (¼ pint) madeira
25 g (1 oz) butter   125 ml (¼ pint) stock
pepper, salt, dash of nutmeg   garnish – croûtons of fried bread

Roast pheasant 1
Season: 1 October to 1 February

Sprinkle the pheasant with salt and pepper to taste and rub well
with butter. Wrap in a thin sheet of larding pork or fat bacon. Roast
in a moderate oven, 190°C (375°F), Gas 5, for 40 minutes
(approximate).

Remove the fat and arrange bird on a dish garnished with
watercress. Arrange pieces of pâté de foie gras over the pheasant on
the dish. Serve with the pan juices, partially free from fat and
strained. Accompany with boiled rice and a tart jelly.
Cumberland

pheasant   watercress
salt and pepper   pâté de foie gras
butter   boiled rice
larding pork or fat bacon   tart jelly

Roast pheasant 2

Put the steak or butter inside the bird and cover it with fat bacon
and thickly greased paper. Place in a roasting pan. Cook in a
moderate oven, 190°C (375°F), Gas 5, for 45–60 minutes according
to the age of the bird. Ten minutes before the bird is ready, froth the
breast. To do this, remove paper and bacon, and baste the breast
with melted dripping or butter, dredge it with flour and baste again.
Return to the oven heated up to 220°C (425°F), Gas 7, and leave
until it is a good brown colour and frothy.

Decorate the cooked pheasant with tail feathers and serve with
accompaniments: gravy, bread sauce, browned crumbs, chipped
potatoes, French salad or watercress.
Gloucestershire

1 pheasant   50 g (2 oz) dripping or butter for
slices of fat bacon   basting
small piece of rump steak or   flour
  butter

Casserole of pigeons with steak and mushrooms

Cut pigeons in halves and steak in neat pieces. Fry pigeons, steak and bacon in fat. Place in casserole with stock, mushrooms (sliced) and seasoning. Cover and simmer 2½ hours.

Add jelly, lemon juice and flour blended with a little milk. Simmer for another 15 minutes. Serves 4.

Durham

2 pigeons	salt and pepper
200 g (8 oz) steak	30 ml (1 tablespoon) redcurrant
1 rasher bacon, chopped	jelly
butter or margarine	15 ml (1 tablespoon) lemon juice
300 ml (½ pint) stock	15 ml (1 tablespoon) flour
50 g (2 oz) mushrooms	milk

Roast pigeon

Draw and truss the pigeon, cover with buttered paper, baste with butter. Roast for 20–30 minutes at 220°C (425°F), Gas 7. Serve with gravy and other accompaniments.

Cumberland

young pigeon	orange salad
butter	redcurrant jelly
gravy	

Roast plover, snipe, quail or woodcock

Roast for 20–30 minutes at 220°C (425°F), Gas 7, and serve with gravy, fried breadcrumbs and chipped potatoes.

Cheshire

Roast ptarmigan

Roast for ½ hour at 220°C (425°F), Gas 7. Serve with gravy, bread sauce, fried breadcrumbs, chipped potatoes.

Cheshire

Roast wild duck
Young

Roast for 40–50 minutes at 190°C (375°F), Gas 5, and serve with gravy, orange salad and chipped potatoes.
Cheshire

Rook pie

Method for skinning
Cut the skin down the centre of the breast, draw the skin off the breast in the direction of the wing, pulling it up to the first joint, cut the wing at the joint and discard the end part, then draw the skin from the legs and cut off at the shank joint; cut the legs off at the joint where they join the body, then insert the first finger of one hand at the breast cavity and take hold of the lower portion of the neck with the other hand and pull apart. This leaves the breast in one hand and the remainder of the body in the other hand – the latter being discarded. Wash the breast and legs thoroughly in cold water and rinse several times in cold water. (The definition of a rook for this purpose is a young bird, recently left the nest and just able to fly.)

Method for cooking
Stew the breasts and the legs gently until tender (a small proportion of steak and a tablespoon of beef dripping is an improvement). When cool, take the meat from the bones and place in a pie-dish, season well with salt and a shake of cayenne, add a little of the gravy and cover with shortcrust pastry and bake until brown and attractive in appearance. This can be made with a pastry base and covering if desired and can be eaten hot (or cold with salad).

   (Rooks are usually available about the second week in May in the North of England.)
Yorkshire

Note for beginners

Quantities usually recommended are 1 rook per person and 100 g (4 oz) steak for 4 rooks.

Hare jugged

Cut hare flesh into pieces size of a small egg – heat 50 g (2 oz) butter, fry pieces of hare brown, put them into stew jar with a little salt, onion, shallot (parsley, thyme, bay leaf, cloves, peppercorns and mace should be tied together in muslin), lemon juice and stock (previously made hot). Cover jar closely – cook in moderate oven, 150–160°C (300–325°F), Gas 2–3, or the jar may be stood in saucepan of water on stove. About ½ hour before serving, knead the remaining 25 g (1 ounce) of butter and the flour together, stir into stock, add wine.

Make the forcemeat, shape into balls, fry in hot fat. Pile hare on hot dish with the strained gravy and forcemeat balls around. Serve jelly separately. Allow 3–4 hours for cooking. Serves 6–8.
Shropshire

1 hare	12 peppercorns
75 g (3 oz) butter	small piece mace
salt	15 ml (1 tablespoon) lemon juice
1 onion	850 ml (1½ pints) good stock
2 shallots	25 g (1 oz) flour
1 small sprig thyme	1 glass port or claret (150 ml)
parsley	forcemeat balls
1 bay leaf	red- or whitecurrant jelly
4 cloves	

Roast saddle of young hare

Roast only the body of the hare – the neck, legs and head can be jugged or converted into soup. Put the stuffing into the saddle, fold skin over and secure well at the ends. The flesh of the back may either be larded or have slices of fat bacon laid over. Cover with greased paper and roast with dripping 30–40 minutes in hot oven. Baste frequently.

Serve with brown gravy and redcurrant jelly. Serves 3–4.
Cheshire

1 young hare	dripping
savoury stuffing	brown gravy
slices of fat bacon or larding fat	redcurrant jelly

Note for beginners

For larding, a special larding needle is used, threaded with thin strips of fat pork. Strips of fat are threaded through the flesh of the hare at close intervals.

Roast the hare at about 200°C (400°F), Gas 6, or at a lower temperature for a longer time.

A suitable stuffing would be Forcemeat (Veal), see page 142.

Hotpot of rabbit and sausages

Joint, flour and lightly fry the rabbit, also sausages and onions (cut up). Pack all these in a fireproof casserole. Make a gravy in the frying pan with flour, pepper and salt and stock or cold water, boil up and pour over the meat. Put in a few forcemeat balls. Cover with potatoes and cook in oven for about 2 hours, 180°C (350°F), Gas 4. About 20 minutes before serving take off the lid and brown the potatoes. Serves 6.

Northamptonshire and Soke of Peterborough

1 rabbit	pepper and salt
flour	stock or water, about 400 ml
fat for frying	($\frac{3}{4}$ pint)
250 g (8 oz) sausages	a few forcemeat balls
2 onions	1 kg (2 lb) potatoes, cut in pieces

Stewed rabbit

Cut the onion in thin slices and fry in a stewpan. Cut up the rabbit, wash well and dry in a cloth. Mix the flour with pepper and salt and dip in the pieces of rabbit. Fry them with the onion until a nice brown colour. Pour off any surplus fat and add the hot stock or water, carrot and bay leaf. Simmer gently for $1\frac{1}{2}$–2 hours. Mix remainder of flour with cold water and add to the stew, stirring well. Arrange the rabbit in hot dish and pour gravy over. Delicious hot or cold. Serves 4–6.

Cheshire

1 large onion	800 ml ($1\frac{1}{2}$ pint) hot stock or
dripping	water
1 rabbit	1 carrot
40 g ($1\frac{1}{2}$ oz) flour	1 bay leaf
pepper and salt	

Roast venison
Season: Buck, June to September; Doe, October to December

Brush the venison with melted butter and wrap it in greased paper, then in a paste of flour and water. Roast haunch will take 4–5 hours in a slow oven, 160°C (325°F), Gas 3. Serve with accompaniments.
Cumberland

venison joint
melted butter
flour and water paste

brown gravy flavoured with red wine
gooseberry or cranberry sauce
green salad

Venison casserole

Brown the meat in the dripping. Remove it and fry the prepared vegetables and bacon with a pinch of sugar. Remove vegetables. Add a tablespoon of flour to the pan, stir it round and add the stock and wine. Let it thicken. Put the venison in the casserole with the vegetables, seasonings and herbs. Pour the liquid over it. Seal closely and cook in a moderate oven, 190°C (375°F), Gas 5, for 2½ hours. Add the redcurrant jelly just before serving.

   Hare, chicken or beef can be cooked like this. It is a good basic casserole. Serves 6.
Hampshire

1 kg (2 lb) venison haunch
50 g (2 oz) dripping
2 onions
3 carrots
50 g (2 oz) bacon
pinch of sugar
15 ml (1 tablespoon) flour
150 ml (1 gill) stock

150 ml (1 gill) red wine
seasoning
bouquet garni
rosemary
allspice (*not* cake spice)
60 ml (2 tablespoons) redcurrant jelly

6 Supper dishes

Appledore
Sausage

Melt butter in pan and fry onions until tender but not coloured.
Add apples and sliced red pepper, cover pan and cook gently until
apples are just soft. Season to taste.

At the same time fry sausage either in oven or pan. Place sausage in
centre of dish with apple sauce around. Cooking time about ¾ hour.
Serves 3–4.
Cumberland

50 g (2 oz) butter	1 large red pepper (from can)
2 large sliced onions	salt and pepper
450 g (1 lb) cooking apples, sliced	500 g (1 lb) Cumberland sausage

Cumberland sausage

Cut lean and fat into small pieces. Add seasoning. Mix well. Mince

fairly finely and fill into prepared skins. Hang for 24 hours before using.
Cumberland

4½ kg (9 lb) lean pork	75 g (3 oz) salt
1½ kg (3 lb) pork fat	25 g (1 oz) pepper

Bacon and apple skewers
May be eaten cold for picnics or useful hot for barbecues

Trim rind from bacon. Mix grated cheese with yolk of egg and seasoning. Spread on rashers. Roll each rasher round quarter of an apple. Stick skewer through and grill for approximately 10 minutes.
(If eaten at home serve on a bed of savoury rice.)
Hampshire

For each person take:	25–50 g (1–2 oz) grated cheese
2 rashers bacon, back or streaky	salt and pepper
half apple	egg yolk

Bacon casserole

Slice potatoes 6 mm (¼ inch) thick. Slice onion. Arrange alternate layers of potatoes and onion, smeared with chutney and seasoning. Pour over egg and milk, add dabs of butter.
Make rolls from the bacon and place on top of casserole. Cover and bake at 180°C (350°F), Gas 4, for 1¼ hours, the last 15 minutes without lid to brown bacon. Serves 4.
Cumberland

350 g (12 oz) potatoes	½ egg beaten in 150 ml
1 large onion	(¼ pint) milk
30–60 ml (2 tablespoons) chutney	15 g (½ oz) butter
seasoning	225 g (8 oz) shoulder bacon rashers

Broccoli with bacon sauce

Cut broccoli into sprigs, wash well and cook in 300 ml (½ pint) boiling salted water.
Cut chopped bacon with onion and cook gently without browning, add curry powder, pepper and flour, cook for 2 minutes. Use water from broccoli and make up to 300 ml (½ pint) with milk, add to

sauce, gently stirring till thick. Pour over broccoli. Serves 4.
Shropshire

1 medium-sized broccoli

Sauce
50 g (2 oz) bacon, chopped
30 ml (1 tablespoon) onion,
chopped

2½ ml (¼ teaspoon) curry powder
pepper and salt
30 ml (2 level tablespoons) flour
a little milk

Cheese and carrot savoury

Cook carrots till tender, preferably in a steamer or a pressure cooker.
Mash well, add fat, breadcrumbs, cheese and seasoning. Place in a
greased pie-dish and bake at 190°C (375°F), Gas 5, till golden brown,
about 20–30 minutes.

It may be steamed for 1 hour.

Serve with jacket potatoes, gravy and Brussels sprouts. Serves 4–6.
Westmorland

1 kg (2 lb) carrots
40 g (1½ oz) fat
50 g (2 oz) brown breadcrumbs

200 g (8 oz) grated cheese
seasoning, mace and nutmeg

Cheese pancakes

Mix and fry as ordinary pancakes. Makes 8 pancakes.
Gloucestershire

100 g (4 oz) self-raising flour
salt and pepper to taste
1 egg

250 ml (½ pint) milk
100 g (4 oz) finely grated cheese

Cheese pinwheels

Sieve the flour with the salt and mustard. Rub in the lard and
margarine until the mixture resembles breadcrumbs. Add the
cheese, grated coarsely. Add 40 ml (approximately 8 teaspoons)
water to bind. Turn out of bowl and knead very lightly. Roll out into
an oblong approximately 30 × 20 cm (11 × 8 inches).

Spread the sausage meat over the pastry, leaving about 2 cm
(¾ inch) at the top edge. Moisten the edges with water, and roll the
pastry up as for a Swiss roll. Firm the roll. Take a sharp knife and

cut about 12 slices from the roll, round them up and place on a baking tray. Bake in a moderately hot oven about a third of the way from the top at 200°C (400°F), Gas 6, for 20–30 minutes, or until lightly browned.

These are delicious eaten hot with baked beans and grilled tomatoes or cold, served with green salad. Makes 12 pinwheels.
Derbyshire

200 g (8 oz) plain soft flour
salt
5 ml (1 teaspoon) dry mustard
50 g (2 oz) lard

50 g (2 oz) margarine
100 g (4 oz) strong cheese
200–300 g ($\frac{1}{2}$–$\frac{3}{4}$ lb) sausage meat

Cheese savoury

Cut crusts from bread and dice. Place in greased ovenware dish 600-ml (1-pint) size, add cheese. Beat eggs with seasonings, add milk, pour over the bread. Leave to soak $\frac{1}{2}$ hour at least. Sprinkle with a little more cheese. Bake in a moderate oven, 190°C (375°F), Gas 5, for about $\frac{1}{2}$ hour until firm and golden brown.

Can be served alone, or with peas, baked beans or spaghetti in tomato sauce, or a thick onion sauce. Serves 4.
Denbighshire

2 rounds of bread, buttered
75–100 g (3–4 oz) grated cheese
2 eggs

pepper, salt and a little made
  mustard
300 ml ($\frac{1}{2}$ pint) milk
a little more grated cheese

Cheese snack

Cut ordinary cheese sandwiches then fry them in pan till both sides are crisp and brown.
Oxfordshire

Cheese whirls

Use the flour and lard to make short pastry in the usual way. Roll out thinly into a rectangle and spread lightly with butter. Cover with grated cheese and roll up as for a Swiss roll. Cut into slices and

place on a baking sheet. Bake in a hot oven, 220°C (425°F), Gas 7, for 15–20 minutes or until the pastry is lightly browned. Serves 4–6.
Westmorland

200 g (8 oz) plain flour	a little butter
100 g (4 oz) lard	grated cheese (about 150 g)

Chicory and ham in cheese sauce

Grease a casserole, put in the washed heads of chicory, pour over the water to which a few drops of lemon juice have been added, cover with a buttered paper and the lid. Braise the chicory in a moderate oven, 180°C (350°F), Gas 4, for 50–60 minutes until tender.

Drain well, then wrap each in a slice of cooked ham. Arrange neatly in a fireproof dish and coat with the cheese sauce. Reheat in a moderate oven for 15–20 minutes, and serve with crisp toast. Serves 4.
Oxfordshire

8 small heads chicory	*Cheese sauce*
150 ml (¼ pint) water	40 g (1½ oz) butter
few drops lemon juice	40 g (1½ oz) flour
8 thin slices cooked ham (approx 200 g (½ lb))	450 ml (¾ pint) milk
	175 g (6 oz) grated cheese
	pinch salt and cayenne pepper

Country flan

Sieve flour, salt and pepper together in a bowl. Rub in margarine. Stir in the cheese. Add egg yolk and water and mix with a knife to a firm dough. Turn out on to a lightly floured board. Roll out thinly and mould into an 18-cm (7-inch) flan ring, placed on a baking sheet. Bake in a fairly hot oven, 200°C (400°F), Gas 6, for approximately 20 minutes.

Prepare the filling by cutting the bacon into small pieces, fry gently. Skin and chop the tomato. Wash, peel and chop the mushrooms. Beat the eggs in a basin. Add tomato, mushrooms, fried bacon, grated cheese, milk and seasoning. Pour into flan case. Return to middle shelf of oven for 15–20 minutes, until golden brown and set. Garnish with parsley. Eat hot or cold. Serves 4–5.
Northumberland

Cheese pastry	Filling
150 g (6 oz) plain flour	2 rashers bacon
pinch salt	1 tomato
pinch cayenne pepper	50 g (2 oz) mushrooms
75 g (3 oz) margarine	2 eggs
50 g (2 oz) grated cheese	25 g (1 oz) grated cheese
1 egg yolk	15 ml (1 tablespoon) top of milk
15 ml or more (1 tablespoon) cold water	parsley

Country omelette

Quantities for one omelette.

Cut the bacon and potato into small dice, fry and keep hot.
Season.

Thoroughly mix the eggs but do not beat to a froth. Add water and seasoning. Put a large piece of butter in a frying pan and make very hot, then pour in the eggs and stir them quickly round and round. Allow to set, keeping in a round shape. When the mixture begins to set, spread the bacon and potato on top. Serve flat and the top should be moist.

Berkshire

1 slice of fat bacon	10 ml (1 dessertspoon) cold water
1 potato	salt and pepper
2 eggs	a large piece of butter

Note for beginners

The potato and bacon will take about 20 minutes to fry until the potato is tender. It is better to do this in a separate pan from that to be used for cooking the eggs.

Durham woodcock

Melt butter in a saucepan, add the beaten seasoned egg. Stir until thickened. Remove from heat. Add cream and stir. Arrange in shapes on toasted bread. Garnish with trellis pattern of anchovy fillets and capers or olives. Arrange on a hot dish on a plain doily and garnish with sprigs of parsley. Serves 2.

Durham

40 g (1½ oz) butter
2 eggs
seasoning
10 ml (1 dessertspoon) cream

toasted bread
anchovy fillets
capers or olives
sprigs of parsley

Egg savoury

Cut for each person a thick piece of bread (this should be at least
2½ cm or 1 inch thick). Toast one side. On the untoasted side, scoop
out a hole and break into that an egg. Cover the egg and bread with
grated cheese and brown under grill.
Herefordshire

thick pieces of bread
eggs

grated cheese

Farm cheese patties
A Kirkcudbright recipe at least 155 years old

Line 18–24 patty tins with pastry. Grate cheese and breadcrumbs,
beat eggs, oil the butter. Mix all together, and put a little into each
patty tin. Bake at 200°C (400°F), Gas 6, for 15 minutes.
   This can be made in a large tin, 20 cm (8 inches), and baked about
25 minutes. A touch of garlic or grated onion can be added.
Northumberland

any type of pastry
200 g (8 oz) mild cheese
2 eggs
30 ml (1 tablespoon) breadcrumbs
15 g (½ oz) butter

75 ml (¼ gill) thick cream or
   evaporated milk
salt, pepper, and a few grains
   cayenne
garlic or grated onion (optional)

Fitchett pie

Make an ordinary plate pie with short pastry and for filling put in a
layer of grated apple, then a layer of grated cheese and finally a layer
of grated onion. If necessary repeat all three layers. It makes a
delicious supper dish.
Cheshire

short pastry
grated apples

grated cheese
grated onion

Gruyère surprise

Line a sandwich tin or flat plate with rough puff pastry. Shave Gruyère cheese all over, as much as you can spare. Scatter a very little shaved butter over and seasoning too, if liked. A few drops of white wine is also added as a tasty extra. Cover with a thin layer of pastry. Seal edges and lightly cut either sections or a pattern on top. Brush over with beaten egg or milk and bake in a hot oven until golden brown, 230°C (450°F), Gas 8, for 15–20 minutes.
Berkshire

This was served to us in a tiny little hotel in the wilds of central France. It makes a tasty luxury supper dish.

rough puff pastry	salt and pepper
Gruyère cheese	few drops white wine
butter	beaten egg or milk for brushing

Italian risotto

Fry the onion in the butter, add the rice and stir carefully over a gentle heat. Season to taste and add the stock by degrees. Cover and cook slowly, stirring frequently to prevent burning. When the rice is soft and all the liquid absorbed remove from the heat and add the grated cheese. Reheat and serve on a hot dish, accompanied if liked by grilled tomatoes or mushrooms, or a green salad. Cooking time about ½ hour. Serves 2–3.
Westmorland

1 onion, chopped finely	600 ml (1 pint) stock or 1 meat cube
25 g (1 oz) butter	dissolved in 600 ml hot water
175 g (6 oz) Patna rice	50 g (2 oz) grated cheese
salt and pepper	

Leek and egg bake

Put eggs into pan of cold water, bring to boil and boil 10 minutes. Wash leek well and cut into 2½-cm (1-inch) lengths. Cook in salted boiling water for 5 minutes. Make a roux sauce and take off the heat and beat in the grated cheese, season with salt and pepper. Shell the hardboiled eggs; drain the leeks and divide between two individual fireproof dishes. Put an egg on top of each and coat them with cheese sauce. Sprinkle the rest of the cheese on top and brown surface quickly under the grill. Serves 2.

Yorkshire

2 eggs	150 ml ($\frac{1}{4}$ pint) milk
1 leek	25 g (1 oz) grated cheese
15 g ($\frac{1}{2}$ oz) margarine	salt and pepper
15 ml (1 level tablespoon) plain flour	little extra grated cheese

Leek pasty
Traditional recipe

Wash the leeks and cut them into $2\frac{1}{2}$- or 5-cm (1- or 2-inch) pieces. Pour boiling water over them and leave for 5 minutes. Drain off water.

Make shortcrust pastry. Grease a Swiss roll tin, then line with pastry.

Cut the ham into small pieces and put a layer into the pastry and add the leeks and beaten eggs. Add seasonings. Cover with pastry, sealing the edges well. Brush with a little milk and egg. Put in a hot oven, 220°C (425°F), Gas 7, for 20 minutes, then reduce heat to 180°C (350°F), Gas 4, but allow plenty of time to cook through, about 40 minutes total. Serves 6.

Northumberland

Short pastry	*Filling*
350 g (12 oz) flour	500 g (1 lb) leeks
5 ml (1 teaspoon) salt	250 g (8 oz) ham or bacon
10 ml (1 teaspoon) baking powder	2 eggs beaten up with 60 ml
175 g (6 oz) lard or $\frac{1}{2}$ lard and $\frac{1}{2}$ margarine	(4 tablespoons) milk
	salt and pepper to taste

Note for beginners

Weigh the leeks after trimming. Allow time for them to cool after blanching and before putting them in the pastry.

Pan Haggerty
Traditional recipe

Cut vegetables into very thin slices and dry in a cloth. Heat dripping in a heavy frying pan, and put vegetables and cheese in the pan in layers. Season each layer. Fry gently until cooked, about 45 minutes, then brown under grill. Serves 4.

Northumberland

225 g (8 oz) onions
450 g (1 lb) potatoes
25 g (1 tablespoon) dripping

100 g (4 oz) grated cheese
pepper and salt

Pizza

Cream yeast with a little water; sieve flour and salt. Add yeast, milk and beaten egg to the flour, blend in softened but not melted butter, beat well with the hand until mixture comes away from the fingers. Cover with a cloth. Leave to prove for 30 minutes in a warm place. Grease a large baking tray. Pat out dough with hands to 23 cm (9 inch) round.

To prepare the filling melt fat, fry chopped onion until tender and golden. Add skinned tomatoes with 2 tablespoons water, purée, sugar, seasoning, bay leaf, oregano. Simmer 10–15 minutes until thick. Cool.

Cover dough to within 1 cm ($\frac{1}{2}$ inch) of edge with filling. Decorate with anchovies thinly sliced, grated cheese and olives. Prove in a warm place for 15 minutes.

Place in centre of oven, 220–230°C (425–450°F), Gas 7–8, for 25–30 minutes. Serve hot or cold. Serves 6.

Lincolnshire

For the dough
15 g ($\frac{1}{2}$ oz) yeast
150 ml ($\frac{1}{4}$ pint) lukewarm water
250 g (8 oz) plain flour
5 ml (1 teaspoon) salt
25 g (1 oz) butter or margarine
1 small egg

Filling
15 g ($\frac{1}{2}$ oz) vegetable cooking fat
  or 1 tablespoon oil

1 small onion
250 g (8 oz) tomatoes
75 g ($2\frac{1}{2}$ oz) tomato purée
5 ml (1 teaspoon) sugar
seasoning
1 bay leaf
pinch of oregano
small tin anchovy fillets (56 g)
25 g (1 oz) cheese
4–6 olives

Note for beginners

Allow at least 1$\frac{1}{2}$ hours for making the pizza from start to finish. The filling can be prepared in advance of making the dough if that is more convenient.

Risotto

Boil rice.

Chop onion and fry lightly in dripping. If using bacon cut into small pieces and fry with onion.

Peel tomatoes, quarter and add to onion and bacon. Cook gently, then add cooked rice, chopped hardboiled eggs and chopped ham, if used instead of bacon. Season. Heat gently till hot through, cover with chopped parsley and serve. Serves 4.
Cumberland

100 g (4 oz) long grain rice	4 tomatoes
1 medium-sized onion	2 hardboiled eggs
dripping	seasoning
100 g (4 oz) bacon or cooked ham	chopped parsley

Sardine pie

Drain off as much as possible of the oil from the sardines. Dip each sardine in flour mixed with the curry powder. Arrange on fireproof plate, about 20-cm (8-inch) size, tails to centre. Cover with pastry and cook in a hot oven until well browned, 230°C (450°F), Gas 8, about 15–20 minutes. Serves 4.
Berkshire

short pastry (one part fat to two parts self-raising flour)	10–20 ml (2 teaspoons) curry powder
2 tins sardines (240 g)	10–20 ml (2 teaspoons) flour

Sardine snack

Remove sardines carefully from the tin so that they remain whole and drain off the oil.

Remove the tails from the fish and then dip each sardine in the melted margarine and then in the cheese.

Place one fish on each finger of fried bread. Brown under the grill. Garnish with paprika and chopped parsley in alternate lines.
Cumberland

1 tin sardines (120 g)
25 g (1 oz) melted margarine
25 g (1 oz) grated cheese

fingers of bread fried in the
  sardine oil
paprika pepper
chopped parsley

Sausage rolls

These are universal favourites, but the following hints may help:
1 If you want your sausage rolls to gain a reputation and to be a little different, try mincing an onion and adding to the sausage meat.
2 They are much quicker to make if you roll the sausage meat into long rolls and wrap it in equally long strips of pastry, and then cut to size required.
3 When making quantities for the Village Do it is a good idea to make the long rolls beforehand and leave them in the fridge or a cool place and cook at the last minute. This makes for fresher rolls, and less rush.
4 Short pastry rolls are easier to handle than the richer pastries.
5 See that your sausage rolls really are *sausage* rolls and not mostly pastry!
Hampshire

Savoury beans
Traditional recipe

Steep beans overnight in boiling water, then parboil for about an hour. Drain.

Lightly fry ham and cut in small pieces.

Chop onion and tomato.

Place all in a casserole with 500 ml (one pint) of stock or water. Season to taste and cook for 1 hour at 180–190°C (350–375°F), Gas 4–5, or until the beans are tender. Ten minutes before serving add golden syrup. Serve hot.

This is a real Durham supper dish and is delicious served with toast. Serves 4.
Durham

225 g (8 oz) butter beans
boiling water
2 rashers ham
1 large onion
2 tomatoes

500 ml (1 pint) water or stock
salt and pepper
20 ml (2 dessertspoons) golden
  syrup

Supper savoury

Put the cheese on the bread, then the seasonings. On the cheese place slices of tomato, then a slice of bacon. Place on a hot baking tin and bake in a hot oven until the bacon is crisp, 200°C (400°F), Gas 6, for about 15–20 minutes.

Herefordshire

For each person:
a thick slice of buttered bread
a thin slice of cheese

salt, mustard and a dash of
 Worcestershire sauce
sliced tomato
a slice of rather fat bacon

Swiss eggs

Grease a gratin dish, cover bottom with cream or top of the milk, and a little grated cheese. Break in as many eggs as required, sprinkle over salt and pepper to taste, and a little more cream or top of milk, and grated cheese. Bake in oven, 180°C (350°F), Gas 4, until set, about 15 minutes.

Gloucestershire

fat
cream or top of milk
grated cheese

eggs
salt and pepper

Tomato and mushroom flan

Line an 18-cm (7-inch) plate or sandwich tin with pastry and bake blind.

Wash and peel mushrooms and skin tomatoes. Put in a small pan and cook in margarine for about 10 minutes, remove mushrooms and mix in flour with remaining margarine and cook 2 minutes. Add 3 tablespoons water and a meat cube and cook till it thickens, add more water if needed to thin the sauce.

Arrange mushrooms and tomatoes over cooked pastry, season and sprinkle with grated cheese. Pour sauce over and bake in moderate oven, 180°C (350°F), Gas 4, for 15 minutes. Serves 4.

Somerset

4 oz rough puff pastry (100 g flour)
100 g (4 oz) mushrooms
2 tomatoes
25 g (1 oz) margarine

10 ml (1 teaspoon) flour
salt and pepper
meat cube
25 g (1 oz) cheese

Tatie stovies

Melt dripping in large stew pan. Add sliced potatoes, meat and onion in layers with seasoning. Almost cover contents of pan with stock or water. Cook slowly until potatoes are soft and floury and moisture almost absorbed, $\frac{1}{2}$–$\frac{3}{4}$ hour. Serves 4.
Northumberland

Diced carrot and/or turnip can be added if desired. A suet crust can also be cooked on top of the mixture.

15 g (1 level tablespoon) meat
  dripping (from roast beef)
4–6 large potatoes
100 g (4 oz) meat (preferably cold
  roast beef in small pieces)
1 large onion

salt and pepper to taste
stock or water
diced carrots and/or turnips
  (optional)
suet crust (optional)

The Cornish pasty

The Cornish pasty is, and has been since time immemorial, the staple dish of the county, and in giving various recipes for making it, it may be noted that the method does not vary, but the nature of the pasty varies according to the filling, or inside.

Therefore, the general method of making has been given, and a list of various kinds of pasties afterwards.

It is said that the Devil has never crossed the Tamar into Cornwall, on account of the well-known habit of Cornishwomen of putting everything into a pasty, and that he was not sufficiently courageous to risk such a fate! However that may be, the Cornish pasty, in its various forms, is a delectable dainty and deservedly world-famous.

When the pasties are being made, each member of the family has his or hers marked at one corner with the initial of the prospective owner. In this way each person's tastes can be catered for.

The true Cornish way to eat a pasty is to hold it in the hand, and begin to bite it from the opposite end to the initial, so that should any of it be uneaten, it may be consumed later by the rightful owner. And woe betide anyone who takes another person's 'corner'!

Pasty

Any good pastry may be used, but it should not be too flaky nor too rich. A very useful pastry is:
500 g (1 lb) flour
250 g (8 oz) lard and suet
5 ml ($\frac{1}{2}$ teaspoon) salt
mix with water

When pastry is made, roll out about 6 mm ($\frac{1}{4}$ inch) thick, and cut into rounds with a plate to the size desired.

Lay the rounds on the pastry board with half of the round over the rolling pin and put in the fillings, damp the edges lightly and fold over into a semi-circle. Shape the pasty nicely and 'crimp' the extreme edges where it is joined between the finger and thumb. Cut a slit in the centre of the pasty, lay on a baking sheet and bake in a quick oven, so that it keeps its shape.

Apple pasty

Peel apples, slice thinly, and lightly sprinkle with brown sugar. In summertime, blackberries are usually mixed with the apple.

Chicken pasty

Chicken cut up in small pieces.

Date pasty

Stone dates and fill in the usual way.

Eggy pasty

Bacon cut in dice, parsley and one or two eggs, according to size of pasty required.

Jam pasty

These are usually made smaller than a savoury pasty, and any kind of jam may be used.

Mackerel pasty

Allow one or two mackerel to each pasty, and clean and boil them in the usual way. Then remove skin and bones, and lay on pastry; fill up with washed parsley, and add pepper and salt. Finish as above.

Meat and potato pasty

Always use fresh steak, potatoes cut small, salt and pepper, flavoured with onion.

Parsley pasty

Parsley and lamb or mutton.

Pork pasty

Fresh pork, and potatoes, flavoured with onion, sage or thyme.

Rabbitty pasty

Use fleshy part of rabbit cut the same as meat, fairly small.

Sour sauce pasty

Gather a quantity of sour sauce (sorrel) leaves. Shrink them by pouring boiling water over and use the leaves in a pasty. Serve with sugar and cream.

Windy pasty

Take the last bit of pastry left over from making pasties, roll it into a round, fold over and crimp as for ordinary pasty. Bake in oven and when done (whilst still hot) open out flat and fill each side with jam. It may be eaten hot or cold.
Cornwall

Note for beginners

500 g (1 lb) flour makes enough pastry for 8 small pasties. For a meat filling allow 500–750 g (1–1½ lb) meat. Cook them at 200–225°C (400–425°F), Gas 6–7, for 30–40 minutes.

Decker sandwiches

These substantial sandwiches, which are made with 3–4 slices of bread and 2–3 different fillings, are very suitable for lunch or supper snacks. To make them, spread one piece of bread and butter with one of the fillings, and cover with a second slice of bread, buttered side down. Butter the top of the piece, spread with the second filling and cover with a slice of bread. Press together.

Good combinations for these sandwiches are:

Ham or bacon with seasoned scrambled egg.
Ham, green salad and sliced hardboiled egg.
Flaked salmon or haddock, moistened with a little mayonnaise, with thin slices of cucumber, seasoned with salt and pepper.
Grilled ham or bacon with sliced sausage, spread with mustard.
Cream cheese with chopped celery, and sliced chopped ham or meat loaf.
Yorkshire

Open sandwiches

The base of these sandwiches is usually brown, rye or white bread; this is thickly buttered, and on it the fillings and garnishes are arranged to give an attractive appearance, as well as an appetizing flavour. The sandwiches may be either made immediately before serving, or the guests may make up their own sandwiches, choosing from amongst a selection of attractively displayed ingredients. Set out a variety of breads and butter, and try to offer some fillings from each of the following groups:

Anchovy fillets
Sliced smoked salmon
Smoked eel
Sardines
Prawns and shrimps

A variety of cheeses
Hardboiled eggs
Scrambled eggs

Cold roast meats
Sliced ham and tongue
Cooked bacon rashers
Salami
Liver sausage
Liver pâté

Sliced cucumber
Sliced tomato
Onion rings
Lettuce
Watercress
Fried apple
Russian salad

Garnishes Orange and lemon slices. Gherkin fans. Sliced pickled beetroot. Radish roses. Celery curls. Red or green pepper rings.
Yorkshire

Toasted sandwiches

Toasted sandwiches are very good. Almost any sandwiches, stale or fresh, can be used. Cheese, egg, sardine, ham are particularly good, but not cucumber. Toast under grill or in electric toaster (flatten well first) and serve at once.
Oxfordshire

Toasted sandwiches

Dutchie mushroom toasties
Toast the bread on one side. Butter other side, cover with sliced Gouda cheese and grill until it melts. Cover with fried sliced mushrooms, season and top with another slice of toast.

Mushroom club sandwich
Toast the bread on one side. Turn and cover with streaky bacon and grill till crisp. Cover with raw sliced mushrooms marinated in lemon juice. Cover with watercress and spread with mayonnaise. Top with second slice of toast.

Buttered shrimps and mushroom toasties
Toast the bread on both sides. Spread one side with buttered shrimps and grill till butter melts. Sprinkle with lemon juice and cover with grilled mushrooms and remaining slice of toast.
Yorkshire

Sandwich fillings

Savoury
1 Chicken chopped and mixed with chopped fried bacon and moistened with mayonnaise.
2 Cream cheese mixed with watercress or chopped chives, chutney, chopped chicken or ham, chopped olives or nuts or both.
3 Mushrooms chopped, dredged with flour, sautéd in butter and moistened with top of milk.
4 Hardboiled egg chopped and mixed with tomato and Worcestershire sauce and chopped parsley.

Sweet

1 Banana mashed with lemon juice, a few dates and honey.
2 Mint and raisins, equal quantities minced and moistened with water.
3 Dates chopped and moistened with lemon juice.
4 Orange marmalade – especially good with nut breads.

Sandwich hint

To cut a tidy sandwich use a very sharp knife and cut from the centre of the pile of sandwiches outward in each direction, having removed the crusts first.
Oxfordshire

Anchovy spread

Melt butter over slow heat, add anchovy essence and stir well, add well-beaten egg. Stir over slow heat until the mixture thickens. Will keep two weeks.
   Delicious in sandwiches, or on toast or crumpets.
Oxfordshire

25 g (1 oz) butter   1 egg
15 ml (1 tablespoon) anchovy
  essence

Sardine spread

Mash together sardines and scrambled egg – adding seasoning to taste.
Oxfordshire

1 scrambled egg   seasoning
1 tin sardines (120 g)

Small savouries for picnic or TV evenings

Mix as for pastry. Roll out to 3 mm ($\frac{1}{8}$ inch) and cut into circles for patty tins and small fancy biscuit shapes. Bake in hot oven, 200°C (400°F), Gas 6, for 15 minutes or until lightly browned.

Fillings for cases
Flaked white or smoked fish bound with a light sauce.
  Chopped shellfish in a light sauce.
  Any kind of diced cooked or canned meat with a little chutney.
  Cooked diced vegetables.
  A little minced curry (think of the scope from left-overs).

Spreads for fancy shaped cheese biscuits
Anchovy paste with a little flaked fish – garnish with parsley.
  Finely chopped egg yolk, chutney and creamed butter.
  Chopped sardine mashed with a little cheese, flavoured with
lemon juice.
  Shrimps pounded in parsley sauce, garnish with parsley and one
shrimp.
  Cream cheese sprinkled with finely chopped mint.
  Diced cold chicken in mayonnaise, garnish with cress.
  Minced fried mushrooms in egg sauce, garnish with parsley.
  Finely chopped celery and cream cheese with creamed cayenne
butter.
Cumberland

Cheese pastry	75 g (3 oz) margarine
100 g (4 oz) plain flour	75 g (3 oz) grated cheese
pinch cayenne	1 yolk of egg
salt and pepper	15 ml (1 tablespoon) milk

Cheese butterflies

Roll out pastry 3-mm (⅛-inch) thick and cut into rounds. Make an
incision right across half the rounds (these form wings). Bake 10
minutes in moderately hot oven, 190°C (375°F), Gas 5.
  Mix filling. Spread biscuits with mixture. Place halves of cut
biscuits, standing up to form wings.
Cumberland

½ cheese pastry recipe above	chopped parsley
	or
Filling	Primula cheese spread
25 g (1 oz) margarine	salt and papper
15 g (½ oz) grated cheese	green colouring if liked
pinch cayenne	

7 Vegetables & Salads

Cooking roots

It is easy to overcook these and to send them sodden to table.
Intelligent cooks dish them at the right moment, send them to table
hot, and either dry, or finished and glazed in a little butter, with the
flavour in the dish instead of in the stock left in the saucepan.
West Kent

Braising root vegetables

Fry them in dripping until lightly browned, then add enough stock
to half cover the vegetables, and a little seasoning. Cover with a lid
and cook gently till the vegetables are tender. Lift them out on to a
hot dish and continue to heat the liquid until it is reduced and of a
glazing consistency. Pour it over the vegetables and garnish with
parsley.
Cheshire

Purée of vegetables

Prepare the vegetables. Cook in boiling salted water until tender.

Strain and pass through a fine wire sieve. Return to a clean saucepan and add butter or margarine. Dry over a gentle heat, shaking well.

Place on a hot dish, arranging neatly and smoothly to fit the shape of the dish.

Berkshire

potatoes, root vegetables or a mixture	25 g (1 oz) butter or margarine per 450 g (1 lb) of purée

Vegetable curry

Fry dripping, onion, curry powder and apple for 10 minutes without burning, add flour, some salt and the liquid, stir till boiling.

Put a mixture of cooked or raw vegetables into a casserole, add the sauce and cook in a moderate oven for 1–2 hours, 180°C (350°F), Gas 4.

Add a little lemon juice and a good tablespoonful sweet chutney before serving. Serve with boiled rice. Serves 4.

Leicestershire and Rutland

Sauce	Vegetables
25 g (1 oz) dripping	¾–1 kg (1½–2 lb) vegetables. A
1 sliced onion	mixture of cooked or raw
20 ml (1 dessertspoon) curry powder	vegetables including a small tin of baked beans if liked
1 chopped apple	a little lemon juice
25 g (1 oz) flour	a good tablespoon sweet chutney
salt	boiled rice
400 ml (¾ pint) vegetable stock or milk and water	

Globe artichokes

A great delicacy which you can grow yourself. 1 per person.

Pick them before they turn into handsome flowers. There are three parts to an artichoke; the leaves, the bottom of which you eat; the firm bottom part, which you eat; and the choke which obviously you do not eat.

To prepare

Cut off the stalk part. Strip off the outer layer or two of coarse leaves. Cut off just the tips of all the leaves with scissors. Soak the artichokes upside down in salted water. All sorts of living creatures then drop out.

To cook
Put them heads down in boiling salted water with some lemon juice in it for about 20–25 minutes. Drain.

To serve hot
Stand the artichoke up and remove the choke. This is easily done with a spoon. Serve on a hot dish with melted butter sauce or Hollandaise.

Note: You pull off the leaves with your fingers and rather messily suck the succulent bit at the bottom. Then you eat the bottom or 'fond' with a knife and fork.
Hampshire

Jerusalem artichokes

Artichokes can be treated like potatoes and boiled in their skins. A sharp cut through the outer layer and the tough part can be pulled away and the vegetable sent to table in the perfection of flavour.
   They are good cut up raw and fried as chips.
West Kent

Asparagus

Scrape white end, tie in bundles. Cook in salted water for 20 minutes. Serve with melted butter.
Gloucestershire

Aubergines
Egg plant

Remove hard stalk and bake in a casserole with a little milk and margarine for about 30 minutes.
Gloucestershire

Broad beans I

If picked very young, both pods and beans can be used. Cook in salted water for approximately 10 minutes.
Gloucestershire

S–DJC–C

Broad beans 2

Gather while quite young. Shell and boil rapidly in a minimum of
salted water until the inner shells begin to crack, about 25 minutes.
Serve with parsley sauce.
Cumberland

Canadian treacle beans

Soak beans overnight, and then simmer gently until cooked
($1\frac{1}{2}$–2 hours).

Cook tomatoes and rub through a sieve, add treacle and fat and
heat together, adding required amount of seasoning.

Strain beans, place in fireproof dish and pour over tomato mixture.
Cover and bake in moderate oven, 190°C (375°F), Gas 5, for
$\frac{3}{4}$–1 hour.

Serve with jacket potatoes and cauliflower. Serves 4.
Westmorland

225 g (8 oz) butter beans	25 g (1 oz) fat
225 g (8 oz) fresh tomatoes or	salt and pepper to taste
170 g (6 oz) tinned tomatoes	jacket potatoes
25 g (1 dessertspoon) black treacle	cauliflower

French and scarlet runner beans

Gather while very young. Wash, remove the stalks and any strings
which come away. Cut if desired, or cook whole. Boil rapidly until
tender. Toss with butter and chopped parsley.
Cumberland

Guernsey bean jar

Soak beans overnight, boil till tender, strain off water. Place all
ingredients in stone jar or earthenware dish, add stock, cover down.
Bake well in slow oven, 120°C (250°F), Gas $\frac{1}{2}$, for 4–5 hours.
Guernsey

500 g (1 lb) small dried beans	parsley and salt to taste
1 pig's trotter or piece of shin of beef	600 ml (1 pint) slightly thickened stock
1 onion	

Small beans like haricot or small red beans usually take about 1 hour to boil until tender.

Beetroot

Beet is very seldom made the most of. Tiny beet look very smart when cooked and served in small moulds in a lemon- or tarragon-flavoured aspic.

Sliced raw beet, just covered with cold water, with a dessertspoon of butter, and boiled furiously for about 10 minutes, makes a good hot vegetable with beef.

A hint to prevent bleeding
Dipping broken beetroot into dry flour before putting into the saucepan to boil will prevent bleeding and retain the colour.
West Kent

Baked beetroot

Wash the beetroot. Wrap in greased paper or foil. Place on a baking tray and put into the middle of a moderate oven, 180°C (350°F), Gas 4. The cooking time varies, according to the size and the age of the beetroot, from 1 to 3 hours. To test for readiness, remove the greased paper and press the beetroot with the fingers, when the skin should come away easily. Baked beetroot may be served as for boiled beetroot.
Shropshire

Beetroot
Hot

Take even-sized small beet. Wash and boil quickly until cooked. Skin whilst hot, put into a serving dish and cover with either a thin parsley sauce or oil and vinegar to which a little sugar has been added.
Shropshire

To cook beetroot
Devon style

Wash and peel beetroot – RAW. Slice or cut into dice. Place in saucepan and just cover with water; add a little salt. Simmer until soft (about 20–30 minutes, according to age of beet).

Remove beet from juice with perforated spoon. To the hot juice add vinegar (about 3 tablespoons) and sugar to taste. Pour the juice back over the beet and allow to cool.

Devon

Polish beetroot

Grate the beetroot. Melt the fat in a strong pan. First fry the onion, then add the beetroot, cover the pan and allow the beetroot to cook gently, shaking the pan occasionally to prevent sticking. If necessary, the vinegar may be added at this stage. Meanwhile, boil the potatoes. When both the vegetables are cooked, beat the potatoes with the beetroot. Add the seasoning and apple. Serve hot with grated cheese or grilled sausages and bacon, or cold, spoonfuls being wrapped in lettuce leaves. Serves 6–8.

Berkshire

500 g (1 lb) raw beetroot	500 g (1 lb) peeled potatoes
40 g (1½ oz) fat	seasoning
1 chopped onion	1 grated apple or 30 ml
30 ml or more (2 tablespoons)	(1 tablespoon) apple chutney
vinegar, spiced if liked	

Cabbage
To cook

Shred cabbage finely, wash thoroughly and place in saucepan without drying. Add seasoning and fat, but no extra water. Simmer gently for about 15 minutes with the lid on; strain, make a sauce with the liquor and pour over the shreds. If liked, add pepper and a little grated nutmeg.

It can also be served with a little tomato sauce round the base and decorated with croûtons of fried bread or toast.

West Kent

savoy or 'drum head' cabbage	*Optional*
pepper and salt	tomato sauce
knob of butter or margarine	croûtons of fried bread
grated nutmeg	

Bavarian cabbage

Wash and quarter the cabbage and shred it finely lengthwise. Chop the onion finely, chop the apple. Melt butter in a thick saucepan, and fry the onion lightly. Add the cabbage, chopped apple, salt, pepper, sugar, stock and caraway seeds. Cover pan tightly and simmer very gently for 1 hour.

Sprinkle in the flour and stir. Add vinegar, stir and bring to the boil. Serves 6–8.

Gloucestershire

1 large red cabbage
1 onion
1 cooking apple
75 g (3 oz) butter
salt and pepper

10 ml (1 dessertspoon) sugar
150 ml (¼ pint) stock or water
a few caraway seeds
30 ml (1 tablespoon) flour
75 ml (⅛ pint) vinegar

Belgian carrots

Melt dripping in a saucepan. Put in carrots, pepper and salt. Sprinkle flour on top and just cover with boiling water. Cook over moderate heat for about 20 minutes or until tender. When cooking old carrots add a teaspoon of sugar. Garnish with chopped parsley. Serves 4–5.

Shropshire

25 g (1 oz) dripping
350 g (1 lb) diced carrots
pepper and salt
15 ml (1 level tablespoon) flour

5 ml (1 teaspoon) sugar for old
  carrots
chopped parsley

Carrots Vichy

Wash and scrape carrots. Put into a saucepan with butter, sugar and seasoning. Just cover with cold water and cook quickly until all the water is evaporated and the carrots are covered with the butter. Pile into a hot dish, sprinkle with parsley and serve. Serves 6–8.

Shropshire

1 kg (2 lb) young carrots
50 g (2 oz) butter
10 ml (1 teaspoon) sugar

seasoning
chopped parsley

Glazed carrots with mint

Blanch the carrots in boiling salted water for 6–7 minutes. Strain and put them in a heavy pan with the butter; after 5 minutes' gentle cooking, add the sugar; simmer gently. When the carrots are tender, season with salt and pepper and stir in the mint.

Thinly shredded older carrots may be used in the same way. Serves 4.

Berkshire

500 g (1 lb) small new carrots
50 g (2 oz) butter
15 ml (1 tablespoon) sugar

salt and ground black pepper
30 ml (1 tablespoon) fresh, chopped mint

Celeriac
Baked

Peel the celeriac, cutting away hard parts, slice thickly and cook in a little water till tender with a pinch of salt. Drain and place in an ovenproof dish with the milk, butter, cheese, pepper and salt. Sprinkle with breadcrumbs and bake 20 minutes at about 190°C (375°F), Gas 5. Serves 3.

West Kent

1 root of celeriac
salt and pepper
15 ml (1 tablespoon) milk

25 g (1 oz) butter
30 ml (1 tablespoon) grated cheese
breadcrumbs

Celery au gratin

Cut the celery into thin slices, put in the saucepan with the water, butter, lemon juice and salt. Bring to the boil and cook gently for 35 minutes with lid on.

Drain the celery, keeping the liquor. Put celery in an ovenproof dish and keep hot, make the sauce, pour over and sprinkle on top the breadcrumbs and cheese, and brown under the grill. Serves 4.

Leicestershire and Rutland

450 g (1 lb) celery, prepared
45 ml (3 tablespoons) water
25 g (1 oz) butter
squeeze lemon juice
salt and pepper
25 g (1 oz) grated cheese
some breadcrumbs

Sauce
25 g (1 oz) butter
25 g (1 oz) flour
300 ml ($\frac{1}{2}$ pint) milk and vegetable liquor

Chestnuts and Brussels sprouts

Peel, blanch and stew the chestnuts in stock very gently. Cook sprouts quickly in a little boiling water and drain well. Melt a large lump of butter in a stew pan and toss sprouts in this until they are thoroughly mixed in the butter. Drain chestnuts and pile them in the centre of a dish and arrange sprouts round them.
Westmorland

500 g (1 lb) chestnuts	500 g (1 lb) Brussels sprouts
well-flavoured stock	a large lump of butter

Braised chicory

Wash and separate chicory. Lightly butter a fireproof dish. Put in chicory, other ingredients and remainder of butter. Cover closely and bake in a moderate oven, 180°C (350°F), Gas 4, for 30–40 minutes.
   Celery or sea-kale can be cooked by the same method.
Shropshire

250 g (8 oz) chicory	a few drops of lemon juice
25 g (1 oz) butter	pepper
salt	a little white stock or water

Courgettes
Tiny young marrows will do

Courgettes are easy to grow and the more you pick the more will come along.

Wash and trim the ends of the courgettes. Cook in boiling salted water for 2–3 minutes. Drain and put in a fireproof dish. Melt the butter and lemon juice in a pan and pour over the courgettes. Sprinkle with herbs and a twist or two of the black pepper mill.
   Cook at 160°C (325°F), Gas 3, for 30–35 minutes. Serves 4.
Hampshire

500 g (1 lb) courgettes	30–50 ml (2 or 3 tablespoons)
50–75 g (2–3 oz) butter	mixed herbs, say, chives, basil
5 ml (1 teaspoon) lemon juice	and parsley
	black pepper

Cucumbers
To cook

Slice them thickly; add pepper and salt, and some thinly sliced
onions, a little stock and a nut of butter. Simmer slowly, and thicken
with a little flour and grated nutmeg.

Another way – fry them with sliced onions till brown in a little
butter, cover with a little good gravy and simmer till tender for
about 20 minutes.
West Kent

Leeks
To clean

Leeks are not difficult to free from grit if they are placed green ends
down in a deep jug full of water. Most of the sand and earth then
falls out, and after they have been split, they are cleaned very
quickly. (This plan works well with dirty celery.)
West Kent

Leeks à la Greque

Trim the leeks carefully, removing the outer tough leaves. Slit the
top into a sort of fringe and wash very well under a running tap.
They are great vegetables for having little bits of sand and grit
hidden in their leaves. Get it all washed out.

Cut the leeks into 2½-cm (1-inch) slices. Put into a saucepan with
the water, oil, tomato purée and sugar. Season with salt and freshly
ground black pepper, cook for 4 minutes with the lid on. Add the
rice, cook for another 5–10 minutes. The liquid should be almost
absorbed by the rice, but the rice should not be soft and mushy.
Leave in the pan with the lid off for another 4 minutes. Add lemon
juice. Taste and check the seasoning. Serve chilled, with the olives
and lemon slices on the top. Serves 4.
Hampshire

3 or 4 medium leeks	salt and freshly ground black
300 ml (½ pint) water	pepper
150 ml (¼ pint) olive oil	50 g (2 oz) long grain rice
30 ml (1 tablespoon) tomato purée	lemon juice and lemon slices
2 or 3 sugar knobs	12 black olives

Stewed leeks

Wash, trim and stew the leeks until tender in just enough milk and water to cover them. Drain the leeks thoroughly and make up the liquid to 300 ml (a full ½ pint). Melt the margarine, add the flour and stir for a minute until well blended. Draw the pan from the heat and add the liquid gradually, beating well to remove lumps. Return the pan to the heat, add seasoning and cook for a minute or two. Add the beaten yolk of egg to the sauce and pour the whole over the leeks. Serve very hot with the crisp fried rashers of bacon as garnish. Serves 4.
Oxfordshire

8 leeks	pepper and salt
milk and water	1 yolk of egg
25 g (1 oz) margarine	small rashers of bacon
25 g (1 oz) flour	

Beurre noisette

For an old marrow cooked in the usual way.

Melt the butter, add the other ingredients. Combine with a spoon for a few seconds and pour while boiling over the cooked marrow. Serves 4.
Hampshire

50 g (2 oz) butter	30 ml (2 tablespoons) chopped
30 ml (2 tablespoons) herb vinegar	fresh herbs
	pepper and salt

Easy cheesy marrow

Cut marrow unpeeled in half, scoop out centre and pile up with crumbled cheese. Put in fireproof dish (no need to grease or add water). Scatter over browned breadcrumbs. Bake in a fairly hot oven, 190°C (375°F), Gas 5, about 1 hour. Serves 4.
Westmorland

1 small marrow, young enough for seeds to be barely formed inside	200 g (8 oz) moist crumbled Lancashire or Cheshire cheese browned breadcrumbs

Stewed marrow

Peel the marrow and onion. Cut the marrow into small thick squares, remove seeds. Chop the onion finely. Put the fat and pepper and salt into a saucepan, when melted add the onion. Shake over the fire, add the marrow and let it cook until it pulps, stirring occasionally to prevent burning.

Arrange in a vegetable dish and serve hot. Serves 4.
Leicestershire and Rutland

1 small marrow	25 g (1 oz) butter or margarine
1 small onion	pepper and salt

Vegetable marrow Hongroise

Peel marrow, cut in two, scoop out seeds, cut into slivers. Heat three-quarters of the butter in a large stew pan or frying pan, add marrow. Cook over moderate heat, shaking the pan frequently and turning over the marrow with a fish slice. When soft and melting lift out with the slice. Put onion into the pan, cook until soft, return marrow to the pan with vinegar, dill, seasoning and sugar, cook for a few minutes. Work remaining butter into the flour, add, and when melted reboil. Turn into a hot serving dish. Serves 4.
Oxfordshire

1 medium marrow ($\frac{3}{4}$–1 kg)	salt and pepper
25 g (1 oz) butter	5–10 ml (1 teaspoon) paprika
30 ml (1 tablespoon) finely chopped onion	pepper
15 ml (1 tablespoon) vinegar	5 ml (1 teaspoon) sugar
a pinch of dill seed finely crushed or chopped dill leaves	15 ml (1 heaped teaspoon) flour

Creamed onions with cauliflower

Peel the onions and cook with the sage leaf in salted water until tender (20 minutes or more). Drain the onions but keep the water. Rub onions through a sieve. Mix the flour with some milk, add about 100 ml (6 tablespoons) of onion liquid. Stir into the onion purée and cook over low heat until it thickens. Stir in the grated cheese and season with pepper and salt. Put the cooked cauliflower in a deep dish and pour over onion cream and serve hot. Serves 4–6.
Westmorland

450 g (1 lb) onions
1 sage leaf
30 ml (1 tablespoon) flour
60 ml (4 tablespoons) milk

30–45 ml (2–3 tablespoons) grated
  cheese
salt and pepper
1 good-sized cauliflower

Stuffed onions

Boil the onions for 20–30 minutes according to size, after removing
the papery outside skins. Do not allow to become too soft.

Combine the grated cheese, breadcrumbs and mustard in a basin.
When the onions are cooked, scoop out the centre portion with a
small spoon and add to the rest of the ingredients. Season to taste.

Fill the cavities in the onions with the stuffing mixture, place in a
greased fireproof dish, dot the tops with margarine and bake in a
hot oven, 220°C (425°F), Gas 7, for about ½ hour, until tender.

Sprinkle the top of each onion with parsley and serve with a good
white sauce, a tomato sauce or gravy.

Alternative stuffing
Minced bacon, breadcrumbs and finely chopped sage.
Derbyshire

4 even-sized onions
50 g (2 oz) grated cheese
50 g (2 oz) white breadcrumbs
2½ ml (¼ teaspoon) dry mustard
salt and pepper

little margarine
chopped parsley
white sauce, tomato sauce or
  gravy

Baked parsnips

These are delicious if after washing and trimming they are baked
round the joint. They will take about an hour. Should your joint be
very small, partly boil the parsnips for about 20 minutes and finish
off around the joint.
Northamptonshire and Soke of Peterborough

Cheese parsnips

Wash and peel parsnips. Cut into chunks and cook in salted boiling
water until just done. Drain well.

Roll chunks in grated cheese. Pack in a fireproof dish and put under

the grill or in the top of hot oven for about 10 minutes until the cheese is browned.
Shropshire

Note for beginners

The parsnips will take from 10 to 15 minutes to boil. Grate the cheese finely and allow about 75–100 g (3–4 oz) per ½ kg (pound) of parsnips.

As a main dish this will serve 2–3; as a vegetable, 4.

Flemish peas

Start the carefully scraped tiny new potatoes cooking in boiling salted water, in which there is a small onion and the parsley. After a few minutes add the peas. Cook until both peas and potatoes are ready. Strain and serve together piled up on a hot dish and pour melted butter over them. Serves 4–6.
Hampshire

about 15–20 very small new potatoes (500 g)
salt
1 small onion

2 or 3 sprigs parsley
500 g (1 lb) green peas, rather older
75 g (3 oz) butter

Pease pudding

Pease pudding has been served for generations in County Durham, generally with ham as the main dish at feasts and celebrations.

Put peas and water into casserole (or saucepan), cover and simmer until soft and water is absorbed, 1–1½ hours. Beat until creamy, add seasoning to taste, butter and milk and beat well. Turn into mould.

Can be eaten hot or cold with ham. Serves 4–6.
Durham

250 g (8 oz) yellow split peas
600 ml (1 pint) water or stock
salt and pepper

knob of butter
20 ml (1 dessertspoon) top of milk

Potatoes

The full flavour and nourishment of potatoes can only be tasted if they are boiled in their skins, baked or, as a second best, steamed.

As a general rule, fresh boiled potatoes are desirable for every kind of 'made-up' potato dish. Even potato salad should be of potatoes which are boiled in their skins, peeled and seasoned lightly with oil or a little melted bacon fat and lemon or vinegar while they are warm.

West Kent

Potatoes
Austrian

Steam potatoes in their skins and peel while still hot, cut into small pieces. Prepare a frying pan with dripping and finely chopped onion.

Let the onion get a golden brown in the dripping, then add the potatoes, salt and fry until a light brown crust forms on the bottom of the pan.

Dish up and serve hot. Do not use cold potatoes for this, as they must be hot and mealy.

Leicestershire and Rutland

potatoes	finely chopped onion
dripping	salt

Duchesse potatoes

Sieve the potatoes. Melt the fat in a pan, add the potatoes and when warm add the beaten egg, about a tablespoon of creamy milk and seasoning to taste. Turn out on to a floured board and divide into small squares. Place these on a greased baking tin, brush over with beaten egg or milk and brown in a hot oven. If preferred, the mixture can be piped through a forcing bag, using a rosette nozzle. Glaze as above. Temperature 230°C (450°F), Gas 8. Serves 4.

Cheshire

500 g (1 lb) hot cooked potatoes	top of milk
25 g (1 oz) margarine	salt and pepper
1 egg	beaten egg or milk to glaze

Potato croquettes

Boil potatoes and dry off well. Push through wire sieve into warm
bowl or pan. Beat in yolk, butter and enough hot milk to make a
fairly firm paste, add seasoning and herbs as desired.

Divide into small even-sized pieces on a slightly floured board and
leave to cool. Form into cutlet or ball shapes, brush over with beaten
egg and roll in the crumbs. Fry in shallow or deep fat. Serves 4.
Cheshire

500 g (1 lb) potatoes	salt and pepper
1 or 2 egg yolks	chopped herbs
15 g (½ oz) butter	dry white breadcrumbs
hot milk	

Roast potatoes

Parboil potatoes, drain. Half fill frying pan with fat, heat, and put in
potatoes. Cover with a lid and cook slowly for about ¾–1 hour, until
crisp.

These can be done in a covered tin in a hot oven.
Cheshire

Note for beginners

This is a very good way of cooking roast potatoes when the oven is
not in use. To parboil the potatoes put them in boiling water and
cook gently for 10–15 minutes according to size. Drain well before
adding to the fat.

Use a foil lid if no other is available; this is important to keep the
fat from splashing. Turn the potatoes over once during cooking, to
brown both sides. Use about the same amount of heat as you would
to keep a pan simmering.

Salsify and scorzonera

Delicious vegetables, with a flavour like oysters.

Scrape salsify and cook like carrots.

Boil scorzonera in its skin and when tender the black skin peels off
easily.

Cooked salsify and scorzonera are both delicious dipped in batter and fried.
West Kent

Spinach

Wash the spinach well, shake and put into a pan without further water. Put lid on and cook gently till tender, about 10 minutes, stirring frequently. When ready, drain well, chop finely or rub through a sieve. Serve very hot with butter and seasoning.
Cheshire

Spinach-beet and seakale-beet

The green part of spinach-beet and seakale-beet cooks up well as greens. The ribs can be chopped and served with it, but, if they are cooked by themselves like celery and served with a little fresh or melted butter, they make an excellent dish, which travellers will remember meeting abroad under the name of Côte de Blette.
West Kent

Spinach
Creamed

Pick all the stalks off the spinach and wash well in several waters. Put in a saucepan with a lid on and boil until thoroughly tender, about 20 minutes. Put through a wire sieve, put back in the saucepan with butter, cream and seasoning, heat thoroughly and serve in a hot dish. Serves 4.
Leicestershire and Rutland

1 kg (2 lb) spinach   75 ml (⅓ gill) cream
50 g (2 oz) butter   salt and pepper

Swede turnip

Prepare turnip by peeling thickly and cutting in pieces. Wash. Boil in salted water until soft. Drain. Squeeze water carefully out of turnip. Mash well or squeeze through the potato ricer. Season with

pepper and stir in 2–3 tablespoons cream or a knob of butter.
Re-heat. Time to cook 20–30 minutes.
Cumberland

Sweet corn

To cook
Put into boiling salted water and cook for 12–15 minutes. Drain.

To remove corn from cob
Use a sharp pointed knife and slit down the middle of each row of
grain. Remove from the top half and then turn round and remove
from the bottom half.
Berkshire

Sweet peppers

Remove a slice from the stalk end and scoop out seeds and veins.
   Parboil the hollowed peppers in boiling water for 15 minutes. Drain
well.
   Fill with a stuffing and finish off in a moderate oven, 190°C
(375°F), Gas 5, for another 15 minutes. Put a little water in the
baking tin while cooking or brush over the surface with melted
butter.
   Many varieties of stuffings may be used, for instance, Risotto is a
good stuffing.
Berkshire

Stuffed peppers

Slice a lid from each pepper and scoop out every seed and the core.
Wash and parboil in salted water for 5 minutes. Drain and cut in
half lengthwise.
   Melt butter in saucepan and lightly fry onion and mushrooms
until onion is clear. Add tomatoes, ham and seasoning and cook for
a further 3 minutes. Add egg yolk and soaked breadcrumbs.
   Pile the mixture into the prepared peppers, and bake in a moderate
oven, 180°C (375°F), Gas 4, until tender, about 20 minutes. Serve
with tomato sauce.
Gloucestershire

3 or 4 peppers

Stuffing
50 g (2 oz) butter
2 chopped onions
2 mushrooms, peeled and chopped
2 medium-sized skinned and
  chopped tomatoes

125–175 g (4–6 oz) lean ham,
  chopped
seasoning
chopped parsley
1 egg yolk
50 g (2 oz) white breadcrumbs,
  soaked in a little milk
tomato sauce to serve with it

Baked tomatoes

Cut a cross in each tomato. Put a small teaspoonful of fresh chopped herbs into each cut, with a pat of butter on top. Bake at 220°C (425°F), Gas 7, until cooked – 20 minutes or so. Serve at once as a garnish or as a separate vegetable.
Hampshire

For each person:
2 tomatoes

2 small teaspoons fresh chopped
  herbs
a pat of butter

Salads

A salad for hot days

Mix finely shredded cabbage with French dressing. Add any of the other ingredients. Pile on to a bed of lettuce or sprigs of watercress.

green or red cabbage
French dressing

Any of the following:
chopped onion or chives
shredded raw carrot
diced tomato and cucumber
chopped parsley

diced orange and apple
raisins
coarsely chopped walnuts
sliced radishes
stoned and halved grapes

For serving:
lettuce or sprigs of watercress

Bean and pea salad

Add cooked vegetables to the sauce and leave until quite cold.
   Line a salad bowl with lettuce leaves and thin slices of cucumber and beetroot and shake in a little finely shredded spring onion. Pour

in the bean and pea mixture and garnish with radishes and small
bunches of mustard and cress. Serves 4.
West Kent

300 ml (½ pint) very good parsley sauce, well seasoned	cucumber
	beetroot
300 ml (½ pint) cooked broad beans	spring onion
300 ml (½ pint) cooked green peas	radishes
lettuce	mustard and cress

Cabbage or Brussels sprouts salad

Prepare the cabbage or sprouts and shred very finely. Chop the nuts,
apple and celery, chop the onion very finely and add these to the
cabbage. Blend lightly with salad dressing and pile in a salad bowl.
Garnish with small sections of tomatoes. Serves 4.
Westmorland

¼ firm green cabbage or savoy heart or 12 firm sprouts	1 celery heart
	1 sliced onion
50 g (2 oz) walnuts	salad dressing
1 sour dessert apple	2 tomatoes

Cream cheese and celery salad

Chop celery and mix with cream cheese. Trim watercress and
arrange on dish. Pile cream cheese and celery on top and sprinkle
with paprika. Sultanas and chopped apple may be added. Serves 4.
Durham

3 sticks celery	paprika
200 g (8 oz) cream cheese	sultanas and chopped apple (if desired)
1 bunch watercress	

Cream salad

Finely chop lettuce and onions. Mix with cream, sugar, salt and
vinegar. Serve with new potatoes and cold beef. Serves 4.
Yorkshire

1 lettuce	1 teaspoon sugar
1 bunch spring onions or chives	salt and vinegar to taste
150 ml (¼ pint) thick cream	

Kidney bean salad

Slice the beans and cook in the usual way. Drain and leave until cold.
  Fry bacon, finely chopped, until slightly browned.
  Dress the beans with some cream or milk, a little vinegar, salt and
pepper, and chopped onion and parsley. Then mix in the fried
bacon. Serves 4.
Herefordshire

500 g (1 lb) kidney beans	salt and pepper
a small cube (2½ cm) of fat bacon	chopped onion
cream or milk	parsley
a little vinegar	

Marinaded beetroot

Mix the marinade until the sugar is dissolved. Cut the cooked
beetroot into small cubes and place in a bowl. Pour over it the
marinade, and leave if possible overnight. Serves 2–4.
Herefordshire

3 tablespoons best vinegar (wine if possible)	4 cloves (cut in halves)
1 tablespoon water	1 clove garlic (cut in half)
2 teaspoons caster sugar	1 medium-sized beetroot

Midinette

Cut equal quantities of the ingredients into strips and mix together.
Dress with mayonnaise diluted with vinaigrette (French dressing).
Leicestershire and Rutland

sour apples	cheese
cold chicken	mayonnaise
celery	vinaigrette

Minted potato salad

Boil potatoes in skins until tender, skin quickly and cut into neat
slices whilst hot. Put mint, sugar and vinegar in a small bowl and
allow to stand for at least an hour. Line a salad bowl with lettuce
leaves, lay in it potato slices in layers, sprinkling mint, sugar and
vinegar over each layer. Decorate with hardboiled egg. Serves 4.
Westmorland

500 g (1 lb) new potatoes
30 ml (1 tablespoon) finely
  chopped mint leaves
15 ml (1 level tablespoon) caster
  sugar

15 ml (1 tablespoon) vinegar, or
  more
1 head of lettuce washed and dried
1 hardboiled egg

Orange salad

Halve oranges and remove pulp with care. Add chopped orange to
apple, celery and nuts and bind with mayonnaise. Line the orange
skins with lettuce and pile in the mixture or place the mixture on the
lettuce leaves. Serves 4.
Yorkshire

2 oranges
60 ml (2 tablespoons) chopped
  apple
60 ml (2 tablespoons) chopped
  pineapple or celery

30 ml (1 tablespoon) nuts
mayonnaise
lettuce

Orange salad for roast duck

Wash oranges and slice thinly – skins and all, removing any pips.
  Peel and slice onions thinly.
  Place alternate layers of orange and onion in a basin with sugar
sprinkled between layers. Cover basin and leave in a cold place
overnight so that the juices will be extracted and the flavours
mingle. Serves 4.
Cumberland

2 thin-skinned oranges
2 onions of equal size to oranges

50 g (2 oz) granulated sugar

Potato salad

Boil potatoes gently in salted water until just cooked. Drain and dry
over a low heat. Cut potatoes into dice, add onion. Add dressing and
flavouring whilst potatoes are still hot. Leave in cool place until
dressing is absorbed. Then add more dressing or mayonnaise; can
be garnished with chopped parsley. Serves 4.
Yorkshire

500 g (1 lb) potatoes
a little chopped onion
150 ml (¼ pint) salad cream or
  142-ml (5-oz) carton yogurt with
  a dash of Worcestershire sauce

mayonnaise (optional)
chopped parsley (optional)

Tomato salad

Slice tomatoes thinly and arrange in a serving dish. Slice very thinly
a few onion rings and arrange on top. Sprinkle with French dressing
or a little lemon juice, sugar and parsley. Leave to stand 1 hour
before serving.
Yorkshire

tomatoes
onion
French dressing or lemon juice

sugar
parsley

Rice and mushrooms

Chop the mushrooms when cold and squeeze some lemon juice over
them. Add the rice, season with salt, cayenne and ketchup.
Leicestershire and Rutland

1 part mushrooms (cooked in
  butter)
lemon juice
2 parts rice (cooked)

salt
cayenne
tomato ketchup

Note for beginners

For a salad for 4 use approximately 200 g of cooked rice (100 g raw)
and 100 g of mushrooms, fried in 15 g of butter.

Winter salad 1

Mix the ingredients, sprinkle with sugar and dress.
Herefordshire

*A very pleasant winter salad can be
  made of:*
well-sliced Brussels sprouts
grated carrots

small amounts of swede and
  turnip, grated
a sprinkling of sugar
French dressing

Winter salad 2

Mix beetroot, celery and cauliflower. Add some green stuff and serve with French salad dressing.
West Kent

small cubes of cooked beetroot
chopped celery
small florets of uncooked
  cauliflower

green stuff
French dressing

Salad Dressings

A simple dressing
Without vinegar

Blend well in a cream-making machine or with an egg-beater.
West Kent

2 parts olive oil
1 part honey

1 part lemon juice (or orange juice)

Canadian mayonnaise

Make a sauce by melting margarine, working in the flour. Add water and cook until thick. In a basin put egg yolks, lemon juice, vinegar, mustard, salt and pepper. Pour oil over. DO NOT STIR. Pour sauce over all whilst still hot. Beat immediately using egg whisk. If too thick add more water or vinegar.
Yorkshire

50 g (2 oz) margarine
50 g (2 oz) flour or cornflour
400 ml ($\frac{3}{4}$ pint) water
2 egg yolks
5 ml (1 teaspoon) lemon juice

30 ml (2 tablespoons) vinegar
5 ml ($\frac{1}{2}$ teaspoon) dry mustard
15 ml (1 teaspoon) salt
shake of cayenne pepper
45 ml (3 tablespoons) salad oil

Cream dressing

Mix mustard, salt and sugar together with vinegar, and add the cream slowly. Serves 8.
Gloucestershire

5 ml (½ teaspoon) dry mustard
pinch of salt
15 ml (1 tablespoon) sugar

30 ml (2 tablespoons) vinegar
150 ml (¼ pint) thin cream

French dressing

Mix seasoning, and if used, garlic with oil, add vinegar and lastly
herbs. Shake or stir until emulsified.
Westmorland

3 parts oil
1 part wine vinegar
crushed garlic (optional)
mustard

salt and freshly ground black
  pepper
chopped herbs, etc, as wished

Hurry-up-mayonnaise

Put egg yolk into a deep bowl. Heat the other ingredients (except
oil) in a small pan. When quite hot, add to yolk of egg and beat with
a rotary egg-beater. Add oil generously and quickly. The mayonnaise
will thicken almost immediately.
Yorkshire

1 egg yolk
30 ml (2 tablespoons) vinegar
2½ ml (½ teaspoon) salt
2½ ml (½ teaspoon) sugar
1 ml (¼ teaspoon) pepper

little paprika
5 ml (1 teaspoon) prepared
  mustard
salad oil – 150 ml (¼ pint)
  approximately

Russian salad dressing

Mix all together.
Northamptonshire and Soke of Peterborough

30 ml (1 tablespoon) mayonnaise
15 ml (1 tablespoon) Heinz tomato
  sauce

15 ml (1 tablespoon) cream
2½ ml (½ teaspoon)
  Worcestershire sauce

Salad dressing
Cooked

Mix mustard, sugar, egg and seasoning in a saucepan – then add,

stirring all the time, the oil, vinegar and milk; cook slowly stirring all the time until it thickens. This will keep for a long time. Makes about 150 ml (¼ pint).
Oxfordshire

15 ml (1 dessertspoon) mustard
15 ml (1 dessertspoon) caster
  sugar
1 egg

salt and pepper
30 ml (2 tablespoons) salad oil
30 ml (2 tablespoons) vinegar
60 ml (4 tablespoons) milk

Summer cream dressing

Half whip the cream and mix with seasoning and lemon juice. Beat up egg white and fold into cream mixture. Serves 4.
Oxfordshire

75 ml (3 tablespoons) cream or
  evaporated milk
pinch of cayenne pepper
1 ml (¼ teaspoon) sugar

pinch of salt
10 ml (2 teaspoons) lemon juice
1 egg white

Thousand island dressing

Mix all together, adding the vinegar last.
Hampshire

300 ml (½ pint) mayonnaise
30 ml (2 tablespoons) tomato sauce
1 very small onion, finely chopped
2 chopped hardboiled eggs
30 ml (1 tablespoon) finely
  chopped sweet pickles

60 ml (2 tablespoons) sliced
  stuffed olives
30 ml (1 tablespoon) chopped
  parsley
15 ml (1 tablespoon) chilli vinegar

Yogurt salad dressings

Yogurt and mint
Add fresh chopped mint and a little honey to yogurt.

Yogurt and orange
Add the juice of a sweet orange to yogurt.
Lincolnshire

8 Herbs & Flavourings

Herbs and their uses

Compiled from information in books from Cheshire, Leicestershire and Rutland, West Kent and Yorkshire.

Angelica
The stems may be candied in May or June, and also small pieces of the stem may be stewed with rhubarb and the leaves, chopped, can improve salads.

Alecost
Use in salads, gives a faint flavour of mint. Useful in bread sauce.

Balm, lemon
Useful in forcemeat, fish sauces and summer drinks; and for making wine.

Basil
With a clove-like flavour, is used to flavour soup, especially turtle and tomato soups; for herb cheeses; calves' liver; in salads; sprinkled on fish.

Bay (*leaves fresh or dried*)
Leaves in a bouquet garni and to flavour soups, stews, sauces; with herrings; also to flavour custards and milk puddings.

Bergamot
Sparingly in salads and summer drinks.

Borage
In claret cup and other drinks.

Capers
Bottled in vinegar or use bottled nasturtium seeds. In sauces, salads, sandwich spreads.

Caraway
Use the seeds for flavouring cakes, breads, sweets, cabbage and other vegetables. The leaves may be used in salads.

Celery seed
In soups, stews, sauces, gravies and savoury dishes, when celery is out of season.

Chervil
As a garnish and in salads, sauces, soused fish, soups, egg and cheese dishes.

Chives
Used fresh from the garden. In salads, egg dishes, rissoles, soups, stews, cheese, sandwiches; and any dish needing onion flavour. Infuse chives in a light cider vinegar and strain off after ten days. The flavoured vinegar is excellent for salads and egg dishes.

Coriander
Seeds used for flavouring sweets and curries. Use leaves for flavouring soups and stews.

Dandelion
Flowers for wine, leaves for salads, and root for dandelion coffee.

Dill
Young leaves used for flavouring. Cucumber salad welcomes this in small quantities with lemon juice instead of vinegar.
   Soak seeds in vinegar for a few days to make dill vinegar.

Fennel
For sauces used with fish, in salads and pickles. A small shoot

added to a bottle of nasturtium capers improves them. The seeds
can be used for fennel tea or dusted over buns or rolls. They have an
aniseed flavour.

Garlic
Each bulb is made up of many 'cloves'. Should be used very
sparingly. Very small amounts in savoury dishes, quarter or half a
small clove is sufficient to flavour a soup or stew for four.

Horehound
Excellent candy may be made with this.

Horseradish
Fresh root or bottled grated. The grated root of this may be made
into a sauce or cream to be eaten with roast beef; may also be added
to white sauce and served hot with fish. Excellent mixed with apple
sauce; also in sandwich spreads and savoury dishes.

Lovage
With a celery flavour, used very sparingly in soups, stews and
stuffings.

Marjoram
Dried or fresh. In sauces, stews, soups, rissoles, forcemeats and in a
bouquet garni. Sprinkled over roast pork it is a tasty addition and
white fish is improved by small amounts of marjoram added as
flavouring. Marjoram and onion when used together will each bring
out the flavour of the other.

Mint
Fresh or dried. In sauces, with vegetables during cooking, in meat
tarts, in stuffings for lamb; and in salads and sandwich fillings. In
juleps and tea. With peas, potatoes, lamb, made into jelly, sprinkled
in salad, the leaves also may be crystallized for cake decorations;
also for mint pasties and syrups and with onion instead of sage for
stuffing; also chopped with sugar for sandwiches.

Nasturtium
Leaves chopped in salads or with egg sandwiches; and the seeds
pickled and used as capers.

Parsley
Fresh or dried (fresh is better). In all savoury dishes; to make parsley
butter.

Rosemary
Chopped and sprinkled on mutton or lamb before roasting and finely ground for dusting fish before frying and can be added to flavour pickles; also in veal stuffing.

Sage
Fresh or dried. In savoury dishes and stuffings but especially with duck, pork and goose; for flavouring cheeses; also with baked beans and bacon; in salads.

Savory
For flavouring broad beans; in stuffings.

Sorrel
Leaves in salads.

Tarragon
A leaf or two in salads and cold sauces; vinegar.

Thyme
Fresh or dried. In stuffings, soups, sauces and savoury dishes. Lemon thyme is super-excellent for stuffings. In salads, cheeses, bouquet garni and *fines herbes*.

Bouquet garni

Soups and stews are improved by adding a bay leaf, piece of parsley, thyme and marjoram, tied up in a piece of clean muslin and taken out before serving.
Or
Bouquet garni consists of sprigs of thyme, marjoram, parsley, basil, balm and a bay leaf, tied together in a bunch to flavour meat dishes, and taken out before serving.
Or
2 stalks celery, 1 sprig of thyme, 1 bay leaf, 1 sprig of marjoram.

Fines herbes

A mixture of chopped fresh parsley, chervil and chives for omelettes and other egg dishes.
Or
Parsley, chives, chervil and tarragon.

Seasonings and flavourings and their uses

Compiled from information in books from Cheshire and West Kent.

Cayenne pepper
In savoury dishes. It is much stronger than ordinary pepper.

Chillies
These are very hot and are used sparingly in sauces, pickles, stews and savoury rice dishes.

Cinnamon
Ground or stick In cakes, puddings, sauces, stews and savoury dishes. Is great with raspberries.
Stick Simmer with fruits for compotes, and use for extra flavour with canned fruits. Use when pickling beetroot.
Ground Sprinkle on whipped cream for lemon, chocolate, butterscotch, banana-cream or apple pie. On baked custards, junkets, melon or a cup of cocoa for novelty. To top breakfast cereals, pears, prunes or peaches. On your breakfast orange or grapefruit. Mixed with cottage cheese. On anything chocolate. Perks up cranberry sauce; adds character to apple sauce.

Cloves
Whole Add to soups, braised meats, dried fruits during cooking. Improves tomato soup or sauce. Peps up prunes and apples. Stick them into the pears you pickle.
Ground On sliced grapefruit, oranges or pineapple. In grapefruit cocktail, apple or peach pie, or chocolate pudding. In potato soups, meat stews and vegetable broths.

Curry powder
A blend of spices. Add to baked beans, lamb or beef stew, hamburgers, gravy for roast chicken, stuffed eggs, French dressing or mayonnaise, savoury butters for sandwiches, creamed onions, buttered cabbage or string beans.
   Curry adds piquancy to made-up fish dishes, or serve fish in an apple, raisin and curry sauce.

Essence
A great variety of flavours can be achieved by using different essences in puddings and cakes. Try vanilla in coffee- and chocolate-

flavoured foods; almond essence in custard to serve with plums; lemon essence with apple.

Ginger
Crystallized Sliced in cakes, puddings and stewed fruits.
Ground Adds new interest to pot roast, apple sauce, creamed chicken, fish dishes and sauces. Sprinkle a bit on peaches, pears, apricots, melons.
Whole pickling (root) In sweet and savoury dishes but is removed before serving.

Lemon
Fresh fruit, dried peel or juice In fish dishes, stuffings, stews, sauces, cakes and puddings.
Rind For many sweet dishes, fish, sauces and cakes.

Mace
Blade or whole Try a piece in milk soups, white stews, rabbit fricassée and chicken pie, chicken soup, shrimp sauce. Mashed, hashed and creamed potatoes taste excellent with it.
Powdered or ground Use in pound cakes, cherry pie, chocolate puddings, fruit jellies. Sprinkle some on bottled or canned cherries, peaches, pears and apricots. Add to pickled damsons. Add to spinach stuffings, stews and fish stock.

Mustard
Whole seed Generally only used in pickles and chutneys.
Ground Used in all savoury dishes.

Nutmeg
Complements vegetables – boiled cabbage, Brussels sprouts, mushrooms, asparagus, cauliflower and especially spinach. Makes delicious spinach or nettle soup, split pea soup, dumplings for chicken stew, hard sauce. Milk puddings, junkets and jellies. Use with fruits – fruit salads, sliced bananas, rhubarb pie and fruit cakes. With stewed rhubarb and sauce for cauliflower.

Orange
Rind or juices of fresh oranges or dried rind In savoury dishes, cakes, pies, puddings and sauces.

Paprika
Ground red pepper (less pungent than cayenne). For sprinkling on dishes to add colour and for flavouring. Used to make goulash.

Pepper
Whole peppercorns or ground. In all savoury dishes. Home ground pepper has the best flavour.

Salt
Cooking In all savoury dishes. A little in all sweet dishes, cakes, etc, improves the flavour.

Sugar
In all sweet dishes. A little in savoury dishes brings out the other flavours.

Vinegar
Malt, tarragon, chilli, garlic, wine, elderflower, etc. A little added to stews, sauces, or other savoury dishes often improves the flavour. Vinegar helps to make meat more tender.

The drying of herbs

When drying herbs, the aim is to preserve the natural colour as nearly as possible whilst retaining the full flavour and aroma.

Herbs just tied into bunches and left to dry soon lose their fresh colour, and naturally, they attract dust. The fine flavour is lost and the finished product is faded and insipid.

To dry herbs satisfactorily, pick them when free from dew or rain, before the full heat of the day, and before they come into flower.

Pick the leaves from the stalks of the larger varieties and tie the smaller ones into sprays.

Lay on shallow trays in thin layers so that the moisture can escape during drying. Do not pack tightly as the trapped moisture will darken the colour of the herbs and detract from the true flavour.

Leave in a cool oven, 45–55°C (110–130°F), until quite dry, or ideally, leave in the airing cupboard or on a rack over the stove until dry. Oven drying takes more care than the other methods and invites singeing should the oven temperature increase suddenly.

Parsley is the one exception to the above methods. Place in a hot oven, 200°C (400°F), Gas 6, for 1 minute then finish off in a cool oven or in the airing cupboard.

When the herbs are dry, roll them down with a rolling pin and pick out any stalks. Rub large-leaved herbs through a wire sieve.

Store all herbs in tins or small jars and keep them in a cool dry place.

Herbs may also be put into deep freeze. Wash, drain and dry, taking care not to bruise. Either lay sprigs of herb flat and wrap in tin foil, or chop ready for use and pack into small plastic containers. To use, either thaw out or grate into the dish they are to flavour.
Yorkshire

A mixed seasoning for stews and soups

Dry thoroughly and put through a sieve. Put in airtight bottle or tin. Always ready. Use sparingly.
West Kent

25 g (1 oz) pepper
15 g (½ oz) powdered cloves, mace, ginger

10 ml (1 teaspoon) powdered mixed herbs
25 g (1 oz) powdered salt

Burnet or cucumber vinegar

Fill a wide-mouthed jar with fresh green leaves of burnet and cover them with vinegar. Let them steep for 10 days; if you wish a very strong essence, strain the vinegar, put it on some fresh leaves and let them steep 14 days more.

The flavour of burnet resembles cucumber so exactly that when infused in vinegar the nicest palate would pronounce it to be cucumber.
Berkshire

Cheese of the seven herbs

Put all ingredients into a double saucepan and stir over a very gentle heat until the mixture is creamy and a pale green in colour. Whilst still warm, put into small pots and use when cold.
Lincolnshire

125 g (4 oz) grated cheese
30 ml (2 tablespoons) thick cream
45 ml (3 tablespoons) sherry or cider

30 ml (2 level tablespoons) herbs consisting of a mixture of finely chopped parsley, sage, thyme, tarragon, chives, chervil and winter savory
seasoning to taste

Mint pastry

Take equal parts fresh finely chopped mint, brown sugar and currants. Mix well and pound together to a soft, thick consistency. Spread between thin layers of pastry and cook until golden.
Lincolnshire

chopped mint   currants
brown sugar   pastry

Note for beginners

Make these with short pastry using 150 g (6 oz) flour and allowing about 50 g (2 oz) each of currants and sugar with 45 ml (3 level tablespoons) finely chopped mint. Bake at 220°C (425°F), Gas 7, for about 20 minutes.

Mint tea

Pour the boiling water on to the dried mint, infuse 4 minutes, strain and add lemon juice and sugar.
  Excellent hot for colds and refreshing as a cold drink.
West Kent

10 ml (1 teaspoon) dried mint   squeeze of lemon juice
250 ml (½ pint) boiling water   sugar to taste

Mint vinegar

Put into a wide-mouthed bottle enough fresh young mint leaves to fill it loosely. Fill up with good vinegar, and infuse for 2 or 3 weeks. Pour off clear into another bottle, and cork down for use.
West Kent

fresh young mint leaves   good vinegar

Omelette with herbs

Make omelette in usual way, but add chopped parsley and chives to egg mixture and water. Serve with sprigs of fresh parsley.
Serves 2–3.
Yorkshire

6 eggs
salt and pepper
30 ml (1 tablespoon) chopped
  fresh parsley

30 ml (1 tablespoon) chopped
  chives
5 ml (1 teaspoon) water
25 g (1 oz) butter
4 sprigs fresh parsley

Rosemary cream

Beat the egg yolks and add to the milk in which a sprig of bruised
rosemary has been infused, stir until the mixture thickens. Put in the
sugar, stir until dissolved, then strain through a sieve to remove
rosemary. Dissolve the gelatine in 30 ml (1 tablespoon) water and
add to the custard. Whip the cream slightly and stir it lightly into the
custard. Pour into prepared mould. Serves 4–6.
Cambridgeshire

500 ml (1 pint) milk
1 sprig rosemary
2 egg yolks

40 g (1½ oz) caster sugar
15 g (½ oz) gelatine
150 ml (¼ pint) cream

Rosemary sugar

Clean and dry sprigs of rosemary. Place in a screw-topped jar, and
fill up with sugar (caster). Shake well and leave 24 hours. Shake
again, and leave for a week.
  The flavoured sugar is unusual, and good with any milk sweet.
  Lavender sugar can be made in the same way.
West Kent

Tarragon vinegar

This is a very agreeable addition to soups, salad sauces and to mix
mustard.

Fill a wide-mouthed bottle with fresh gathered tarragon leaves.
(They should be gathered on a dry day between Midsummer and
Michaelmas, just before the plant flowers.) Pick the leaves off the
stalks and dry them a little before the fire; cover them with the best
vinegar, let them steep for 14 days, and then strain through a flannel
jelly bag and pour into bottles; cork them carefully and keep them
in a dry place.
Berkshire

To preserve capers
Nasturtium seeds

Wash nasturtium seeds in cold water and soak overnight in cold salted water. Cover with cold spiced vinegar. Seal and keep for 12 months before using.

Mix together.
West Kent

nasturtium seeds
salted water
spiced vinegar

Spiced vinegar
1¼ l (1 quart) vinegar

50 g (2 oz) salt
a dozen peppercorns
a small piece of horseradish
2 cloves
3 or 4 tarragon leaves

9 Sauces & Stuffings

Savoury sauces

A superior sauce – béchamel
Quick method

Scald the milk, pour over vegetables and spices. Cover and leave to infuse for 30 minutes, then strain. Melt the butter, add the flour and cook without browning, add the flavoured milk and simmer, stirring all the time. Strain, add salt to taste and cream. Re-heat before using if necessary.

This sauce can be flavoured and coloured as desired. Serves 4.
Berkshire

300 ml (½ pint) milk
slice of carrot and turnip
5 cm (2 inches) celery
1 small onion stuck with cloves
1 blade mace

6 white peppercorns
25 g (1 oz) butter
25 g (1 oz) flour
salt
15 ml (1 tablespoon) cream

Sauce mornay

Beat the cheese thoroughly into the hot sauce off the fire. Add seasonings.

The cheese thickens the sauce considerably, and extra liquid may have to be added. The amount of flour in the basic sauce may be reduced to 15 g to 300 ml ($\frac{1}{2}$ oz to $\frac{1}{2}$ pint) of milk.

Re-heat the sauce, taking care not to boil it or the sauce will curdle.

Use for eggs, vegetables, gratins, fish, spaghetti and gnocchi.
Serves 4.
Berkshire

300 ml ($\frac{1}{2}$ pint) béchamel sauce
25–40 g (1–1$\frac{1}{2}$ oz) grated cheese
 (Gruyère or Parmesan)
pepper and salt

5 ml (1 small teaspoon) French
 mustard
cream or the top of the milk

Barbecue sauce

Melt butter. Add onion, sauté. Mix remainder of ingredients in saucepan and bring to boil.

Alternative uses
1 This sauce can be used with lamb chops that have been cooked for 6–10 minutes. Remove chops. Drain fat, pour sauce over and cook 30–40 minutes in slow oven.
2 Alternatively place slices of cold cooked lamb into an ovenproof dish and gently warm through – one way of using the remains of the Sunday joint. Serves 4.
Yorkshire

25 g (1 oz) butter
1 small chopped onion
60 ml (4 tablespoons) tomato sauce
30 ml (2 tablespoons) vinegar
30 ml (2 dessertspoons) chutney

10 ml (1 teaspoon) made mustard
5 ml (1 level teaspoon) sugar
15 ml (1 tablespoon)
 Worcestershire sauce

Bitter sweet sauce

To serve with boiled ham.

In a small saucepan blend the mustard and vinegar. Add the sugar and cloves. Set in a warm place to melt.

When the ham is cooked, add 4 tablespoons of the liquor in which it has been boiled. Stir well, heat thoroughly, strain, and serve with the ham. Serves 4.
Berkshire

5 ml (1 level teaspoon) mustard
30 ml (2 tablespoons) vinegar
100 g (4 oz) demerara or soft
  brown sugar

6 or 8 cloves
60 ml (4 tablespoons) liquor from
  boiled ham

Cranberry sauce

Heat water and sugar until sugar dissolves, bring to boil, add the washed and drained cranberries. Simmer for 7–10 minutes until tender. Sieve and test for sweetness. Serve with turkey or capon. Serves 4–6.
Yorkshire

75 ml ($\frac{1}{8}$ pint) water
50 g (2 oz) sugar

250 g (8 oz) cranberries

Cumberland sauce

Chop the shallots very finely, parboil for 2 minutes and drain. Peel and cut finely the orange and lemon. Cover with water and boil for 5 minutes. Drain well.

Place the shallots with the peel in a bowl and add the juice of the orange and half that of the lemon. Add ginger, cayenne and the jelly (melted) and the port. Mix well.

Suitable for cold meat or venison. Serves 6.
Cumberland

3 shallots
1 orange
1 lemon
pinch of powdered ginger

pinch of cayenne pepper
90 ml (6 level tablespoons)
  redcurrant jelly
75 ml (5 tablespoons) port

Curry sauce

Soak coconut in boiling stock for 15 minutes. Strain. Melt butter in pan, fry chopped onion, then chopped apple until soft. Add curry powder, fry 1 minute. Add flour, mix well. Remove from heat, stir in stock, stir over heat until boiling, add chutney and sultanas. Cover, but stir occasionally and cook for 30 minutes. Add lemon juice, add salt.

Any cold meats or vegetables may be added, and if served with boiled rice, makes a substantial meal. Serves 4.

Yorkshire

20 ml (1 dessertspoon) coconut
300 ml (½ pint) stock
25 g (1 oz) butter
1 medium onion
1 medium apple
20 ml (4 level teaspoons) curry powder

25 g (1 oz) flour
20 ml (1 dessertspoon) chutney
20 ml (1 dessertspoon) sultanas
10 ml (1 dessertspoon) lemon juice
salt to taste

Dutch sauce

Melt butter, stir in flour, add water or stock and boil for 2 minutes. Remove from heat, cool and stir in oil, capers, salt, cayenne and vinegar. If added before the sauce has cooled, the oil, etc, will float on the top. Stir in the yolks gradually, beat over the heat until the sauce thickens, but do not boil. If necessary, thin with a little more stock or water. Serves 4.

Surrey

15 g (½ oz) butter
15 g (½ oz) flour
150 ml (¼ pint) chicken stock or cold water
30 ml (2 tablespoons) salad oil
15–30 ml (1 tablespoon) chopped capers

1 ml (¼ teaspoon) salt
cayenne pepper
15 ml (1 tablespoon) tarragon vinegar
2 egg yolks

Espagnole sauce

Cut up the ham or bacon and sauté in the butter or dripping. Slice the vegetables and fry them until beginning to brown. Add the flour and fry all slowly till a rich brown colour. Add the stock and bring to boiling point. Simmer for about 2 hours. Add the tomato pulp when the sauce is half cooked. Pass through a very fine strainer or a tammy cloth. Add the sherry. Re-heat the sauce and season.
Serves 4–6.

Cheshire

50 g (2 oz) ham or bacon
50 g (2 oz) butter or dripping
1 onion
1 small carrot
1 shallot
50 g (2 oz) mushrooms

50 g (2 oz) flour
600 ml (1 pint) brown stock
150 ml (¼ pint) tomato pulp
75 ml (⅛ pint) sherry
pepper and salt

Hollandaise sauce

Put water, egg yolks and vinegar into the top of a double boiler.
Stir till thick. Remove top pan to side of stove, stir in butter bit by
bit, then lemon juice, salt and pepper to taste.

Serve with fish, meat loaf, asparagus or cauliflower. Serves 2–4.
Westmorland

30 ml (2 tablespoons) water
2 egg yolks
10 ml (2 teaspoons) white vinegar

50 g (2 oz) butter
squeeze of lemon juice
salt and pepper

Horseradish sauce that will keep

Grate the horseradish and bottle with a small quantity of vinegar
and a little salt. This will keep for 6 months and can be used with
roast beef.
Leicestershire and Rutland

horseradish
vinegar

salt

Horseradish sauce cold

Whisk the cream lightly and add the horseradish and seasonings.
Serves 4.
Leicestershire and Rutland

25 g (1 oz) grated horseradish
125 ml (1 gill) cream

a little pepper, salt, mustard,
   vinegar and caster sugar

Horseradish and cucumber cream

Beat all ingredients into cream taking care not to overbeat. Serve
with cold chicken or game, cold fish, etc. Serves 4.
Westmorland

150 ml (¼ pint) lightly whipped
  cream
30 ml (1 tablespoon) grated
  horseradish
60 ml (2 tablespoons) finely
  chopped cucumber (remove skin
  and pips)

a very small piece of onion very
  finely chopped
pepper and salt
10 ml (1 dessertspoon) tarragon
  vinegar

Hot beetroot sauce

Dice beetroot. Peel and finely chop onion and apple. Put onion
and apple in a saucepan with dripping and allow to cook
and glaze without browning. Add diced beetroot, and keep
stirring using a wooden spoon. Make a sauce with cornflour, water,
vinegar and sugar. Add sauce just before serving. Serve with
pork chops, ham or gammon. Serves 4.
Durham

450 g (1 lb) cooked beetroot
1 medium onion
1 large green apple
dripping size of a walnut
15 ml (1 level tablespoon)
  cornflour

45 ml (3 tablespoons) water
45 ml (3 tablespoons) vinegar
10 ml (1 teaspoon) brown sugar
seasoning

Lord Welby's sauce

A delicious substitute for horseradish sauce.

Mix all ingredients together and serve in a sauce boat. The parsnip,
being sweet, requires no sugar.
The story of this recipe is that Lord Welby used to dine frequently
at Christ Church College and on one occasion there was no
horseradish sauce. The cook made a substitute sauce with parsnip
and Lord Welby said that it was the best horseradish sauce he had
ever tasted! Serves 4.
Yorkshire

30 ml (2 tablespoons) cream
30 ml (1 tablespoon) mustard
15 ml (1 tablespoon) vinegar

60 ml (1 tablespoon) grated parsnip
a little salt

Mint sauce that will keep

Boil vinegar and sugar together. Withdraw from heat and add
chopped mint. Bottle when cold and seal.

When required for use, add more vinegar, as the sauce should be
very thick when made.
Leicestershire and Rutland

150 ml (1 teacup) finely chopped mint	150 g (6 oz) white sugar
	250 ml (½ pint) vinegar

The perfect mint sauce.

Pound down the leaves, preferably with pestle and mortar. Cover
with caster sugar to take up all juice. Add just a little boiling water
as will dissolve the sugar. Sharpen with strained lemon juice,
home-made wine vinegar, or shop vinegar if you must.
West Kent

fresh mint leaves	boiling water
caster sugar	lemon juice or wine vinegar

Sauce Indienne

A very favourite sauce with the French. Can be used with fish,
hard- or softboiled eggs, and is particularly good with chicken.
Plain boiled rice should be served with the chicken, eggs or fish.

Make your sauce in the ordinary way and be sure to cook your curry
powder dry with the flour – very important. If you do not want to
use cream, use more milk.

This sauce is excellent cold in the summer – then put a tablespoon
of aspic in the sauce, as it gives a more glazed look. Enough for 4
people.
Berkshire

75 g (3 oz) butter	300 ml (½ pint) milk
25 g (1 heaped tablespoon) plain flour	150 ml (¼ pint) cream
10 ml (1 teaspoon) curry powder	salt

Sweet-sour sauce
Chinese

Heat a very little cooking oil in a heavy frying pan and cook the
crushed clove of garlic and the onion tops for a few seconds. Next
add the vinegar and sugar.

When the sugar is melted add the chopped ginger and sweet pickles and the soya sauce.

Thicken with cornflour mixed with a little water. Stir for a minute or two and then serve. Serves 4.

Devon

a little oil for cooking
1 clove garlic
the finely chopped tops of 1 or 2
  spring onions if available
170–200 ml (1–1¼ teacups) malt
  vinegar
75 g (½ teacup) brown sugar

20 ml (1 dessertspoon) chopped
  preserved ginger (or ginger
  marmalade)
20 ml (1 dessertspoon) chopped
  Chinese sweet pickles
3–4 drops soya (Chinese) sauce
20 ml (1 dessertspoon) cornflour

Tomato sauce

Melt the butter in a saucepan. Add the finely chopped onion and cook for a few minutes, but do not allow to brown.

Add the tomatoes cut in halves, the sweet basil, sugar and seasoning. Cover with lid and simmer until the vegetables are quite cooked and pulpy.

Next rub the whole through a fine sieve. Return to the pan and thicken with a little plain flour. Cook for a moment or two and serve.

This makes approximately 250 ml (½ pint) of sauce.

With the addition of a little good stock it can be served as soup. Serves 4.

Devon

15 g (½ oz) butter
1 medium-sized onion
500 g (1 lb) tomatoes (tinned
  tomatoes can be used)

5 ml (1 teaspoon) dried sweet basil
5 ml (1 teaspoon) sugar
pepper and salt to taste
a little plain flour

Sweet sauces

Clotted cream

Use new milk and strain at once as soon as milked into shallow pans. Let it stand for 24 hours in winter and 12 hours in summer. Then put the pan on the stove, or, better still, into a steamer containing

water, and let it slowly heat until the cream begins to show a raised ring round the edge. When sufficiently cooked place in a cool dairy and leave for 12 or 24 hours. Great care must be taken in moving the pans so that the cream is not broken, both in putting on the fire and taking off. When required, skim off the cream in layers into a glass dish for the table, taking care to have a good 'crust' on the top. Clotted cream is best done over a stick fire.
Cornwall

Devonshire clotted cream

Put fresh milk into a wide bowl and leave to stand for approximately 12 hours in summer and 24 hours in winter.

Stand the bowl over a pan of water and heat this *very slowly* so that the water never boils.

Leave until the surface of the milk has formed a thick crust.

Stand in a cool place until next day, then carefully skim the scalded cream from the top of the milk.
Devon

Cornflour or arrowroot sauce
Sweet white sauce

Mix cornflour or arrowroot with some milk, heat remainder with lemon rind. Stir on to cornflour or arrowroot, return to pan and boil for 5 minutes, remove lemon rind and add sugar. Serves 4.
Herefordshire

10 ml (1 teaspoon) cornflour or arrowroot
250 ml (½ pint) milk

strip of lemon rind
10 ml (1 dessertspoon) caster sugar

Custard sauce
Economical

Blend cornflour with a little of the milk. Add beaten egg, sugar, salt and the rest of the milk. Put into a pan and cook thoroughly, stirring all the time until it thickens. Cook another 5 minutes without allowing it to boil. Flavour if liked. Serves 4.
Cheshire

5 ml (½ teaspoon) cornflour   10 ml (1 dessertspoon) sugar
300 ml (½ pint) milk   pinch of salt
1 egg   flavouring if desired

Custard sauce
Rich

Heat milk (boil in summer) with lemon rind. Beat eggs and sugar
together. Pour milk over eggs, stirring at same time. Strain into pan
and stir over gentle heat until custard thickens. Remove instantly.
Serve hot or cold. Serves 8.
Cheshire

600 ml (1 pint) milk   sugar to taste
lemon rind   flavouring
3 eggs or 5 yolks

Jam and marmalade sauce

Boil water and sugar for 3–4 minutes, stir in jam or marmalade,
bring to boiling point and strain if jam is used. Serves 2–3.
Herefordshire

150 ml (1 gill) water   few drops lemon juice for jam
40 g (1½ oz) loaf sugar   sauces and cochineal to improve
30 ml (1 tablespoon) jam or   colour when red jam is used
  marmalade

Melba sauce

This can be made at the end of the raspberry season. Stew the
raspberries with very little water. Sieve and sweeten. Ready to serve.
  To store, cool, pour into cartons, seal, label and freeze.
  Yorkshire

raspberries   sugar
water

Rum butter

Melt butter, add sugar and nutmeg. Pour in rum, mix well until it

starts to thicken. Pour into an attractive old chainbowl and leave to set. Serves 8 or more.
Cumberland

450 g (1 lb) butter	10 ml (2 teaspoons) grated nutmeg
700 g (1½ lb) soft brown sugar	100 ml (1 wineglass) rum

Stuffings

Apple and prune stuffing

Bind all together. Good for pork.
Hampshire

12 prunes soaked, stoned and chopped	2 large apples cored, peeled and rough chopped
50 g (2 oz) cashew nuts, chopped	175 g (6 oz) breadcrumbs
50 g (2 oz) melted butter	grated rind and juice of lemon
1 egg, beaten	seasonings

Chestnut stuffing

Make a split in both ends of the nuts and boil them in water for 10 minutes, then skin. Put them into a pan with stock or milk to cover and simmer gently until tender. Mash or sieve the nuts.

Chop ham and add with other ingredients to the chestnuts. Bind with the beaten egg.

Use to stuff turkey, chicken, etc.
Northumberland

500 g (1 lb) chestnuts	a little grated lemon rind
300 ml (½ pint) stock or milk	10 ml (1 teaspoon) sugar
50 g (2 oz) ham or bacon	seasoning
100 g (4 oz) breadcrumbs	25 g (1 oz) margarine, melted
10 ml (1 teaspoon) chopped parsley	1 egg

Forcemeat
Veal

Mix all the ingredients together thoroughly and bind with the beaten egg and a little milk.
Yorkshire

250 ml (8 tablespoons)
  breadcrumbs
30 ml (1 tablespoon) chopped
  parsley
60 ml (2 tablespoons) shredded suet
20 ml (2 teaspoons) chopped bacon
5 ml (½ teaspoon) chopped onions

10 ml (1 teaspoon) powdered herbs
grated rind of lemon
dash of pepper
5 ml (½ teaspoon) salt
1 egg
little milk
(the bacon and onion may be
  omitted)

Orange stuffing

Four or five oranges will be needed. Combine all ingredients and
use for duck really, but it is a delicious stuffing for turkey.
Hampshire

150 ml (¼ pint) orange pulp
100 g (4 oz) breadcrumbs.
5 ml (½ teaspoon) grated lemon
  rind
15 g (½ oz) butter, melted

45 ml (3 tablespoons) orange juice
the grated rind of an orange
15 ml (2 teaspoons) chopped mint
salt

Raisin and nut stuffing

A good stuffing for vegetables.

Mix all the ingredients together.
Berkshire

150 g (6 oz) fresh breadcrumbs
50–75 g (2–3 oz) chopped stoned
  raisins
50–75 g (2–3 oz) chopped nuts
50 g (2 oz) melted butter, not oiled

45 ml (1 heaped tablespoon)
  chopped parsley
1 egg, beaten
seasoning if liked

Sage and onion stuffing

Boil the onions for 5 minutes. Add to the other ingredients after
chopping finely. Add the melted fat and mix well together.
Yorkshire

3 large onions
200 ml (6 tablespoons)
  breadcrumbs
20 ml (1 dessertspoon) chopped
  parsley

dash of pepper
2½ ml (small half teaspoon) salt
50 g (2 oz) butter or margarine

Sweet corn stuffing

Melt the butter in a saucepan, add the chopped onion and cook over gentle heat until beginning to soften. Stir in the salt, pepper and sweet corn and cook for 2–3 minutes. Remove from the heat, add the lemon rind and juice, the parsley and beaten egg. Mix thoroughly and fill loosely into the bird.

Sufficient to stuff a 1½ kg (3–4 lb) bird.

Surrey

26 g (1 oz) butter
1 small onion, finely chopped
salt and pepper
½ can sweet corn kernels, drained
  (140 g or 5 oz)

finely grated rind of ½ a lemon
squeeze lemon juice
30 ml (1 tablespoon) chopped
  parsley
1 egg

To serve with a fowl

Grate the suet and add to the other ingredients finely chopped. Bind together with beaten egg.

Yorkshire

50 g (2 oz) suet
100 g (4 oz) breadcrumbs
1 small onion, chopped finely
30 ml (1 tablespoon) chopped
  parsley

10 ml (1 teaspoon) chopped mint
2½ ml (½ teaspoon) chopped thyme
4 nasturtium leaves, chopped
salt and pepper
1 egg

Unusual stuffing for turkey

Mix all together. This quantity is sufficient to stuff the crop of the bird.

Pembrokeshire

100 g (4 oz) fresh breadcrumbs
100 g (4 oz) diced apple
50 g (2 oz) chopped onion

25 g (1 oz) raisins
25 g (1 oz) melted margarine
pepper and salt

10 Hot Puddings

Apple and almond pancakes

Peel, core and slice apples, toss in lemon juice. Melt butter in pan,
add sugar and stir in apples, juice and cinnamon. Cook gently,
stirring occasionally until soft. Stir in ground almonds and sultanas.

Cook pancakes – spread filling along centres, roll up and arrange
in an ovenproof dish. Sprinkle almonds on top – re-heat in oven and
dredge with icing sugar before serving. Serves 4.
Yorkshire

Pancakes
100 g (4 oz) plain flour
1 egg
pinch salt
250 ml (½ pint) milk

Filling
500 g (1 lb) cooking apples
juice 1 lemon

50 g (2 oz) butter
50 g (2 oz) caster sugar
5 ml (⅛ teaspoon) cinnamon
25 g (1 oz) ground almonds
25 g (1 oz) sultanas
50 g (2 oz) flaked or nibbed
  almonds
icing sugar

Apple crisp

Peel, core and slice apples and stew with 50 g (2 tablespoons) sugar until soft.

Sieve baking powder and ground rice together, add coconut.

Cream margarine and caster sugar until light, adding almond essence slowly.

Beat egg and add alternately with dry ingredients to the creamed mixture.

Grease a shallow fireproof dish and spread the jam over the bottom.

Place stewed apples over the jam then cover the apples with the creamed mixture.

Bake in a fairly hot oven, 200°C (400°F), Gas 6, for 15–20 minutes or until top is crisp. Serves 4.

Devon

500 g (1 lb) Bramley or other cooking apples	50 g (2 oz) desiccated coconut
50 g (2 tablespoons) sugar	50 g (2 oz) margarine
25 g (1 oz) ground rice	50 g (2 oz) caster sugar
5 ml (1 level teaspoon) baking powder	2½ ml (½ teaspoon) almond essence
	1 egg
	60 ml (2 tablespoons) jam

Apple flan

Line a greased flan tin with short pastry. Into this put grated apple, raisins, sprinkled sugar and a little powdered cinnamon in layers, finishing with apple. Pour over this a few tablespoons of (melted) golden syrup. Put a few knobs of butter on top, and bake for about 20 minutes at 220°C (425°F), Gas 7.

(My own invention and well liked.)

Devon

short pastry	cinnamon
grated apple	golden syrup, melted
raisins	a few knobs of butter
sugar	

Apple soufflé

Peel, core and slice apples, cook with sugar and a little water if necessary. When tender add butter, cinnamon and beaten yolks.

Whisk whites stiffly and fold into apple mixture. Turn into well-buttered soufflé dish, sprinkle with almonds. Place in oven, 190–200°C (375–400°F), Gas 5–6, for about 30 minutes. Serve with whipped cream. Serves 4.
Durham

2 medium apples (350 g or ¾ lb)	3 egg whites
50 g (2 oz) caster sugar	25 g (1 oz) chopped almonds
25 g (1 oz) butter	whipped cream
pinch cinnamon	1-l (1½-pint) soufflé dish
2 egg yolks	

Apple streusel

Make pastry and line an 18–20-cm (7–8-inch) flan ring. Peel, core and slice apples, toss in lemon juice and arrange in pastry shell. Sprinkle with sugar and spices. For topping mix together flour, sugar and lemon rind. Cut up softened butter or margarine into mixture using pastry blender or two knives until crumbly. Sprinkle mixture over apples.

Bake in hot oven 230°C (450°F), Gas 8, for 15 minutes. Reduce to 180°C (350°F), Gas 4, and cook for 20 minutes. Serves 6.
Yorkshire

Note: Pastry shell can be omitted and sweet made in a pie-dish.

Pastry	1 ml (¼ level teaspoon) nutmeg or
150 g (6 oz) flour	allspice
75 g (3 oz) lard	
water to mix	*Topping*
	75 g (3 oz) sifted plain flour
Filling	75 g (3 oz) brown sugar
450 g (1 lb) cooking apples	grated rind of lemon
slice of lemon	75 g (6 tablespoons) softened
25 g (1 oz) sugar	butter or margarine
1 ml (¼ level teaspoon) cinnamon	

Baked lemon whip

Sift sugar, flour and salt together, beat in egg yolks, lemon juice and rind and milk. Melt butter and stir in mixture. Beat egg whites then fold into mixture.

Pour into a dish and stand in baking tin with hot water half-way up. Bake at 190°C (375°F), Gas 5, for 30–40 minutes. Sprinkle top with caster sugar. Serves 3–4.

Yorkshire

175 g (6 oz) sugar
15 ml (1 level tablespoon) plain flour
good pinch of salt
2 eggs

rind and juice of 1 large or 2 small lemons
150 ml (¼ pint) milk
25 g (1 oz) butter
light sprinkling of caster sugar

Blackcurrant flan

Sieve the flour and cinnamon, rub in the margarine, mix in ground almonds and sugar.

Sprinkle with the lemon juice, beat in the egg to a firm paste. Reserve ¼ of the paste to form a lattice topping on the flan. Roll the remaining paste and line an 18-cm (7-inch) flan ring (preferably fluted).

Prepare the blackcurrants, half fill the case with the fruit, sprinkle on the sugar, fill the case with the remaining fruit. With the trimmings and reserved paste, cut strips 1 cm (⅓ inch) wide and arrange in a lattice pattern on the top. Brush the lattice with water and sprinkle with caster sugar to produce a glaze.

Bake at 200°C (400°F), Gas 6, for approximately 20–25 minutes. Serves 4.

Cumberland

125 g (4 oz) plain flour
10 ml (¾ dessertspoon) cinnamon
70 g (2½ oz) butter or margarine
20 g (¾ oz) ground almonds
20 g (¾ oz) caster sugar

5 ml (1 teaspoon) lemon juice
15 ml (1 tablespoon) beaten egg
350 g (12 oz) blackcurrants
75 g (3 oz) sugar

Bread pudding de luxe

Grease the pie-dish. Put milk into a saucepan and bring to the boil, then add lard and stir until melted. Crumble bread into greased dish and add fruit and sugar. Beat egg and salt and add to boiled milk and melted lard. Pour over bread and mix well together.

Bake in oven, 200°C (400°F), Gas 6, for 30 minutes. Serves 4.

Berkshire

300 ml (½ pint) milk
50 g (2 oz) lard
100 g (4 oz) bread (not crust)
50 g (2 oz) currants
50 g (2 oz) sultanas

50 g (2 oz) raisins
50 g (2 oz) moist brown sugar
1 egg
pinch of salt

Caramelled rice

Cook rice in milk with vanilla and sugar, very slowly, for 1–1½ hours. Stir in peel and cherries while hot. When cool, fold in cream.

Put in a dish, and sprinkle with brown sugar and crisp under grill for 1 minute. Serve with cream or ice-cream.

Northumberland

75 g (3 oz) rice
600 ml (1 pint) milk
vanilla essence
50 g (2 oz) sugar
50 g (2 oz) candied lemon peel

25 g (1 oz) glacé cherries
75 ml (½ gill) thin cream or
  evaporated milk
50–75 g (2–3 oz) brown sugar

Note for beginners

The best way of cooking the rice is in a double boiler, cooking until the rice is soft and the mixture creamy.

It makes enough for 4, more if served with ice-cream.

Cheese surprise

Make pastry and line a 20-cm (8-inch) flan ring. Bake in a moderate oven, 190°C (375°F), Gas 5.

Mix cheese, egg yolks, sugar, rind and milk or cream together thoroughly. Add the stiffly beaten egg whites and pour into the already cooked pastry case. Bake for 15–20 minutes at 180°C (350°F), Gas 4.

Decorate with more orange rind cut into strips. Serves 4–6.

Cumberland

cooked pastry flan made with
  100 g (4 oz) flour and 50 g (2 oz)
  butter
150 g (6 oz) cream cheese
2 eggs

100 g (4 tablespoons) sugar
grated rind of ½ orange
125 ml (¼ pint) cream or top of
  milk
little orange rind to decorate

Coconut apple pudding

Peel and stew the apples in the water until tender, and beat with a wooden spoon until smooth. Stir in the coconut, sugar, breadcrumbs, lemon rind, butter and beaten egg. Mix all together thoroughly and turn into a greased fireproof dish.

Bake in a moderate oven, 180°C (350°F), Gas 4, until set, about 25 minutes. Lower the heat if the pudding shows any tendency to boil. Serves 4.
Isle of Ely

500 g (1 lb) cooking apples
250 ml (½ pint) water
40 g (2 tablespoons) desiccated coconut
50 g (2 tablespoons) sugar

25 g (1 oz) breadcrumbs
grated rind of 1 lemon
25 g (1 oz) butter or margarine
1 egg

Coffee and walnut pudding

Cream butter and sugar, add beaten egg and flour gradually. Add ground rice and walnuts, coffee and vanilla essence and baking powder. Mix well and put into a greased basin, 600-ml (1-pint) size, and steam for 1½ hours. Serve with hot custard. Serves 4.
Northumberland

50 g (2 oz) butter
50 g (2 oz) sugar
2 eggs
50 g (2 oz) plain flour
25 g (1 oz) ground rice

50 g (2 oz) chopped walnuts
10 ml (1 dessertspoon) coffee essence
vanilla flavouring
10 ml (1 teaspoon) baking powder

Cornish burnt cream

Put a layer of baked custard in the bottom of a pie-dish, then a layer of clotted cream, then more layers of custard and cream until the dish is full. Slice some citron very thin and put on top. Sprinkle with caster sugar and lightly brown.
Cornwall

baked custard
clotted cream

citron peel
caster sugar

Devonshire omelette

Peel, core, slice and cook the apples in a pan with 3 tablespoons of water, and the sugar, until it is a soft pulp. Add the butter and mix thoroughly, also the powdered cinnamon, macaroons and the beaten yolks.

Whisk the whites to a stiff froth and stir lightly into the other ingredients.

Thickly butter a 600-ml (1-pint) fireproof dish and pour in the mixture. Dredge the surface with caster sugar, and place the dish in a hot oven, 200°C (400°F), Gas 6, for about 20 minutes until it is puffed up and brown. Serves 4.
Devon

3 large cooking apples
50 g or more (2 tablespoons) caster
  sugar
15 g (½ oz) fresh butter
powdered cinnamon

50 g (2 tablespoons) powdered
  macaroons
2 eggs
caster sugar for sprinkling

Elizabeth Raffald's apple pudding
18th Century

Line an 18-cm (7-inch) flan tin with pastry and bake blind.

Cream the butter and add to the warm stewed apple. Beat well. Beat the eggs and add to the apple mixture with the sugar and lemon rind. Fill pastry case and bake in a moderate oven for about 30 minutes, 190°C (375°F), Gas 5. Serves 4.
Yorkshire

shortcrust pastry
100 g (4 oz) stewed apples
100 g (4 oz) butter

75–100 g (3–4 oz) soft brown sugar
3 eggs
grated rind of 1 lemon

Grenadier's pudding

Mix well and steam in a 425-ml (¾-pint) greased basin for 2 hours. Serve with custard sauce. Serves 4.
Northumberland

100 g (4 oz) breadcrumbs
75 g (3 oz) red jam (any variety)
2½ ml (½ teaspoon) bicarbonate of
  soda

50 g (2 oz) sugar
50 g (2 oz) butter, melted
1 well-beaten egg

Isle of Wight pudding

Roll out pastry to a rectangle. Spread with golden syrup and sprinkle
with cleaned dried fruit. Roll up into a neat roll leaving ends
unsealed. Put into pie-dish and pour milk over the roll to glaze and
until the milk is about half-way up the side of the roll. Bake for
¾–1 hour in a moderate oven, 190°C (375°F), Gas 5. Serve hot.
Serves 4.
Oxfordshire

4 oz pastry (short or flaky) (100 g   75 g (3 oz) dried fruit
  flour)   250 ml (½ pint) milk (approx)
50 g (2 tablespoons) golden syrup

King George First's Christmas pudding

Mix the dry ingredients. Moisten with eggs beaten to a froth, and
the milk, lemon juice and brandy mixed. Stand for at least 12 hours
in a cool place, then turn into buttered moulds. Boil for 8 hours at
first, then for 2 hours before serving.

    This quantity makes three puddings of about 1½ kg (3 lb) each.
Berkshire

700 g (1½ lb) finely shredded suet   15 ml (1 heaped teaspoon) mixed
450 g (1 lb) dried plums, stoned   spice
  and halved   ½ nutmeg, grated
450 g (1 lb) mixed peel cut in long   10 ml (2 teaspoons) salt
  strips   450 g (1 lb) eggs, weighed in their
450 g (1 lb) small raisins   shells
450 g (1 lb) sultanas   300 ml (½ pint) new milk
450 g (1 lb) currants   juice of one lemon
450 g (1 lb) sifted flour   a very large wineglass of brandy
450 g (1 lb) sugar   (170 ml)
450 g (1 lb) brown breadcrumbs

Note for beginners

For the dried plums use large plump prunes. For just one large
pudding make a third of the recipe. Cook it in the same way as any
ordinary steamed pudding, making sure it does not boil dry during
the long cooking.

Marmalade pudding

Mix thoroughly the flour, sugar, breadcrumbs, suet and salt, add marmalade and mix together with beaten egg and milk. Dissolve bicarbonate of soda in a little milk and mix well with the batter. Pour into a well-greased mould coated with brown sugar, 1-l (1½–2-pint) size, cover with greased paper and steam 2 hours. Turn out and serve with marmalade sauce or white sauce. Serves 6.
Northamptonshire and Soke of Peterborough

100 g (4 oz) flour
100 g (4 oz) demerara sugar
100 g (4 oz) breadcrumbs
100 g (4 oz) suet
pinch of salt

175 g (6 oz) marmalade
1 egg
about 150 ml (¼ pint) milk.
2½ ml (½ teaspoon) bicarbonate of soda

Pineapple upside-down pudding

Melt the margarine and brown sugar in the bottom of a cake tin, place the pineapple rings over the surface, placing a cherry in the centre of each. Place the cake crumbs and ground almonds into basin, pour on milk and add some small pieces of pineapple. Cream the butter and caster sugar and beat in yolks of eggs. Add the crumb mixture and fold in the stiffly whisked egg whites. Put on top of pineapple and bake in moderate oven. Turn out on to a hot dish with the pineapple uppermost. Serves 4–6.
Cheshire

25 g (1 oz) margarine
50 g (2 oz) brown sugar
1 tin pineapple rings (4–6 rings)
cherries
100 g (4 oz) cake crumbs

50 g (2 oz) ground almonds
60 ml (4 tablespoons) milk
50 g (2 oz) butter
50 g (2 oz) caster sugar
2 eggs

Note for beginners

Use either a round tin large enough to take 4 rings of pineapple or a larger oblong tin to take 6 rings. In the latter case the cake mixture will be thinner and cooking time a little less. Bake at 190°C (375°F), Gas 5, for 30–45 minutes.

Pumpkin pie

Cut one pumpkin into small cubes. Cover with water and simmer
until tender. Strain and put into pie-dish. Add brown sugar,
currants, grated nutmeg and a little lemon juice. Cover with
shortcrust pastry and bake in a moderate oven, 200°C (400°F), Gas 6,
for 30–45 minutes. Serve with cream or custard.
Devon

pumpkin	a little lemon juice
brown sugar	shortcrust pastry
currants	cream or custard
grated nutmeg	

Rhubarb and banana tart

Prepare rhubarb and cut in pieces, peel and chop bananas, put in a
600-ml (1-pint) pie-dish with water and sugar to taste. Cover with
pastry and bake in oven as for any fruit pie, about 40 minutes at
220°C (425°F), Gas 7. Serves 4.
Isle of Ely

shortcrust pastry (150 g flour)	30 ml or (2 tablespoons) water
500 g (1 lb) young rhubarb	sugar to taste (50 g)
3 large or 4 medium bananas	

Rhubarb charlotte

Toss the crumbs in the melted butter, shaking the pan as they
absorb it evenly. Spread a thin layer of these over the bottom of a
buttered 1-l (2-pint) ovenproof dish. Cover with rhubarb cut into
$2\frac{1}{2}$-cm (1-inch) lengths. Mix together the sugar and spices and the
grated orange rind. Sprinkle some of this over the rhubarb. Repeat
the layers until the dish is full, ending with a layer of crumbs.

Heat the syrup with the fruit juices and the water. When melted
pour over the charlotte. Cover with a piece of greaseproof paper and
bake in the centre of the oven, 200°C (400°F), Gas 6, for 20–30
minutes, depending on the age and thickness of the rhubarb, then
uncover and cook for a further 10 minutes approximately until the
top is golden and crisp. Serve with thin cream. Serves 4.
Derbyshire

150 g (6 oz) white breadcrumbs
50 g (2 oz) melted butter
450 g (1 lb) rhubarb
50 g (2 oz) brown sugar
5 ml ($\frac{1}{2}$ teaspoon) ground ginger
2$\frac{1}{2}$ ml ($\frac{1}{4}$ teaspoon) cinnamon
2$\frac{1}{2}$ ml ($\frac{1}{4}$ teaspoon) grated nutmeg

grated rind of 1 orange
30 ml (2 tablespoons) golden
  syrup
10 ml (1 dessertspoon) orange
  juice
10 ml (1 dessertspoon) lemon juice
thin cream

Rochester pudding

Cream butter and sugar until light and fluffy, add yolks of eggs,
beat well. Stir in the flour, then fold in the stiffly beaten whites of
eggs.

Grease a basin, 1-l (1$\frac{3}{4}$-pint) size, put in golden syrup (and a little
lemon juice if liked), put the mixture on top. Cover and steam for
2 hours. Serves 4–6.

Gloucestershire

100 g (4 oz) butter or margarine
100 g (4 oz) sugar
2 eggs

100 g (4 oz) self-raising flour
100 g (4 oz) golden syrup
a little lemon juice (optional)

Saxon pudding

Butter an 850-ml (1$\frac{1}{2}$-pint) basin, spread with the almonds. Slice
sponge cakes and fill basin in layers with ratafias. Beat eggs, add
sugar, milk, cream and sherry. Pour over the sponge cake. Let soak.
Steam for $\frac{1}{2}$ hour. Serve hot or cold. Serves 4.

Shropshire

40 g (1$\frac{1}{2}$ oz) butter
25 g (1 oz) toasted split almonds
4 sponge cakes
50 g (2 oz) ratafias
3 eggs

25 g (1 oz) sugar
250 ml ($\frac{1}{2}$ pint) milk
150 ml ($\frac{1}{4}$ pint) cream
45 ml (3 tablespoons) sherry

Tipsy strawberry meringue

Wash and hull strawberries, if large cut in half and place in
attractive ovenproof dish. Pour brandy over strawberries. Whisk the
egg whites until stiff. Whisk in half the sugar lightly, the other half
of the sugar is then folded in with a metal spoon. Cover the fruit
with the meringue mixture, and cook in centre of pre-heated oven

until lightly browned, about 10–15 minutes, 200°C (400°F), Gas 6. Can be served hot or cold. Serves 4–6.

Isle of Ely and Pembrokeshire

500 g (1 lb) strawberries	3 egg whites
15 ml (1 tablespoon) brandy	175 g (6 oz) caster sugar

Treacle George

Butter a pie-dish and line the bottom with thin short pastry. Spread with a good layer of golden syrup and fine white breadcrumbs. Add a sprinkle of lemon juice.

Fill up the dish with layers of pastry, syrup and crumbs, sprinkling each layer with a few drops of lemon juice. Bake in a fairly quick oven, 200°C (400°F), Gas 6, for ¾ hour. Serve hot or cold with clotted cream.

Devon

a little butter	fine white breadcrumbs
short pastry	lemon juice
golden syrup	clotted cream

11 Cold Sweets

Apple soufflé

Boil the milk with the lemon rind and strain on the egg yolks which
have been worked with the sugar.

Add the gelatine and thicken over the fire without boiling.

Strain, and when cool fold in lightly the stiffly whipped egg whites,
apple purée and two-thirds of the cream.

Put into small dishes and decorate with the rest of the cream when
quite cold. Serves 4–6.

Devon

400 ml (¾ pint) milk
the rind of 1 lemon
2 eggs
50 g (2 oz) sugar

15 g (1 dessertspoon) gelatine
250 ml (4 tablespoons) apple purée
30–45 ml (2–3 tablespoons) cream,
 whipped

Breadcrumb mousse

Put the egg yolks in a basin with the sugar and add the gelatine
dissolved in a little water. Beat over a pan of boiling water until the
mixture is thick and creamy. Remove from the heat and add the
breadcrumbs. Allow to cool a little and then add the whipped cream

and sherry. When almost cold add the beaten whites of the eggs and pour into a mould to set. Serve with clear fruit juice. Serves 4–6.
Yorkshire

2 eggs
50 g (2 oz) caster sugar
10 ml (¼ oz) powdered gelatine
30 g (2 heaped tablespoons)
  wholemeal breadcrumbs

150 ml (1 gill) cream, whipped
little sherry (15 ml)
clear fruit juice

Caramel d'orange

Make a caramel with the sugar and water and pour it on to an oiled baking sheet, leaving it to cool.

Whip your cream, peel and quarter the oranges, and pound the caramel very fine in a mortar. Arrange in layers in a glass dish, and serve with ginger snaps. Serves 6.
Northamptonshire and Soke of Peterborough

400 g (1 lb) loaf sugar
250 ml (½ pint) water
500 ml (1 pint) cream

6 oranges
ginger snaps

Note for beginners

To make the caramel, heat and stir sugar and water until the sugar dissolves, then boil rapidly until it turns a deep amber colour.

An alternative method for crushing the cold caramel is to break it into small pieces and process it in the electric blender.

Chestnut cream

Boil the chestnuts, skin and pass through a wire sieve. Mix a liberal supply of grated chocolate with the chestnuts. Put into a glass dish and spread over a thin layer of whipped cream.

Cover the surface with little divisions of carefully peeled sweet oranges and overlay them neatly.

Just before serving sprinkle over with a little grated chocolate not to be made wet with the cream. Serves 4.

Northamptonshire and Soke of Peterborough

500 g (1 lb) chestnuts
grated chocolate

whipped cream
sweet oranges

Note for beginners

To boil chestnuts Wash, cut a slit in the rounded sides of the shells, cover with water and boil for about 30 minutes. Drain and peel off shell and skin.

Chocorum cold dessert

Melt the chocolate in a basin over a pan of hot water, then cool slightly. Beat the egg yolks into the chocolate then add the rum. Whisk egg whites stiff and carefully fold into chocolate mixture. Divide between individual glasses (6), chill and decorate with cream and nuts. Serves 6.
Yorkshire

175 g (6 oz) plain chocolate
4 eggs, separated
30 ml (2 tablespoons) rum

150 ml ($\frac{1}{4}$ pint) double cream,
  whipped
25 g (1 oz) chopped nuts

Coffee ice-cream

Dissolve the sugar in the water in a thickish pan. Bring to the boil and boil fast for 5 minutes. Cool slightly. Pour on to the beaten egg yolks in a thin stream beating all the time. Put the bowl over hot water and beat until thick. When cold fold in the whipped cream and the coffee dissolved in the water. Freeze. Beat when just beginning to set and re-freeze. Serves 6–8, about $1\frac{1}{4}$ l (2 pints).
Hampshire

175 g (6 oz) caster sugar
150 ml ($\frac{1}{4}$ pint) water
5 egg yolks
300 ml ($\frac{1}{2}$ pint) cream

25 ml ($1\frac{1}{2}$ level tablespoons)
  instant coffee
10 ml (2 teaspoons) water

Cold chocolate soufflé

Separate eggs. Whisk yolks and sugar over hot water until thick and pale. Dissolve the chocolate in the milk and the gelatine in a little hot water; add both strained to the yolks, the lemon juice and vanilla. When nearly set, add whipped cream and lastly the stiffly beaten egg whites. Serves 6.
Berkshire

3 eggs
50 g (2 oz) caster sugar
50 g (2 oz) chocolate meunier
75 ml (½ gill) milk

15 g (½ oz) gelatine
juice of 1 lemon
300 ml (½ pint) cream
vanilla essence

Note for beginners

Warm the milk gently to dissolve the chocolate. Use about 3 tablespoons hot water to dissolve the gelatine. Be careful not to let the chocolate mixture set before adding cream and egg whites or the soufflé will be lumpy instead of smooth. Pour it into a large soufflé dish or individual dishes and leave in a cold place to set.

Custard jelly

Warm the milk, add the beaten egg yolks and sugar and flavouring. Stir over gentle heat until creamy. Pour into a basin.

Dissolve the gelatine in the water and add to the contents of the basin.

Lastly stir in the stiffly beaten egg whites. Pour into a wetted 1-l (2-pint) mould and leave until set. Turn out. Serves 4.
Leicestershire and Rutland

500 ml (1 pint) milk
2 eggs
50 g (2 tablespoons) sugar
few drops vanilla essence or other
  flavouring

15 g (½ oz) powdered gelatine
30 ml (1 tablespoon) water

Fruit and hazelnut galette

Brown the nuts in the oven at 180°C (350°F), Gas 4, until husks can be rubbed off (approx 7–8 minutes when nuts should be a deep golden brown). Reserve a few nuts for decoration and pass the remainder through a mincer or work until fine in a blender.

Soften butter, add sugar and beat together until light and fluffy.

Sift flour and salt and stir into mixture with the prepared nuts. Chill for at least 30 minutes.

Divide pastry into three and place each piece on a lightly floured baking sheet. Roll or pat into very thin rounds approximately 18 cm

(7 inches) in diameter. Bake for about 10 minutes in the oven at
190°C (375°F), Gas 5.

When cooked cut one round into six individual portions, cool on a
rack.

Whisk cream until thick. If fresh fruit is used sprinkle on the 25 g
(1 oz) sugar.

To finish, sandwich the layers together with cream and fruit
alternately, placing the cut portions on top. Dust with icing sugar.
Pipe a rosette of cream on each portion and decorate by placing a
whole hazelnut on each rosette.

The cooked pastry rounds will freeze well if carefully packed into
a container. Serves 6.
Derbyshire

75 g (3 oz) shelled hazelnuts
75 g (3 oz) butter
50 g (2 rounded tablespoons) caster
  sugar
100 g (4½ oz) flour
pinch of salt

Filling
fresh or tinned fruit
300 ml (½ pint) double cream
icing sugar (for dusting)
25 g (1 oz) sugar if fresh fruit is used

Fruit flan

Line an 18-cm (7-inch) cake tin or flan ring with the pastry. Beat the
sugar and butter to a cream, add the beaten egg, mix in the ground
almonds, then the other ingredients. Bake in a moderate oven,
160°C (325°F), Gas 3, for ½ hour or till brown on top. Serves 4.
Northumberland

shortcrust pastry
50 g (2 oz) butter
50 g (2 oz) sugar
1 egg

50 g (2 oz) ground almonds
50 g (2 oz) chopped walnuts
50 g (2 oz) glacé cherries
50 g (2 oz) sultanas

Fruit sorbet

Beat egg until frothy, then whisk in syrup. Add the orange and lemon
juice and the smoothly mashed banana. Stir in water. Turn into
refrigerator tray, freezing until firm and beat up well when half
frozen. Serves 4.
Durham

1 egg
100 g (4 oz) golden syrup
juice of 1 orange

juice of 1 lemon
1 banana
200 ml (1½ gills) cold water

Ginger mould

Dissolve the gelatine in the hot water, add it to the milk, sugar, butter and well-beaten egg yolks. Stir over heat in a double saucepan until thick, but do not boil. Add ground ginger and, when nearly set, fold in stiffly beaten egg whites and lemon juice. Pour into a wetted mould, 700–850-ml (1¼–1½-pint) size and leave to set. When set turn out and serve with preserved ginger and syrup. Serves 4.
Herefordshire

15 g (½ oz) gelatine
30–45 ml (2–3 tablespoons) hot
  water
300 ml (½ pint) milk
50 g (2 oz) caster sugar
75 g (3 oz) butter

2 eggs
5 ml or more (½ teaspoon) ground
  ginger
juice of 1 lemon
preserved ginger and syrup

Gooseberry velvet

Cook 450 g (1 lb) gooseberries with 300 ml (½ pint) water and 75 g (3 oz) sugar. Pass through a very fine sieve or muslin – make up to 600 ml (1 pint) with water. Sprinkle gelatine over the warm liquid – stir until dissolved. Tint to a delicate green. Cool, then pour into 6 sundae glasses – leave to set.

Cook the remaining gooseberries in 30 ml (2 tablespoons) water and 100 g (4 oz) sugar until fruit is soft. Sieve and leave to cool.

Make the custard – leave to cool, covered to prevent skin forming. Lightly whip the cream.

Fold the custard into the gooseberry purée, add colouring to colour of jelly – fold in whipped cream. Pour on to the jelly in the glasses. Leave to set.

Decorate with crystallized ginger, poached whole berries and grated chocolate. Serves 4–6.
Cumberland

1 kg (2 lb) gooseberries
200 g (7 oz) sugar, or to taste
approximately 300 ml ($\frac{1}{2}$ pint)
  water
15 g ($\frac{1}{2}$ oz) gelatine
green colouring
150 ml ($\frac{1}{4}$ pint) double cream
crystallized ginger

grated chocolate
poached whole berries for garnish

Custard
150 ml ($\frac{1}{4}$ pint) milk
15 ml (3 level teaspoons) custard
  powder
15 ml (3 level teaspoons) sugar

Honey cream

Dissolve the jelly in 400 ml ($\frac{3}{4}$ pint) hot water, add lemon juice.
Allow to cool.

When starting to set, whisk until light and frothy, add finely
grated lemon rind, honey and cream. Blend thoroughly, pour into
mould and allow to set. Serves 4.
Cumberland

lemon jelly
juice of 1 lemon
grated rind of $\frac{1}{2}$ lemon

30 ml (2 tablespoons) honey
150 ml ($\frac{1}{4}$ pint) cream, whipped

Ice-cream

Whip egg whites until very stiff. Whip milk lightly, adding the sugar
and vanilla essence. Gradually whip egg whites into milk. Pour into
ice drawer and freeze. (The mixture is sufficient to fill about two
trays.)

* egg whites
*140 ml ($\frac{1}{4}$ pint) prepared
  evaporated milk

4 level tablespoons icing sugar
  (about 40 g or 1$\frac{1}{2}$ oz)
5 ml (1 teaspoon) vanilla essence

* *To prepare evaporated milk* Place unopened tin of milk in saucepan
of cold water. Bring to the boil and boil for 15 minutes. Leave to
cool and when cold store in refrigerator until next day. It is then
ready for use. Several cans may be prepared at the same time and
stored indefinitely in the refrigerator. Serves 6–8.
Yorkshire

Lemon cream
Homburg crème

Beat yolks with sugar. Add lemon juice and finely grated rind. Heat

over boiling water till thickened, stirring constantly. When cold add stiffly beaten egg whites. Serve at once. Serves 3.
Cumberland

2 eggs   1 lemon
100 g (4 oz) sugar

Note for beginners

The egg yolk mixture can be cooked in advance and this and the unbeaten egg whites stored in a cold place. Whip the whites and combine the two just before the meal is to be served.

Lemon ginger crunch

Peel and slice bananas into the bases of 4 or 5 sundae glasses. Sprinkle on half the ginger crumbs.

Whip cream until thick, reserving a little for decoration, fold the rest into the lemon yogurt. Spoon the lemon cream over the ginger crumbs, and cover the cream with the remaining crumbs.

Top with the reserved cream and decorate with the lemon slices. Chill well before serving.

This recipe was also tested using pineapple yogurt; it was delicious. Serves 4.
Derbyshire

2 bananas   two 142-ml (5-oz) cartons lemon
50 g (2 oz) ginger biscuits   yogurt
  (crushed)   garnish: 4 thin slices lemon
150 ml (5 oz) cream

Martinique egg

Place on a slice of pineapple a round coffee ice-cream and cap with half a peach. Arrange whipped cream or whipped evaporated milk all round to resemble fried egg. Pour over a little rum and serve cold.
Oxfordshire

pineapple slices   whipped cream or whipped
coffee ice-cream   evaporated milk
peach halves   rum

Orange cream

Beat yolk and sugar. Add juice of orange. Heat over boiling water till thickened. Dissolve gelatine in the boiling water in which the rind has been soaking. Add to mixture and when it has cooled fold in stiffly beaten whites. Put into dish or individual glasses and allow to set. Serves 3.
Cumberland

2 eggs
50 g (2 oz) sugar
1 orange

7½ ml (⅛ oz) gelatine
150 ml (¼ pint) boiling water

Orange jelly soufflé

Soak the gelatine in the orange juice for a short time, then add the sugar and heat very gently in a saucepan (do not boil). Remove from the stove and pour gently over the beaten yolks of eggs. Stir well and leave to cool. Add the stiffly beaten egg whites and fold them into the soufflé. Leave to set and put whipped cream, flavoured with a little sherry, on top. Decorate with slices of blanched almonds.

A small tin of mandarin oranges added to the soufflé makes a delicious flavour. Serves 6–8.
Oxfordshire

15 g (1 tablespoon) powdered
  gelatine
600 ml (1 pint) orange juice
  (canned or fresh)
50 g (2 tablespoons) sugar
3 eggs

whipped cream
sherry
blanched almonds
a small tin of mandarin oranges
  (optional)

Quick ice-cream

Whip the cream. Separate egg and whisk yolk and white separately. Fold all together with sugar and vanilla.

Pour into trays and freeze till firm. No stirring is needed.

Flavourings can be varied by using a little fresh fruit purée instead of vanilla. It makes sufficient for 4–6.
Cumberland

150 ml (¼ pint) cream
1 large egg

50 g (2 oz) caster sugar
vanilla essence

Stone cream

Dissolve the gelatine in hot, not boiling water (about 60 ml or 4 tablespoons). Tear laurel leaves in half and simmer in milk for a few minutes. Remove leaves from milk. Pour on to eggs – add sugar and return to saucepan. Stir until it coats the spoon – do not boil – allow to cool, add gelatine, put jam at bottom of glass bowl and strain contents of saucepan over. Allow to set and serve with cream. Decorate with split almonds. Serves 4.

Oxfordshire

gelatine to set 600 ml (1 pint)
2 or 3 laurel leaves
600 ml (1 pint) milk
3 eggs (yolks only)

25 g (1 oz) caster sugar
a little apricot jam
a few almonds if liked
cream

Strawberry ice-cream

Whip the cream lightly and fold in the sieved icing sugar and the strawberry purée. Whisk the egg whites stiffly and fold into the mixture. Put in containers in the ice box compartment and freeze until solid. Bring out and beat until it is smooth and creamy. Return until needed. About another 2 hours to freeze again.

If you brush the container out with glycerine it will prevent the ice-cream from sticking. Serves 4.

Hampshire

300 ml (½ pint) cream
50 g (2 oz) icing sugar

225 g (8 oz) strawberries or a tin
of strawberries, puréed
2 egg whites

Note for beginners

If using canned strawberries you will need enough drained strawberries to give about 150 ml (¼ pint) of purée.

Strawberry mousse

Drain strawberries and make juice up to 300 ml (½ pint) with water. Heat liquid and pour over the jelly, allow to become cold but not set.

Whisk egg whites, whisk cream and reserve some for decoration.

Fold cream into jelly mixture, followed by egg whites and strawberries – reserve 4 for decoration. Pour mixture into a glass dish, and allow to set.

Decorate with piped cream and strawberries. Serves 6–8.
Cumberland

454-g (1-lb) can of strawberries
1 packet strawberry jelly

2 egg whites
300 ml (½ pint) double cream

Surprise roll

Dip biscuits one by one in sherry, upend and coat with whipped cream. Place coated biscuits together forming a long roll on the plate, cover with more whipped cream and then with grated chocolate.

Place the sweet in the refrigerator overnight so that it sets firmly before serving. Serves 4.
Cumberland

1 packet Maryland cookies or
  biscuits with chopped chocolate,
  about 170 g (6 oz)
sweet sherry

200 ml (⅓ pint) cream (to be
  whipped)
grated plain chocolate

Syllabub

Finely grate rind of lemon, squeeze juice. Put rind, juice, sherry, sugar and brandy in bowl and stir until sugar is dissolved. Pour in cream and whisk until thick. Spoon into individual glasses, leave in cool place. Can be made one day in advance. Serves 6.
Shropshire

1 large lemon
150 ml (¼ pint) medium sweet
  sherry

50 g (2 oz) caster sugar
30 ml (2 tablespoons) brandy
300 ml (½ pint) double cream

12 Fruit

Apple hedgehog

Very useful for windfalls. Can be stored for several months. Ready to turn out and serve.

Place prepared apples in a preserving pan with enough water to prevent burning. When cooked, beat to a smooth pulp, return to pan and add sugar and lemon juice. Stir over gentle heat until sugar is dissolved, then boil for 30 minutes. Place in small moulds, cover and tie down.

To serve, turn out and decorate with whipped cream and chopped nuts or with custard sauce.

Westmorland

2 kg (4 lb) apples, weighed after   1½ kg (3 lb) sugar
  paring and coring   lemon juice if liked

Honey apples

Mix together half the chopped walnuts, raisins, honey and breadcrumbs, fill apples with the mixture. Bake until apples are tender, at 180°C (350°F), Gas 4, for 45 minutes.

Prepare the glaze, heat together in a saucepan jam, water and lemon juice. Bring to the boil and keep on the heat for 3 minutes. Remove from heat and pass through sieve. Brush cooked apples with the glaze and coat sides with remaining walnuts. Decorate with angelica and cherries.

Serve hot with custard sweetened with honey.

Honey may be used instead of jam for glaze.

Yorkshire

100 g (4 oz) chopped walnuts	*To glaze*
25 g (1 oz) raisins	60 ml (2 tablespoons) apricot jam
30 ml (2 tablespoons) honey	30 ml (2 tablespoons) water
25 g (1 oz) fine breadcrumbs	little lemon juice
4 large apples, washed and cored	
	Decoration
	angelica
	cherries

Portuguese apples

Peel and core some apples, stand them on some paper in a baking tin, fill centres with raspberry jam, bake till the apples are quite tender. Pour custard sauce over and serve when cold.

Northamptonshire and Soke of Peterborough

apples	egg custard sauce, 300 ml or (1
raspberry jam	pint) for 2–3 apples

Note for beginners

A piece of foil can be used instead of paper. When cooked transfer apples to serving dish before pouring the custard over them.

Baking temperature can be 180–200°C (350°–400°F), Gas 4–6, time about 40 minutes depending on temperature and size of apple.

Stuffed baked apple

Remove the centre of the apple with a corer and make a cut round the middle. Put the apple in a heatproof dish and fill the hole with any of the suggested fillings. Place a small piece of butter or margarine on the apple and pour two tablespoons water round it.

Bake in a moderately hot oven about 45 minutes until the fruit is quite tender, 190–200°C (375°–400°F), Gas 5–6.

Derbyshire

1 large cooking apple

Alternative fillings
demerara sugar and crystallized
  ginger

chopped dates with lemon juice
stoned raisins or sultanas
marmalade or mincemeat

Apricot ambrosia

Choose the finest dried apricots and soak for at least an hour in just
enough water to cover them. Cook slowly with an orange finely
shredded (rind and pulp) until most of the water is absorbed. Rub
through a fine sieve, add a little honey and a few spoonfuls of any
good orange liqueur. The mixture should be a thick purée but not
solid.

Scoop out the pulp of lemons and make cups of the half rinds,
cutting the edges into scallops. Fill these shells with the ambrosia
and sprinkle with finely cut almonds. Serves 6–8.
Lincolnshire

450 g (1 lb) dried apricots
1 orange
honey

orange liqueur
lemon skins
blanched almonds

Apricots in port wine

Fill the jar with chopped dried apricots, pressing well down. Fill jar
to brim with port wine and cover tightly. Top up with port wine
from time to time, keeping at least 6 months.

Serve with ice-cream or Christmas pudding.
Pembrokeshire

dried apricots
inexpensive port wine

large jar with well-fitted lid

Baked bananas in raisin sauce

Simmer raisins in 300 ml ($\frac{1}{2}$ pint) cold water for 10 minutes. Strain
and save the liquid. Stir in the honey, lemon juice and the blended
cornflour. Cook together until the mixture thickens. Return the
raisins to the sauce.

Halve the peeled bananas lengthwise and lay in a 1-l (2-pint)
fireproof dish in which the butter has been melted. Pour over the

hot sauce and cook at 190°C (375°F), Gas 5, for 25 minutes.

Serve hot or cold with thick cream. Serves 4–6.

Cambridgeshire

50 g (2 oz) seedless raisins	6 bananas
40 g (1½ oz) honey	25 g (1 oz) butter
juice of 1 large lemon	thick cream
7½ ml (1½ level teaspoons) cornflour blended in a little cold water	

Banana bake

Place a banana in its skin on the shelf of the oven at about 180°C (350°F), Gas 4, until the skin turns black, about 20 minutes. Open out on to the serving dish.

This tastes quite delicious on its own, and the addition of the rum and whipped cream turns it into a party dish.

Derbyshire

1 banana	15 ml (1 tablespoon) cream,
15 ml (1 tablespoon) rum (optional)	whipped (optional)

Banana sweet

Allow these quantities for each person. Slice bananas into a shallow dish or individual dishes. Cover thickly with grated chocolate. Decorate with whipped cream and/or glacé cherries.

Berkshire

1 banana	whipped cream
25 g (1 oz) chocolate	glacé cherries

Blackberry and banana

Put the blackberries in a basin, sprinkle with caster sugar, leave a few hours and press several times.

Peel the bananas, cut into 4 or 8 pieces each, lengthwise. Put a layer of blackberries into a dish, then one sliced banana. Repeat with blackberries and second sliced banana. Serves 4–6.

West Kent

500 g (1 lb) blackberries	2 bananas
caster sugar	

Blackberry apples

Scoop out cores without breaking the apples. Mash the blackberries with the sugar and fill apple centres. Place the stuffed apples on a baking tin and pour round golden syrup mixed with an equal quantity of water. Bake in a slow oven, baste frequently with the syrup.
West Kent

6 large cooking apples
125 g (4 oz) blackberries
sugar to taste

45 ml (3 tablespoons) golden
  syrup

Note for beginners

For baking apples in a slow oven use a temperature of 160°C (325°F), Gas 3, and allow an hour or more depending on the size and variety of apple. Test the centres with a fork to see when they are soft.

Cherries stewed without water

Place the cherries in a double boiler with the sugar and lemon juice. Cook until tender. The rich juice produced makes a very colourful dish.
West Kent

500 g (1 lb) ripe dark cherries,
  stoned

100 g (4 tablespoons) demerara
  sugar
juice of 1 lemon

Iced currants

Select fine clusters of red-, white- or blackcurrants. Well beat the egg whites and mix with the water. Take the currants, a cluster at a time, and dip them in. Drain for a moment, then roll or shake them in the caster sugar. Let them dry on clean kitchen paper, when the sugar will crystallize round each currant, giving a very pretty effect.

All fresh fruit may be prepared in this way and attractively arranged on one dish makes an excellent summer dessert.
Devon

currants
2 egg whites

150 ml (¼ pint) water
caster sugar

Cream, mixed fresh fruit

Boil currants and cherries for 10 minutes quickly with sugar, skim often, add raspberries and strawberries, simmer 2 minutes longer. Press through a sieve.

Stir in the cream and whisk quickly until it thickens. Serve in glasses.

Make 2 hours before serving. Keep in a very cool place or refrigerate. Serves 6.

West Kent

85 ml (½ teacup) whitecurrants
170 ml (1 teacup) redcurrants
85 ml (½ teacup) Kentish cherries
400 g (1 lb) loaf sugar

170 ml (1 teacup) raspberries
170 ml (1 teacup) strawberries
600 ml (1 pint) cream

Fresh fruit jelly

Dissolve the gelatine in 2 or 3 tablespoons of water, heated very gently. Mix the syrup, water and lemon juice together, and add the dissolved gelatine. Stir thoroughly and pour into a wet mould, 1-l (1½-pint) size. Serves 4.

Leicestershire and Rutland

15 g (½ oz) powdered gelatine
300 ml (½ pint) fruit syrup

300 ml (½ pint) water
juice of ½ lemon

Fresh fruit salad

Make an hour or two before serving. Prepare any fruit, sprinkling well with caster sugar. For a special occasion add wine, cider or ginger ale. A dash or two of angostura bitters develops the flavour of the fruit.

If bananas or pears are included add a tablespoon of lemon juice. Sprig of mint and frosted grapes at the end add a party air.

Lincolnshire

Quick fruit salad

Scrub the apple and peel the orange. Remove any pith left on the orange. Slice it down in rings, then cut roughly into cubes. Place it in a basin.

Cut apples into quarters, peel each quarter and remove the core. Cut into slices and then into cubes again. Put in the basin.

Sprinkle with sugar and leave to mature for at least 1½ hours. Serves 2–3.

Derbyshire

1 Cox's orange pippin apple	30 ml (2 level tablespoons) sugar
1 large orange	

Filled melon

Scoop out inside of melon with a ball scoop. Mix the fruit and ginger together with a small amount of syrup. Put all inside the melon case and pour over cointreau or brandy.

Pembrokeshire

1 melon	apricots
apples, pears (cut small)	sugar syrup
grapes (pipped)	2 tablespoons cointreau or brandy
ginger (stem or crystallized)	

Peaches in wine

Melt sugar in water and simmer for a few minutes. Skin the peaches by dipping them in boiling water like tomatoes. Simmer them in the syrup for 4 minutes. Remove.

Slice the peaches into goblets, pour in just enough Sauterne to cover and put a very large blob of soured cream on the top of that. Serve with the 'langues de chat'.

Hampshire

100 g (4 oz) caster sugar	Sauterne
250 ml (½ pint) water	soured cream
6 peaches	plain chocolate 'langues de chat'

Pears baked in syrup

Make a thick syrup of brown sugar and water. Peel, halve and core the pears. Place in a baking dish with 1 cm (½ inch) of syrup. Bake

slowly, and baste often until the pears are cooked and coated with a thin layer of brown syrup.
West Kent

brown sugar   pears
water

Note for beginners

To make a thick syrup dissolve about 100 g (4 oz) sugar in 300 ml (½ pint) water. Cook the pears at about 160°C (325°F), Gas 3; time depending on the type of pears used, average about 1 hour.

Pear hedgehogs

Peel and core some pears, cook in a little water (plus some red wine) until soft. Sweeten, add rind of lemon too.

When cooked stuff the stalk end of fruit with sliced almonds. Fill the cavity with a spoon of Devonshire cream and decorate with a few more almonds.
Isle of Ely

pears   rind of lemon
red wine   almonds
sugar   Devonshire cream

Pears in red wine

To make syrup – dissolve sugar, water, wine and flavourings slowly in a pan, bring to the boil, boil 1 minute.

Keeping stalks on pears, remove peel and the 'eye' from each base and place in the prepared syrup.

Poach pears in the pan, covered, until tender, allow 20–30 minutes to prevent them discolouring around the cores. Remove pears and strain syrup.

Mix the arrowroot with a little water before adding to syrup and stir until boiling, cook until the liquid is clear.

Arrange pears in a serving dish, spoon over the wine sauce and finish by scattering the browned and shredded almonds on top. Serve cold, hand round a bowl of whipped cream separately.

175

To shred and brown almonds
Blanch, skin and split, cut each lengthways in fine pieces and brown
quickly in the oven at 180°C (350°F), Gas 4.
Cumberland

125 g (5 oz) lump sugar (gives a
  crystal clear liquid)
150 ml (¼ pint) water
150 ml (¼ pint) red wine
strip of lemon rind
small piece of cinnamon stick

5–6 ripe dessert pears
10 ml (1 teaspoon) arrowroot
25 g (1 oz) almonds (shredded and
  browned)
whipped cream (optional)

Prunes with a difference

Wash the prunes and cover them with a solution of half water and
half tea (poured from the teapot after tea is over). Leave the prunes
to soak in the usual way.
    Place in the oven in a fireproof dish. Add syrup about ½ hour before
prunes are cooked.
Yorkshire

prunes
tea

25 g (1 tablespoon) golden syrup
  to 450 g (1 lb) prunes

Note for beginners

If modern soft prunes are soaked overnight they will only need ½
hour in the oven after they have come to simmering point, so add the
syrup at the beginning of the cooking time. Cook at 180°C (350°F),
Gas 4.

New twist
Prunes

Stew prunes in the usual way, then dissolve a blackcurrant jelly in a
little hot water and make up to 500–600 ml (1 pint) with the prune
juice.
    Leave jelly until the point of setting, then gently drop the prunes
into it, and leave till jelly is firm.
Yorkshire

100–200 g (4–8 oz) prunes
500 ml (1 pint) packet blackcurrant
  jelly

Poached quinces

Quinces are worth looking for. They have a delicious flavour and
scent.

Peel the fruit and leave whole – with their stalks still on. Stand
upright in a fireproof dish containing the water. Pour honey over
each quince and put cloves in the dish. Cover tightly and cook in a
very slow oven, 140°C (275°F), Gas 1, for 2 or even 3 hours. Serve
cold with mountains of whipped cream.
Hampshire

quinces
35 ml (¼ gill) water
15–20 ml (1 tablespoon) honey for
  each quince

1 or 2 cloves
whipped cream

Dream raspberries

Place the raspberries straight into a dish in which a little caster sugar
has been sprinkled. Cover over with the rest of the sugar and pour
the rum on top. Put in a cool place for an hour or two or longer.
Serve with the cream whipped, sweetened slightly and flavoured
with almond essence.
  A plate of sponge cakes or sponge fingers makes a pleasant
accompaniment. Serves 4.
Northamptonshire and Soke of Peterborough

500 g (1 lb) ripe raspberries
100 g (4 oz) caster sugar (or more
  if desired)
10 ml (1 dessertspoon) rum

75 ml (½ gill) cream
sugar
5 drops almond essence
sponge cakes or sponge fingers

Röde gröde

A Scandinavian cold sweet (loosely translated means 'Red Gruel').

Summertime
1¼ l (2 pints) raspberries or raspberries and redcurrants
A good 300 ml (½ pint) water

Boil together gently for an hour, then strain. Measure 600 ml
(1 pint).

Wintertime
1 large tin (426 g) Scottish raspberries sieved and made up to 600 ml
(1 pint)

To thicken
25 g (1 oz) cornflour
A little extra sugar (about a heaped tablespoon)

Put measured 600 ml (pint) of purée (less a little to blend cornflour)
into saucepan and bring to boil. Add sugar and cornflour previously
mixed to a smooth paste with a little of the cold purée. Continue to
cook for a further 3 minutes. Pour into dish to set.

To garnish
Whipped cream
Blanched almonds

Serve with whipped cream all over it and with blanched almonds
standing up in the cream. Serves 3–4.
Cambridgeshire

Rhubarb compote

Rhubarb invariably keeps whole without any attention.

Wipe rhubarb and cut it into short lengths. Spread a layer of jam in
the bottom of a casserole. Cover thickly with rhubarb and add a little
more jam. Fill up with rhubarb and finish with the rest of the jam.
Cover and cook in a moderate oven for ½ hour, 180°C (350°F), Gas 4.
Serves 6.
Oxfordshire

750 g (1½ lb) rhubarb
175–250 g (3–4 tablespoons) jam

If raspberry jam is used warm it
first and rub it through a sieve to
remove pips

Stewed rhubarb

Cut rhubarb into 2½-cm (1-inch) lengths. Put into pan with water to cover. Cook until a fork will pierce (like potatoes). Drain well. Put rhubarb into dish, cover well with sugar and then add grated lemon rind and juice of a lemon. Leave to stand about an hour. This method is much better than stewing in the usual way.
Yorkshire

rhubarb   1 lemon
sugar

To stew rhubarb

Cut up in 2½-cm (1-inch) pieces. Place in a fireproof dish (that has a cover). Add the sugar. Leave overnight. Then carefully cook in own juice, in a slow oven, 160°C (325°F), Gas 3, for about ¾ hour.
Devon

500 g (1 lb) rhubarb   200 g (1 cup) sugar, approximately

13 Cakes

Banbury cakes

Cream the butter and sugar together until soft. Add the beaten egg
and mix thoroughly. Add cake crumbs or ground almonds, mixed
peel, currants and spice. Mix well together.

Roll out the pastry thinly. Cut into 12-cm (5-inch) rounds. Damp
half-way round the edge of each round. Put 1 spoonful of filling in
the centre of each round. Draw the edge up over the filling, taking
care to put the damped edge on to the top of the other edge. Press
lightly together. Form into an oval shape, turn over, flatten slightly
with the hand or rolling pin, reshape into an oval. Glaze with a little
milk. Sprinkle with sugar.

Put into a flat baking tin and bake in a hot oven for 20–25 minutes,
220°C (425°F), Gas 7. Cool on wire tray. Makes 10–12 cakes.
Oxfordshire

8 oz rough puff pastry (using 200 g flour)

Filling
25 g (1 oz) butter
50 g (2 oz) brown sugar
½ beaten egg

25 g (1 oz) cake crumbs or ground almonds
50 g (2 oz) mixed peel
100 g (4 oz) currants
2½ ml (½ level teaspoon) mixed spice
milk for brushing
sugar to sprinkle on top

Barm brack

Put fruit and sugar in a bowl, pour tea over and leave overnight.

Next day, line a 15-cm (6-inch) square tin with greaseproof paper and grease.

Add flour and egg to soaked fruit, mix well. Turn mixture into prepared tin and smooth over.

Bake in centre of oven, 180°C (350°F), Gas 4, for 1 hour, then reduce heat to 150°C (300°F), Gas 2, for a further ¾ hour.

Cut next day. Excellent eaten with butter.

Cumberland

100 g (4 oz) cleaned currants
25 g (1 oz) chopped mixed peel
100 g (4 oz) cleaned sultanas
100 g (4 oz) soft brown sugar

200 ml (7½ fl oz) warm strained tea
225 g (8 oz) self-raising flour
1 large egg, beaten

Belgian chocolate cake

Grease and line an 18-cm (7-inch) cake tin with a detachable base.

Melt chocolate over heat.

Melt margarine in pan. Beat eggs well; add sugar and pour in margarine very slowly, stirring all the time. Add melted chocolate and beat well. Fold in broken biscuits (about 6-mm or ¼-inch size). Add nuts and flavouring and brandy.

Transfer mixture to cake tin. Decorate with nuts or ½ walnuts. Cover with paper and put aside to set. One hour is required in a fridge or up to 6 hours otherwise. Remove from tin by pushing up base.

Cambridgeshire

200 g (8 oz) plain chocolate
200 g (8 oz) margarine
2 eggs
20 ml (2 level dessertspoons) sugar
200 g (8 oz) Marie biscuits

15 g ($\frac{1}{2}$ oz) chopped walnuts
vanilla or almond essence or 5 ml
 (1 teaspoon) liquid coffee
plus a drop of brandy
more nuts for decoration

Border tart
Traditional recipe

Make the pastry and line an 18-cm (7-inch) plate or sandwich tin.

Beat margarine and sugar to a cream. Beat the egg and add to the mixture. Add the dried fruit, almonds and essence. Put the mixture into the pastry case, and smooth the top. Roll out the pastry trimmings, cut into strips, and cover the mixture in a trellis pattern. Bake at 200°C (400°F), Gas 6, for 15 minutes, then reduce to 180°C (350°F), Gas 4, for a further 15 minutes.

Ice top of the tart while warm, adding a few drops of water to make the icing thin.
Northumberland

Pastry
125 g (5 oz) plain flour
25 g (1 oz) lard
40 g (1½ oz) margarine
pinch of salt
cold water to mix

1 egg
50 g (2 oz) currants
25 g (1 oz) cut peel
25 g (1 oz) ground almonds or
 chopped nuts
few drops almond essence

Filling
50 g (2 oz) margarine
50 g (2 oz) caster sugar

Icing
75 g (3 oz) icing sugar
10 ml (2 teaspoons) lemon juice

Buttery Dick

Line a Swiss roll tin with shortcrust pastry. Prick with a fork.

Cream margarine and sugar, add egg, ground rice and currants. Spread evenly over pastry.

Bake in a moderate oven, 190°C (375°F), Gas 5, until golden brown, about 30 minutes. Cut in pieces.
Cumberland

shortcrust pastry (using 100 g
   flour)
100 g (4 oz) margarine

100 g (4 oz) sugar or soft brown
1 egg
25 g (1 oz) ground rice
100 g (4 oz) currants

Cheese cake 1

Mix biscuit crumbs and sugar into melted margarine. Press into the
base of a 20-cm (8-inch) flan ring. Sieve cottage cheese and mix with
cream cheese. Add sugar and vanilla essence. Beat eggs and add to
cheese mixture, beating well until smooth. Pour on to biscuit base,
cook for 20 minutes, 190°C (375°F), Gas 5. Remove from oven and
increase to 230°C (450°F), Gas 8. Mix topping and pour over cheese
cake, bake at new heat for exactly 5 minutes. Leave overnight in cool
place. The topping is optional.
Yorkshire

Biscuit base
100 g (4 oz) crushed digestive
   biscuits
40 g (2 oz) melted margarine
15 ml (1 level tablespoon) sugar

100 g (4 oz) Philadelphia or cream
   cheese
50 g (2 oz) caster sugar
2 eggs
3 drops vanilla essence

Cheese mixture
200 g (8 oz) cottage cheese

Topping
150 ml (¼ pint) cream
5 ml (1 teaspoon) lemon juice

Cheese cake 2

Make up the pastry and mould a 20-cm (8-inch) flan ring. Keep
trimmings for decorating the top.
   Prepare the mixture for filling as follows. Mix the margarine and
sugar, add the beaten egg, cheese, peel, currants and grated lemon
rind, add vanilla essence, mix thoroughly and fill prepared flan ring.
Decorate the flan with pastry strips and brush with beaten egg. Bake
for 30–35 minutes at 180°C (350°F), Gas 4 or until lightly browned
and filling set.
   A variation of the basic recipe is to place sliced drained mandarin
oranges on the top of the cooked cheese cake just before serving.
Yorkshire

Pastry
200 g (8 oz) flour
100 g (4 oz) butter
40 g (1½ oz) sugar
pinch of salt
1 egg
milk and water

Filling
50 g (2 oz) margarine
25 g (1 oz) caster sugar
275 g (10 oz) curd cheese
1 egg
25 g (1 oz) currants
25 g (1 oz) chopped peel
lemon rind
vanilla essence
egg for brushing

Chocolate orange drizzle cake

Set oven to 180°C (350°F), Gas 4. Grease 1-kg (2-lb) loaf tin and line with greased greaseproof paper.

Cream margarine and sugar until light and fluffy. Beat in eggs one at a time. Fold in sifted flour and add milk or orange juice with last tablespoon of flour. Add orange rind. Put cake mixture in tin and cook 1 hour. Turn cooked cake out to cool and when nearly cold make slits in top of cake and drizzle orange syrup across top. To make syrup mix orange juice with sugar.

Break the chocolate into small pieces in bowl with butter and allow to melt over steaming water. Mix well and use immediately.
Cambridgeshire

175 g (6 oz) margarine
175 g (6 oz) caster sugar
3 eggs
175 g (6 oz) self-raising flour
30 ml (2 tablespoons) milk or juice
  of 1 orange
finely grated rind of 2 oranges

Orange syrup
strained juice of 2 oranges

100 g (4 oz) sugar
or
juice of 1 orange and 50 g (2 oz)
  sugar if juice of 1 orange is used in
  cake mixture

Chocolate topping
125 g (4 oz) block plain chocolate
15 g (½ oz) butter

Christmas cake

Line an 18–20-cm (7–8-inch) tin with double greaseproof paper.

Cream butter and sugar together. Beat eggs lightly with fork. Add small quantities to the butter and sugar. Beat thoroughly. Add black treacle if liked with last of egg. Beat thoroughly. Add chopped nuts and beat again. Add ground almonds and glacé cherries. Again beat. Add spice, orange and lemon rind, also vanilla and fruit. Give a final beating and then fold in flour using a metal spoon. Add sherry to make a nice dropping consistency. Put mixture in tin and level. Brush top with a little milk or sherry.

Cook at 150°C (300°F), Gas 2, for 2 hours, 140°C (275°F), Gas 1, for 1 hour, 120°C (250°F), Gas ½, for 1 hour. Allow cake to cool in tin.

Almond paste
Mix almonds and sugar together. Mix to a soft dough with liquids. Well cover cake all over (first brushing cake with melted jelly).

White icing
Beat together egg whites, lemon juice and glycerine. Add sifted icing sugar gradually. Beat thoroughly all the time. The icing should be stiff but not too stiff for fancy icing. It should retain its shape while beating.

Quantities for a 24–26-cm (9–10-inch) tin
285 g (10 oz) butter
285 g (10 oz) brown sugar
6–8 eggs
100 g (4 oz) ground almonds
About 1½ kg (3 lb) fruit
350 g (12 oz) self-raising flour
Continue as for 20-cm (8-inch) tin

Add ½ hour cooking time to each of the lower temperatures, making 5 hours in all.
Cambridgeshire

175 g (6 oz) butter
175 g (6 oz) brown sugar
5 eggs
50 g (2 oz) chopped nuts
50 g (2 oz) ground almonds
50–100 g (2–4 oz) glacé cherries
½ grated nutmeg
10 ml (1 teaspoon) ginger
10 ml (1 teaspoon) mixed spice
grated rind of orange and lemon
vanilla essence
about 900 g (2 lb) fruit – currants,
  sultanas, and raisins
50 g (2 oz) candied peel
225 g (8 oz) self-raising flour
30 ml (eggcup) brandy, sherry or
  rum

25 g (1 tablespoon) black treacle
  if liked

Almond paste
350 g (12 oz) ground almonds
350 g (12 oz) caster sugar (or ½
  caster, ½ icing sugar)
1 egg
juice of 1 orange and 1 lemon,
  approximately
10 ml (2 teaspoons) brandy or
  sherry

White icing
3–4 egg whites
10 ml (2 teaspoons) lemon juice
5 ml (1 teaspoon) glycerine
900 g (2 lb) icing sugar

Christmas cake
80-year-old recipe

Beat the butter and sugar to a cream, then add the eggs, beating well
between each one. Mix all the dry ingredients together and mix well
into the butter, sugar and eggs.

Line a 19-cm (7½-inch) tin with paper, put the mixture into the
tin and bake in a moderate oven for 3 hours, 140–150°C (275–300°F),
Gas 1–2.

This cake is better for keeping a week or two.

After it is baked and cooled down, make a hole with a knitting
needle and put in the brandy and it will keep for months in an airtight
tin.

Cheshire

225 g (8 oz) butter
225 g (8 oz) brown sugar
5 eggs
100 g (4 oz) almonds
225 g (8 oz) cherries
100 g (4 oz) currants

225 g (8 oz) sultanas
100 g (4 oz) candied peel
350 g (12 oz) flour
10 ml (¼ oz) baking powder
½ wineglass brandy (75 ml)

Coffee almond cake

Line and butter a 15-cm (6-inch) cake tin.

Cream butter and sugar, beat in eggs and a little flour. Fold in sifted flour and ground almonds, add coffee essence and 1 tablespoon sherry. Place in tin and sprinkle with chopped almonds and place in centre of moderate oven, 160°C (325°F), Gas 3. Bake for 1½ hours.

Leave cake in tin for 15 minutes, then turn out and cool on a wire tray.

When cold pour rest of sherry over cake; when it has soaked through, wrap cake in greaseproof paper and place in tin. It can be made a week before using and will keep.

Cambridgeshire

100 g (4 oz) butter or margarine
100 g (4 oz) caster sugar
2 eggs
135 g (5 oz) self-raising flour

50 g (2 oz) ground almonds
30 ml (2 tablespoons) liquid coffee
 essence
45 ml (3 tablespoons) sherry
15 g (½ oz) finely chopped almonds

Cornish heavy cake

Rub lard into flour as for pastry, add fruit, sugar, salt, mix with milk (not too light). Roll out fairly long. Flake small pieces of butter over the top two-thirds of the pastry. Fold the bottom third upwards and the top third down on it. Give it a half turn and roll out, repeat this. Form into circle or square 1 cm (½ inch) thick. Lightly mark in squares with a knife, brush with egg. Bake about ½ hour in a hot oven, 220°C (425°F), Gas 7.

Makes about 48 squares. Recipe can be divided by 2 or 4.

Cornwall

900 g (2 lb) flour
225 g (8 oz) lard
350 g (12 oz) fruit and peel
175 g (6 oz) sugar
2½ ml (½ teaspoon) salt

600 ml (1 pint) milk (more if
 required)
spice if desired
225 g (8 oz) butter
egg for brushing

Gingerbread
Family

Grease an oblong tin measuring approximately 23 × 19 cm (9½ × 7½ inches) and line the bottom.

Sift together flour, salt and spices, and mix in the demerara sugar. Melt fat and treacle together, stir into dry ingredients with the beaten eggs and beat until the mixture is quite smooth. Mix in the milk, raisins and walnuts if used, and turn the batter into the prepared tin.

Bake for 1–1½ hours at 180°C (350°F), Gas 4. Sprinkle top with icing sugar.

Gloucestershire

275 g (10 oz) self-raising flour
5 ml (1 level teaspoon) salt
7½ ml (1½ level teaspoons) ground ginger
10 ml (2 level teaspoons) cinnamon
2½ ml (½ level teaspoon) nutmeg
225 g (8 oz) demerara sugar
175 g (6 oz) fat (lard and margarine, mixed)

225 g (8 oz) treacle
2 eggs
150 ml (¼ pint) milk
75 g (3 oz) chopped raisins
50 g (2 oz) chopped walnuts (optional)
sifted icing sugar to sprinkle on top

Hot Durham parkin
Traditional recipe

Grease and line an 18 × 26 cm (7 × 10½ inch) tin.

Sift flour, salt, ground ginger, mixed spice and bicarbonate of soda in a bowl. Mix in oatmeal.

Place dripping, treacle and brown sugar in large pan and heat gently until melted. Stir in milk and dry ingredients. Blend well. Pour into prepared tin and bake in moderate oven, 180°C (350°F), Gas 4, for about 30–45 minutes, until firm. When cold cut into 15 pieces.

Durham

200 g (8 oz) plain flour
pinch of salt
10 ml (2 level teaspoons) ground ginger
5 ml (1 level teaspoon) mixed spice
10 ml (2 level teaspoons) bicarbonate of soda

100 g (4 oz) medium oatmeal
100 g (4 oz) dripping
100 g (4 oz) treacle
150 g (6 oz) soft brown sugar
125 ml (¼ pint) milk

Maids of honour

Line 12 small tins with pastry, saving a little for decoration. Put a little raspberry jam in each pastry case.

Whip up the white of egg and add ground almonds, caster sugar and ground rice which have previously been mixed together. Fold in gently and place a teaspoonful of the mixture on top of each case.

Cut the remaining pastry into thin strips and place a cross on each one.

Bake in a moderate oven, 180–190°C (350°–375°F), Gas 4–5, for 15–20 minutes.
Cheshire

4 oz short pastry (using 100 g flour)
raspberry jam
white of an egg

50 g (2 oz) ground almonds
100 g (4 oz) caster sugar
25 g (1 oz) ground rice

Manse cake

Boil all except the soda, flour and egg together for 3 minutes and when cold add the soda and flour. If the egg is used, add it before the flour. Put in a lined 18–20-cm (7–8-inch) tin and bake in a moderate oven, 180°C (350°F), Gas 4, for 1½ hours.

It is better kept for a few days before cutting.
Devon

200 g (1 breakfast cup) sugar
250 ml (1 breakfast cup) cold water
250 g (1½ breakfast cups) raisins, currants or sultanas
50 g (1 tablespoon) treacle
100 g (4 oz) lard or butter
5 ml (½ teaspoon) cinnamon or ground ginger

5 ml (½ teaspoon) allspice
a pinch of salt
5 ml (1 teaspoon) bicarbonate of soda dissolved in a little warm water
250 g (2 cups) flour
1 egg (optional)

Note for beginners

This recipe can be started the day before and the boiled ingredients left overnight to cool; or prepare in the morning for an afternoon baking.

Marmalade gingerbread

Sieve flour with spices. Melt syrup and margarine together gently.
Pour into dry ingredients. Stir in marmalade, hot water and well-
beaten egg. Mix well and pour into a greased 20-cm (8-inch) square
cake tin.

Bake for approximately 50 minutes at 160°C (325°F), Gas 3.

Cumberland

225 g (8 oz) self-raising flour
5 ml (1 level teaspoon) cinnamon
10 ml (2 level teaspoons) ground
  ginger
175 g (6 oz) golden syrup

75 g (3 oz) margarine
225 g (8 oz) thick orange
  marmalade
30 ml (2 tablespoons) hot water
1 egg

Mocha gâteau

Beat margarine and sugar to a cream. Mix dry ingredients together.
Add to creamed mixture alternately with well-beaten eggs and
coffee essence. Bake in a 20-cm (8-inch) greased cake tin, in
moderate oven, 160°C (325°F), Gas 3, for about 45 minutes.

Filling
Stir milk, chocolate and coffee essence over a gentle heat until
chocolate is melted. Leave to cool. Beat margarine, add sieved icing
sugar and cooled chocolate mixture. Beat well. Split the cold cake
and fill.

Chocolate coating
Break chocolate, add milk, essence, and oil. Heat over pan of hot
water until warm. Beat well, then pour over cake.

Durham

100 g (4 oz) margarine
100 g (4 oz) sugar
100 g (4 oz) plain flour
50 g (2 oz) ground rice
10 ml (1 level dessertspoon) cocoa
25 g (1 oz) drinking chocolate
10 ml (1 teaspoon) baking powder
3 eggs
5 ml (1 teaspoon) coffee essence

Filling
30 ml (2 tablespoons) milk

60 ml (2 tablespoons) drinking
  chocolate
5 ml (1 teaspoon) coffee essence
75 g (3 oz) margarine
75 g (3 oz) icing sugar

Chocolate coating (to be used if
  desired)
125 g (4 oz) plain chocolate
20 ml (2 dessertspoons) milk
2½ ml (½ teaspoon) coffee essence
2 or 3 drops salad oil

Old English cider cake

Sift dry ingredients, except sugar. Cream butter and sugar until fluffy. Beat in eggs, stir in half dry ingredients. Add cider (previously whisked till frothy). Add rest of dry ingredients; beat well.

Cook in a well-greased shallow tin, 20 × 15 cm (8 × 6 inches). Bake in centre of oven at 160°C (325°F), Gas 3 for 45 minutes.

Leave at least 1 day before cutting.

Devon

225 g (8 oz) plain flour
5 ml (½ teaspoon) ginger
2½ ml (½ teaspoon) bicarbonate of soda
pinch of nutmeg

100 g (4 oz) butter
100 g (4 oz) caster sugar
2 eggs
150 ml (¼ pint) cider

Ooozie-woozie tart

Line a 20-cm (8-inch) pie plate with pastry, spread with mincemeat, peel, core and cut apples into thin slices and overlap to cover mincemeat, trickle the lemon curd over the apples.

Damp pastry edges and arrange lattice strips over top.

Bake near top of oven, 200°C (400°F), Gas 6, for 30 minutes.

Serve hot or cold for 4–6 people.

Lincolnshire

8 oz shortcrust pastry (200 g flour)
100 ml (2 large tablespoons) mincemeat

2 large cooking apples
60 ml (2 tablespoons) lemon curd

Orange honey cake

Cream fat and sugar and beat in the eggs gradually. Stir in the flour and baking powder with the warm honey and marmalade. Place in a greased 18-cm (7-inch) tin and bake in a slow oven for approximately 1–1¼ hours, 150°C (300°F), Gas 2.

Yorkshire

75 g (3 oz) fat
75 g (3 oz) sugar
2 eggs
225 g (8 oz) flour

10 ml (1 teaspoon) baking powder
100 g (4 oz) honey
50 g (2 oz) marmalade

Simnel cake

Make almond paste by beating eggs with lemon juice and adding dry ingredients. Knead well but do not over handle.

Into large pan put all cake ingredients, except flour and bicarbonate of soda. Bring slowly to the boil, stirring occasionally. Simmer 3 minutes, remove from heat and cool to just warm. Sift flour and bicarbonate together and stir into cooled mixture and mix well.

Put half into prepared tin, about 20 cm (8 inches), and level. Roll one-third almond paste about 6 mm ($\frac{1}{4}$ inch) thick and put on top of the cake mixture, cover with rest of mixture. Level out and bake in a cool oven, 150°C (300°F), Gas 2, for 1 hour and 140°C (275°F), Gas 1, for another 1–1$\frac{1}{4}$ hours.

Sieve apricot jam into pan, add water and bring to boil. Remove from heat; when cake is cold, brush top with glaze and cover with remaining paste and brown under pre-heated grill.

This is a traditional cake for Mothering Sunday, but can be an Easter Cake by putting part of paste on top and decorating with the rest made into eggs, etc, and browned under grill.
Durham

Almond paste
2 small eggs
15 ml (1 tablespoon) lemon juice
275 g (10 oz) icing sugar
275 g (10 oz) caster sugar
275 g (10 oz) ground almonds

Glaze
30 ml (1 tablespoon) apricot jam
15 ml (1 tablespoon) water

Cake
225 g (8 oz) butter

150 ml ($\frac{1}{4}$ pint) water
150 g (6 oz) sweetened condensed milk
75 g (3 oz) peel
150 g (6 oz) sultanas
150 g (6 oz) currants
75 g (3 oz) glacé cherries
50 g (2 oz) ground almonds
50 g (2 oz) chopped almonds
grated rind of 1 orange and 1 lemon
225 g (8 oz) plain flour
2$\frac{1}{2}$ ml ($\frac{1}{2}$ level teaspoon) bicarbonate of soda

Sly cakes

Roll out some flaky pastry thin, cover half with currants and chopped peel to taste; fold over the remainder of pastry and lightly

roll. Sprinkle top with sugar, then cut into various shapes and bake at 220°C (425°F), Gas 7, for 15–20 minutes.
Cornwall

flaky pastry
currants

chopped peel
sugar to sprinkle on top

Somerset apple cake

Rub fat into flour, add sugar and spice and chopped apples, mix with a little milk or beaten egg to make a stiff mixture.

Spread in a greased 20-cm (8-inch) pie plate or any fairly shallow dish or tin – bake till nicely brown in a fairly hot oven, 200–220°C (400–425°F), Gas 6–7. Serve hot sprinkled with sugar.

A very great winter tea time favourite in this family.
Somerset

200 g (8 oz) flour
75–100 g (3–4 oz) fat
75–100 g (3–4 oz) sugar (according to apple used)
a little mixed spice if liked

450 g (1 lb) cooking apples, chopped
a little milk or beaten egg
sugar for sprinkling

Yorkshire parkin

Melt the margarine in the syrup and treacle and add to the dry ingredients. Add the milk, pour the mixture into a lined 20-cm (8-inch) square baking tin.

Bake at 160°C (325°F), Gas 3, for 2 hours.
Yorkshire

75 g (3 oz) margarine
225 g (8 oz) golden syrup
25 g (1 tablespoon) black treacle
225 g (8 oz) medium oatmeal
100 g (4 oz) plain flour and
5 ml (1 level teaspoon) baking powder or 4 oz self-raising flour

100 g (4 oz) moist brown sugar
10 ml (1½ level teaspoons) ground ginger
200 ml (⅓ pint) milk

14 Biscuits & Cookies

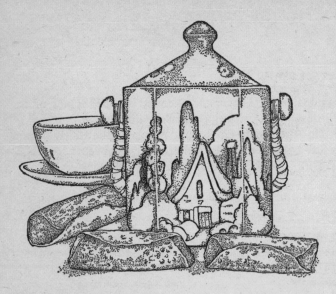

Afternoon tea biscuits

Cream the butter or margarine and sugar together, beat in three parts of the egg with one tablespoon of flour, add the remainder of the flour, and if necessary, the remaining egg. Mix to a stiff paste, roll out to about 6 mm ($\frac{1}{4}$ inch) thick, cut into rounds, bake in a moderate oven, 180°C (350°F), Gas 4, until a golden brown. Coat with jam while hot and stick two together. Decorate with the lemon icing.

Using a 5-cm (2$\frac{1}{2}$-inch) cutter this makes 12 finished biscuits.
Northamptonshire and Soke of Peterborough

75 g (3 oz) butter or margarine
50 g (2 oz) sugar
1 small egg
150 g (6 oz) flour
jam

Lemon icing
100 g (4 oz) icing sugar
juice of lemon to mix

Almond biscuits

Cream sugar and margarine with the hand, add flour and ground

almonds. Make into a roll about 5 cm (2½ inches) thick and cut into slices about 6 mm (¼ inch) thick, or roll out and cut in rounds. Put a split almond on each biscuit. Bake in a moderate oven, 180°C (350°F), Gas 4, for about 20–25 minutes. Makes about 30 biscuits.
Gloucestershire

100 g (4 oz) caster sugar	100 g (4 oz) ground almonds
100 g (4 oz) margarine	split almonds
100 g (4 oz) plain flour	

Almond slices

Rub butter into flour, mix in sugar, mix with beaten egg yolks. Roll out and line Swiss roll tin, spread with jam.

Filling
Beat egg whites stiff, add sugar and ground almonds, mix well. Spread over the jam and put a few chopped almonds on top. Bake in moderate oven, 180°C (350°F), Gas 4, for 25–30 minutes. Cut in slices.
Yorkshire

150 g (6 oz) self-raising flour	*Filling*
75 g (3 oz) butter	2 egg whites
20 ml (2 teaspoons) sugar	75 g (3 oz) icing sugar
2 yolks of egg	50 g (2 oz) ground almonds
jam	a few chopped almonds

Australian Jack

Roll pastry into one thin sheet, put on a baking sheet, spread with jam. Cream butter and syrup, work in Quaker oats, and add flavouring essence. Spread this mixture over the jam, and fold over the edges of pastry. Bake ¾ hour in a hot oven, 190°C (375°F), Gas 5, cool and cut into fingers. Makes about 30 fingers.
Northamptonshire and Soke of Peterborough

short pastry using 6 oz (150 g) flour	200 g (8 oz) Quaker oats
jam	2½ ml (½ teaspoon) essence of
200 g (8 oz) butter or margarine	almonds
150 g (3 tablespoons) golden syrup	

Brandy snaps

These Brandy Snaps have been a traditional sweetmeat on sale at Hull Fair for many years.

Melt the fat, sugar and syrup in a pan. Remove from the heat and add the other ingredients and mix well.

Drop in teaspoons on a greased baking sheet at least 8 cm (3 inches) apart as they will spread in cooking.

Bake in a moderate oven, 180°C (350°F), Gas 4, for 7–10 minutes until golden brown.

Remove the baking sheet from the oven and allow to stand a moment on the stove top until the biscuits can be easily lifted from the sheet with a knife. Roll the biscuits round a wooden spoon handle and leave for a minute to set.

Yorkshire

50 g (2 oz) butter or margarine	5 ml (1 level teaspoon) ground ginger
50 g (2 oz) sugar	
50 g (2 tablespoons) golden syrup	5 ml (1 teaspoon) brandy
50 g (2 oz) flour	1 ml (¼ teaspoon) grated lemon rind

Note for beginners

Bake these in relays, a few at a time; the mixture will not spoil with keeping. Use more than one wooden spoon handle if possible and roll the biscuits with the upper surface on the outside. Removal is easier if the trays have been floured as well as greased. If the last ones in a batch become too hard to roll, return to the oven for a minute.

Canadian shortbread

Cream butter and sugar, add other ingredients, knead well together. Divide into two and press into two 18-cm (7-inch) sandwich tins. Bake 15–20 minutes at 190°C (375°F), Gas 5. (Watch carefully as it soon burns.)

As soon as it is cooked mark the shortbread into triangles, using a small sharp knife. Leave in the tins to cool before turning out.

Each will cut into 8–12 triangles.

If polka dots are not available other similar tiny plain chocolate sweets may be used.

Yorkshire

100 g (4 oz) butter
100 g (4 oz) soft brown sugar
150 g (6 oz) plain flour

25 g (1 oz) broken walnuts
25 g (1 oz) polka dots

Cheese biscuits

Rub all the ingredients together till they form a firm paste (add no liquid). Roll out thin and cut into shapes. Bake in a moderate oven, 180°C (350°F), Gas 4, till pale gold, about 10 minutes. Makes about 24 biscuits, approximately 4-cm (2-inch) size.
Yorkshire

50 g (2 oz) grated cheese
50 g (2 oz) margarine

50 g (2 oz) plain flour

Chocolate crisps

Rub well together, knead and work in the palms of your hands, 1 dessertspoonful at a time, till a round flat cake is formed. Place well apart on a greased tin and bake slowly, 160°C (325°F), Gas 3, till crisp and *hard in centre*. This last is important. Makes 24 crisps.
Devon

200 g (8 oz) self-raising flour
50 g (2 oz) cocoa
125 g (5 oz) granulated sugar

75 g (3 oz) margarine
50 g (2 oz) lard

Chocolate petits fours

Mix all dry ingredients together and bind with the beaten egg. Divide into 16 pieces, roll in balls and put an almond or cherry on top of each. Bake for 15 minutes at 190–200°C (375–400°F), Gas 5–6.
Yorkshire

25 g (1 oz) drinking chocolate
100 g (4 oz) sugar
25 g (1 oz) chopped walnuts

75 g (3 oz) ground almonds
1 small egg
almonds or cherries for decoration

Coconut macaroons

Mix the flour, coconut and sugar together in a bowl. Bind with the whites of eggs, and place in rough heaps on a greased baking sheet

lined with rice paper. Bake for 20 minutes at 160°C (325°F), Gas 3.
Makes about 16 macaroons.
Yorkshire

25 g (1 oz) flour	150 g (6 oz) sugar
150 g (6 oz) desiccated coconut	2 whites of eggs, beaten

Note for beginners

As the size of egg whites varies, you may need to use some more to
bind the ingredients. It should be a very stiff mixture which can be
moulded into heaps using your hands.

Coconut shortbread

Melt butter and mix into other ingredients. Press mixture down into
an 18–20-cm (7–8-inch) flan tin. Bake in a slow oven, 150°C (300°F),
Gas 2, about ¾ hour.
    Cut when warm but leave in the tin until quite cold. Cuts into 8–10
pieces.
Yorkshire

100 g (4 oz) butter	5 ml (1 teaspoon) vanilla essence
100 g (4 oz) coconut	pinch of salt
100 g (4 oz) rolled oats	10 ml (1 teaspoon) baking powder
50 g (2 oz) sugar	

Date flapjacks

Put dates through a mincer. Cream margarine and sugar and work
in rolled oats. Grease a small tin, about 12–15 cm (5–6 inches)
square and press in smoothly half the mixture and spread with the
dates. Sprinkle with a very little lemon juice, cover with the rest of
the mixture. Bake in a moderate oven, 160°C (325°F), Gas 3, for
about 40 minutes and cut in oblongs.
Shropshire

125 g (4 oz) stoned dates	100 g (4 oz) rolled oats
50 g (2 oz) margarine	lemon juice
50 g (2 oz) moist brown sugar	

Fruit and treacle cookies

Sift the flour, salt and cinnamon into a bowl. Cream the margarine
in another bowl until very soft. Add sugar and cream again until
mixture is light and fluffy. Stir in the treacle, then the beaten egg
thoroughly. Fold in the sifted flour, and then stir in the raisins and
nuts. Put heaped teaspoonsful of the mixture on greased baking
sheets and bake at 220°C (425°F), Gas 7, for 12–15 minutes.
Makes 24 cookies.
Isle of Ely

200 g (8 oz) plain flour
5 ml (1 level teaspoon) salt
10 ml (2 level teaspoons) cinnamon
  or mixed spice
100 g (4 oz) margarine
75 g (3 oz) demerara sugar

15 ml (1 tablespoon) treacle (black
  if available or molasses)
1 beaten egg
100 g (4 oz) seedless raisins or
  sultanas or currants
50 g (2 oz) chopped nuts

Ginger biscuits
Traditional recipe

Put all ingredients except the flour into a pan. Bring to boiling point
until golden brown. Add plain flour until it can be rolled out and
cut into biscuits. Place on greased baking sheet, bake in a moderate
oven, 180°C (350°F), Gas 4, for about 15 minutes.
   This mixture absorbs approximately 450 g (1 lb) flour.
   When rolled about 6 mm ($\frac{1}{4}$ inch) thick and cut with a 1-cm
($2\frac{1}{2}$-inch) cutter it will make about 4 dozen biscuits.
Durham

100 g (4 oz) lard
200 g (8 oz) sugar
200 g (8 oz) syrup
20 ml (1 dessertspoon) ginger

10 ml (1 dessertspoon) bicarbonate
  of soda
pinch of salt
plain flour (approximately 450 g or
  1 lb)

Ginger crispies

Sieve flour, salt and ginger. Cream margarine and sugar, beat in egg,
then ginger. Fold in flour mixture. With floured hands pinch out
pieces the size of a walnut, roll into a ball then roll in the cornflakes

and lay on lightly greased tin, well apart. Bake 20 minutes at 180°C (350°F), Gas 4. Makes about 18 crispies.
Lincolnshire

125 g (4 oz) self-raising flour	75 g (3 oz) caster sugar
pinch of salt	1 egg
5 ml (1 level teaspoon) ground ginger	25 g (1 oz) crystallized ginger cornflakes
75 g (3 oz) margarine	

Grasmere shortbread
Traditional recipe

Cream fat and sugar, add syrup and then sifted dry ingredients. Put into greased Yorkshire pudding tin (about 16 × 22 cm or 6½ × 8½ inches). Spread evenly and press down lightly with the back of a spoon. Cook in a slow oven, 150–160°C (300–325°F), Gas 2–3, for 30–40 minutes. Leave in the tin to cool but mark in squares before cold. Makes 16–20 squares.
Westmorland

100 g (4 oz) butter or margarine	pinch of salt
100 g (4 oz) brown sugar	2½ ml (½ teaspoon) bicarbonate of soda
15 ml (1 tablespoon) golden syrup	
200 g (8 oz) flour	2½ ml (½ teaspoon) cream of tartar
10 ml (½ dessertspoon) ground ginger	

Hazelnut and honey biscuits

Cream butter and sugar, sift flour and stir into mixture with ground nuts. Knead into a ball, roll out thinly, and cut into rounds. Bake in a moderate oven for 12 minutes, 180°C (350°F), Gas 4. Cool on tray.

Sandwich together with honey.

Break up chocolate, and melt over a pan of hot water. When smooth roll edges of biscuits in the chocolate, then in ground nuts. If there is any chocolate left over put through an icing tube, and decorate tops of biscuits.

With a 5-cm (2½-inch) cutter it makes 12–18 completed biscuits.
Northumberland

100 g (4 oz) butter	*Filling*
70 g (2½ oz) caster sugar	a little honey
125 g (5 oz) plain flour	
75 g (3 oz) ground hazelnuts	*Decoration*
	75 g (3 oz) plain dessert chocolate
	40 g (1½ oz) ground hazelnuts

Hungarian nut cookies

Cream margarine and sugar together, add flour and lastly chopped nuts. Roll in pieces about 5 cm (2 inches) long, press flat with a fork. Bake in a moderate oven, 180°C (350°F), Gas 4, for about 15 minutes or until lightly browned. Leave them to set for a few minutes before removing from the trays. Makes about 30 cookies.
Oxfordshire

100 g (4 oz) margarine	125 g (5 oz) plain flour
100 g (4 oz) soft brown sugar	50 g (2 oz) walnuts

Melting moments

Beat butter and sugar to a cream, add other ingredients. Put into a forcing bag and force into about 24 rosettes. Bake until very pale brown, 180°C (350°F), Gas 4, for 10–12 minutes. Cool on the tray, then join in pairs with a little butter icing.
Herefordshire

100 g (4 oz) butter or margarine	50 g (2 oz) cornflour
25 g (1 oz) icing sugar	a little vanilla essence
50 g (2 oz) self-raising flour	butter icing

Nut brownies

Whisk eggs well, add sugar, vanilla and whisk again till stiff. Add flour and baking powder and mix well. Add dates and nuts. Spread mixture evenly on small greased tin, 23 × 18 cm (9 × 7 inches). Bake in a moderate oven, 160°C (325°F), Gas 3, for 30–35 minutes. While still hot cut into 16 fingers and roll in icing sugar.
Cumberland

2 eggs
150 g (6 oz) soft brown sugar
few drops vanilla essence
100 g (4 oz) brown flour and 10 ml
(1 teaspoon) baking powder
or

100 g (4 oz) self-raising brown
 flour
125 g (5 oz) chopped dates
100 g (4 oz) chopped walnuts or
 hazelnuts
icing sugar for dusting

Peanut shortbread biscuits

Roast the peanuts golden brown, rub to remove skins, and crush.
   Cream the sugar and margarine, add the egg yolk and dry
ingredients. Knead the dough well and leave for an hour. Roll out
about 6 mm ($\frac{1}{4}$ inch) thick and cut into shapes. Bake for 30 minutes
in a slow oven, 140–150°C (275–300°F), Gas 1–2. Makes 18 biscuits
using a 5-cm (2½-inch) cutter.
Northumberland

50 g (2 oz) roasted peanuts, crushed
50 g (2 oz) caster sugar
100 g (4 oz) margarine

1 egg yolk
150 g (5 oz) plain flour
pinch of salt

Shortbread

Cream butter and sugar by hand and gradually add flour. Roll out
on a floured board into two round cakes about 1 cm ($\frac{1}{2}$ inch) thick.
Put on trays.
   Mark each cake in triangles and bake at 160°C (325°F), Gas 4, for
35 minutes. Allow to cool a little before lifting the shortbread off
the baking trays.
Yorkshire

Variations

Pitchaithly Bannock
Add 1 tablespoon chopped peel and 1 tablespoon chopped almonds.

Huby Bannock
Add 1 tablespoon chopped preserved ginger and 1 tablespoon
chopped almonds.
Yorkshire

100 g (4 oz) butter
50 g (2 oz) caster sugar

125 g (5 oz) flour
75 g (3 oz) rice flour

Shortbread creams

Beat the margarine and sugar to a soft cream. Sift the flour and cornflour and work it gradually into the creamed mixture. Using a vegetable star pipe, force in finger lengths on a greased baking tray or roll into balls and press with a fork. Bake for about 20 minutes at 180°C (350°F), Gas 4. When cool, sandwich with jam or cream and dust with icing sugar. Makes about 24 completed creams.
Cheshire

200 g (8 oz) margarine
75 g (3 oz) icing sugar
175 g (7 oz) plain flour

75 g (3 oz) cornflour
butter cream or raspberry jam
icing sugar for dusting

Spiced Finnish biscuits

Put margarine and sugar with syrup into a saucepan. Melt over gentle heat. Sieve dry ingredients into a bowl. Dissolve bicarbonate in water and add to the margarine, sugar and syrup. Pour into dry ingredients and mix. Leave in a bowl overnight or place in refrigerator until firm enough to use.

Roll out 3 mm ($\frac{1}{8}$ inch) thick and cut into shapes. Bake at 150°C (300°F), Gas 2, for 12–20 minutes. Using a 5-cm (2-inch) cutter it makes about 30 biscuits.
Durham

40 g (1$\frac{1}{2}$ oz) margarine
25 g (1 oz) sugar
50 g (2 oz) golden syrup
100 g (3$\frac{1}{2}$ oz) self-raising flour
2$\frac{1}{2}$ ml ($\frac{1}{4}$ teaspoon) cinnamon

5 ml ($\frac{1}{2}$ teaspoon) ginger
1 ml ($\frac{1}{4}$ teaspoon) bicarbonate of soda
15 ml (1 tablespoon) water

15 Quick Bread & Scones

Quick Breads

Banana loaf

Brush a ½-kg (1-lb) loaf tin with melted fat and line the base with greaseproof paper. Sift flour, bicarbonate of soda, baking powder and salt into a bowl. Rub lard and margarine in with tips of fingers. Add sugar and chopped walnuts. Skin and mash the bananas and add to the mixture to form a stiff dropping consistency. Turn the mixture into the prepared tin and bake in a moderately hot oven, 190°C (375°F), Gas 5, for ½ hour. Reduce heat to 160°C (325°F), Gas 3, for ¾ hour until loaf is well risen and firm in centre.
Durham

200 g (7 oz) plain flour
2½ ml (½ teaspoon) bicarbonate of
  soda
5 ml (1 level teaspoon) baking
  powder
pinch of salt

25 g (1 oz) lard
25 g (1 oz) margarine
100 g (4 oz) caster sugar
75 g (3 oz) chopped walnuts
3 bananas – if small add 15 ml
  (1 tablespoon) milk

Borrowdale tea loaf

Put fruit and sugar in a basin and barely cover with water. Leave overnight.

Next day put flour into a basin and add beaten egg, fruit, sugar and water. Mix well. Put into greased ½-kg (1-lb) loaf tin and bake for 1–1¼ hours at 180°C (350°F), Gas 4, (middle shelf of oven).

When cold cut into slices and spread with butter.

Durham

100 g (4 oz) currants
100 g (4 oz) raisins
25 g (1 oz) mixed peel
100 g (4 oz) sugar, brown preferred

water
200 g (8 oz) self-raising flour
1 egg

Date and walnut loaf

Grease and line a ½-kg (1-lb) loaf tin with greaseproof paper. Sift flour and other dry ingredients. Mix in sugar, dates and walnuts.

Warm black treacle, butter and milk until melted. Stir into flour mixture and beat until the batter is smooth. Pour into tin.

Bake at 180°C (350°F), Gas 4, for 1–1½ hours.

This cuts into approximately 8 slices.

Gloucestershire

175 g (6 oz) plain flour
2½ ml (½ level teaspoon)
  bicarbonate of soda
15 ml (2 teaspoons) baking powder
40 g (1½ oz) soft brown sugar
100 g (4 oz) dates, chopped

40 g (1½ oz) shelled walnuts,
  chopped
40 g (1½ oz) black treacle
20 g (¾ oz) butter or margarine
150 ml (¼ pint) milk

Farmhouse loaf

Mix flour, fruit, peel and spice. Melt sugar, margarine and syrup and stir into dry ingredients with beaten egg and milk. Put in a greased 15-cm (6-inch) tin or a loaf tin.

Bake 1 hour 10 minutes at 160°C (325°F), Gas 3.

Durham

225 g (8 oz) self-raising flour	75 g (3 oz) margarine
175 g (6 oz) mixed dried fruit	75 g (3 oz) golden syrup
50 g (2 oz) chopped peel	1 egg
5 ml (½ teaspoon) mixed spice	60 ml (4 tablespoons) milk
75 g (3 oz) soft brown sugar	

Lincolnshire plum bread

Cream butter and sugar together, beat in eggs and brandy, sift in the flour and salt, stir in the fruit.

Well grease a ½-kg (1-lb) loaf tin. Bake for 3 hours at 140°C (275°F), Gas 1.

Lincolnshire

100 g (4 oz) butter	pinch of salt
100 g (4 oz) demerara sugar	100 g (4 oz) sultanas
2 eggs	50 g (2 oz) cut peel, if liked
15 ml (1 tablespoon) brandy	100 g (4 oz) chopped prunes
200 g (7 oz) self-raising flour	100 g (4 oz) currants

Note for beginners

Plum breads are best made about a week in advance of using. Keep in an airtight box.

Luncheon spice loaf

Sift flour and spice together. Rub in fat, add all other ingredients, bicarbonate of soda and vinegar last and milk if needed. Bake in a greased ½-kg (1-lb) loaf tin in a moderate oven, 180°C (350°F), Gas 4, approximately 1¼ hours.

This is nice served with cheese.

Oxfordshire

200 g (8 oz) plain flour	75 g (3 oz) currants
10 ml (1 teaspoon) sweet spice, cinnamon or ginger	5 ml (1 level teaspoon) bicarbonate of soda
50 g (2 oz) dripping	10 ml (1 dessertspoon) vinegar
50 g (2 oz) margarine	30–45 ml (2–3 tablespoons) milk, if required
75 g (3 oz) brown sugar	

Malt loaf

Grease and line a 1-kg (2-lb) loaf tin with greaseproof paper.

Sieve flour and bicarbonate of soda into a bowl, add dates and walnuts. Warm malt and syrup gently in the milk, add the lightly beaten egg to dry ingredients and also the milk mixture. Turn into the prepared tin.

Bake at 190°C (375°F), Gas 5, for about 1¼ hours, until loaf is well risen.

When cold, store in a tin for at least a day before cutting, then serve spread with butter.

Durham

200 g (8 oz) plain flour
5 ml (1 level teaspoon) bicarbonate of soda
50 g (2 oz) chopped dates
50 g (2 oz) chopped walnuts

250 ml (½ pint) milk
45 ml (3 tablespoons) golden syrup
45 ml (3 tablespoons) malt extract
1 egg

Mrs O'Flanagan's brown bread

Put the wholemeal flour in a bowl. Sift in the white flour and other dry ingredients. Mix to a stiffish dough with the milk. Turn on to a floured board and form into a compact shape.

Bake in a hot oven, 220°C (425°F), Gas 7, for exactly ¾ hour.

The proportions of brown to white flour may be altered to suit individual tastes. A very little extra milk is needed for an entire brown loaf.

Devon

300 g (10 oz) plain wholemeal flour
175 g (6 oz) plain white flour
10 ml (1 teaspoon) sugar
5 ml (1 teaspoon) bicarbonate of soda

5–10 ml (1 teaspoon) salt
10 ml (1 teaspoon) cream of tartar
300 ml (½ pint and 1 tablespoon) of sweet milk

Orange tea bread

Sift flour and salt into a bowl and add sugar and orange rind. Make a well in the middle and stir in the marmalade, oil, egg and milk. Mix well.

Put in a greased ½-kg (1-lb) loaf tin. Bake 40–45 minutes in an oven, 180°C (350°F), Gas 4.

Allow to cool. Cut in slices and butter.

Derbyshire

175 g (6 oz) self-raising flour
2½ ml (½ level teaspoon) salt
75 g (3 oz) caster sugar
grated rind of 1 medium orange

30 ml (2 level tablespoons) coarse
  cut marmalade
15 ml (1 tablespoon) cooking oil
1 egg, beaten
45 ml (3 tablespoons) milk

Scones

Alton tea cakes

Rub the butter into the flour and sugar, and add the baking powder. Beat the egg in a little milk and add to the other ingredients, making the mixture rather moist. Bake in two buttered, shallow 12-cm (5-inch), cake tins about 20 minutes at 190–200°C (375–400°F), Gas 5–6.

Cut and butter like ordinary tea cakes and serve very hot.

Northamptonshire and Soke of Peterborough

150 g (6 oz) flour
75 g (3 oz) sugar
75 g (3 oz) butter

10 ml (1 teaspoon) baking powder
1 egg
a little milk (50 ml)

Apple scones

Sift flour and baking powder together, rub in lard, add sugar. Add the apple, finely chopped. Beat the egg and add to the dry ingredients to make a stiff elastic dough, using a very little milk if necessary. Turn the dough on to a board and divide into the number of scones required. Shape and flatten by hand, about 2½ cm (an inch) thick and bake in a moderate oven, 200°C (400°F), Gas 6, for about ½ hour. Dredge with sugar and serve hot – buttered.

Yorkshire

170 g (6 oz) flour
10 ml (1 teaspoon) baking powder
50 g (2 oz) lard
25 g (1 oz) sugar

1 large cooking apple
1 egg
milk if necessary

Note for beginners

A large cooking apple weighs about 225 g ($\frac{1}{2}$ lb). If more convenient, self-raising flour may be substituted for the plain flour and baking powder. If the mixture is made into 6 large scones the baking time needs to be about $\frac{1}{2}$ hour, for small ones a little less.

Cheese scones

Sieve flour, rub in butter and grated cheese. Beat up egg with a little milk, add to flour and mix to a soft dough. Turn out on to a floured board and roll out to 2 cm ($\frac{3}{4}$ inch) thick, cut into rounds and place on greased baking sheet in a hot oven, 230°C (450°F), Gas 8, for about 10 minutes. Makes 8 scones using a 6-cm (2$\frac{1}{2}$-inch) cutter.
Gloucestershire

175 g (6 oz) self-raising flour
25 g (1 oz) butter
75 g (3 oz) grated cheese

1 egg
milk to mix

Cheese and bacon scones

Sift flour, salt and mustard into bowl. Rub fat in gently. Stir in bacon and cheese. Mix to a soft dough with milk. Turn out on to a floured board. Roll into 1 cm ($\frac{1}{2}$ inch) thickness. Use 5–7-cm (2–2$\frac{1}{2}$-inch) cutter to cut into rounds. Put on a greased baking tray and bake towards top of hot oven, 220°C (425°F), Gas 7, for 10 minutes or until golden brown and cooked through. Serve with butter. Makes approximately 12 scones.
Yorkshire

225 g (8 oz) self-raising flour
2$\frac{1}{2}$ ml ($\frac{1}{2}$ teaspoon) salt
2$\frac{1}{2}$ ml ($\frac{1}{2}$ level teaspoon) dry
  mustard
40 g (1$\frac{1}{2}$ oz) margarine

50 g (2 oz) bacon, cooked and cut
  up finely
50 g (2 oz) grated cheese
just under 150 ml milk (just under
  $\frac{1}{4}$ pint)

Cornish sandwiches

Rub the jam through a sieve, split the scones and remove part of the soft inside. Spread a little jam on each half of the scone, and a teaspoonful of thick cream on the lower half of each, press each

scone together. These are best prepared only a short time before
they are to be eaten.
Cornwall

2 spoonsful of damson,
   whortleberry or blackberry jam
2 spoonsful of clotted cream

8 or 9 little scones, very fresh, but
   cold

Fat rascals

Rub margarine into flour and salt, add sugar and currants. Mix with
milk. Roll out 1 cm ($\frac{1}{2}$ inch) thick. Cut into rounds with pastry
cutter. Bake second shelf from top at 220°C (425°F), Gas 7, for 15–20
minutes. Makes 12 scones using a 5-cm (2$\frac{1}{2}$-inch) cutter.
Yorkshire

200 g (8 oz) self-raising flour
pinch of salt
100 g (4 oz) margarine

25 g (1 oz) sugar
50 g (2 oz) currants
90 ml (7 tablespoons) milk to mix

Finger scones

Put flour, baking powder, sugar and salt in basin and rub in butter.
Moisten with beaten egg and milk enough to make a soft dough.
Divide into 24 pieces and shape into fingers. Dip in milk and roll in
caster sugar.

   Bake for 10–15 minutes in quick oven on greased sheet, 220°C
(450°F), Gas 8.
Oxfordshire

200 g (8 oz) flour
10 ml (1 teaspoon) baking powder
25 g (1 tablespoon) sugar
pinch of salt

50 g (2 oz) butter or margarine
1 egg
milk
caster sugar

Note for beginners

Self-raising flour can be used instead of the flour and baking
powder.

Girdle cakes

Rub the lard and margarine into the flour, add other dry ingredients and mix well. Mix with sufficient cold milk to form a soft dough. Roll out, cut into small round cakes and bake on a hot girdle until golden brown on both sides.

Split open and butter whilst hot.

Northumberland and Durham

225 g (8 oz) plain flour	50 g (2 oz) currants
50 g (2 oz) lard	25 g (1 tablespoon) sugar
50 g (2 oz) margarine	a little milk (100 ml)
10 ml (1 teaspoon) baking powder	butter

Note for beginners

This mixture will make approximately 18 girdle cakes if rolled 6 mm (¼ inch) thick and a 5-cm (2½-inch) cutter is used. Cooking time will be 8–10 minutes.

Instead of using a girdle the cakes can be cooked in an electric frying pan at about 190°C (375°F). Grease the pan lightly with lard or oil.

Light splitters

Add the salt and sugar to the flour, rub in the lard lightly with tips of fingers, form a soft dough with milk and water, roll out about 1 cm (½ inch) thick, cut in rounds with fluted cutter, brush over with a little milk and bake about 15 minutes in a moderate oven, 220°C (425°F), Gas 7. Makes 12 splitters using 5-cm (2½-inch) cutter. Split through the centre, butter with salt butter and serve hot.

Northamptonshire and Soke of Peterborough

200 g (8 oz) self-raising flour	100 g (4 oz) lard
a good pinch of salt	milk and water to mix (about
25 g (1 dessertspoon) caster sugar	125 ml)

Sweet scones

Add salt to flour. Rub in margarine, add sugar and sultanas. Mix together with beaten egg and milk. Cut into rounds 1 cm (½ inch) thick. Bake in hot oven, 230°C (450°F), Gas 8, for 7–10 minutes. Makes 12 scones, using 5-cm (2½-inch) cutter.

Durham

200 g (8 oz) self-raising flour
pinch of salt
75 g (3 oz) margarine
75 g (3 oz) sugar

50 g (2 oz) sultanas
1 egg
10 ml (1 dessertspoon) milk

Welsh cakes

Rub margarine into flour and sugar. Add fruit. Mix to a stiff paste with beaten egg and milk. Roll out, cut in rounds and put in frying pan. Cook till sides are done. Cooking time – 10 minutes.

If rolled about 6 mm ($\frac{1}{4}$ inch) thick and cut with a 5-cm ($2\frac{1}{2}$-inch) cutter the mixture makes about 4 dozen cakes.

Durham

450 g (1 lb) self-raising flour
225 g (8 oz) sugar
225 g (8 oz) margarine

225 g (8 oz) mixed fruit
1–2 eggs
milk to bind

16 Yeast cookery

Yeast cookery

The breads, buns and cakes made by the use of yeast are a feature of
local recipes and of the English tea table.

Notes on yeast

Compressed baker's yeast
When bought, this should be pale fawn in colour, have a fresh smell
and crumble easily. It will keep well if stored in a cool place and

closely wrapped in waxed paper or in foil. All yeast is apt to dry out and discolour if exposed to the air. The length of keeping varies, but if the yeast is in good condition when bought and is carefully stored it should keep a week or two.

Dried yeast

This is dehydrated and usually in the form of pellets. It is more concentrated than compressed yeast and is used in about half the quantity of fresh yeast normally referred to in recipes. It requires 'reconstituting' in a little warm water sweetened with sugar – 15 g ($\frac{1}{2}$ oz) sugar to 300 ml ($\frac{1}{2}$ pint) warm water – before use. It is generally somewhat slow in action. Dried yeast is usually a 'branded' product and any manufacturer's directions should be followed.
Berkshire

Method of making a plain bread dough

Mixing the dough

Choose a strong plain flour which will have a high gluten content.

Add the yeast liquid all at once, using the fingers stretched open, until all the flour has been absorbed (add a little more liquid or flour at this stage if necessary). Work quickly including all the flour from the side of the bowl as well. The dough should feel firm but soft at this stage and the basin should be clean.

Kneading the dough

This is necessary to strengthen the dough and get a good rise.

The dough may at first feel soft and sticky but do not add more flour. It will improve with further kneading. Kneading is a process in which the dough is pulled, stretched, squeezed and folded in a rhythmic manner. The fingers will be clean and the dough firm and elastic when ready.

If you have a mixer the kneading can be done at a low speed using the dough hook, until the mixture collects in one piece leaving the bowl quite clean.

Rising the dough

All yeast doughs MUST be risen before baking.

The dough must be covered to prevent a hard skin from forming and to ensure the dough remains moist. Greasing the container will prevent the dough sticking.

Suggestions:

Large oiled polythene bag which can be loosely tied.
Plastic storage jar with a lid (large enough to allow for rising).
Casserole or saucepan with lid.
Cloth or tea towel.

How long will it take?

The temperature will affect the time taken

The rising time can be made to suit your convenience. Remember a
long slow rising gives a stronger dough and a better result. Warm
rising gives a weaker dough and it is inclined to become dry. When
risen the dough is double its original volume.

Possible rising times:

1 hour in a warm kitchen or other warm place.
2 hours in a cooler room.
4–6 hours in a cool place.
12 hours in a refrigerator. Good for overnight rising if warm rolls
are needed for breakfast. Allow to come to room temperature before
shaping, proving and baking.

   Surplus dough can be stored about 2 days in a refrigerator or
longer in a deep freeze if well wrapped to prevent drying. Thaw
before shaping, proving and baking.

Knocking back the dough

A process whereby the air bubbles the yeast has produced are
'knocked out'. The big bubbles of gas would make large holes in the
dough if baked and the action of the yeast will have softened the
dough, so kneading is again necessary to strengthen it.

   The dough should regain its elasticity and firmness.

   The mixer can be used for this process on a low speed.

Shaping

The dough is ready for shaping according to instructions or can be
adapted for various recipes by the addition of further ingredients.

Proving or second rising

The dough recovers and puffs up to twice its size as the yeast
becomes active again and 'proves' itself. The dough must not be

allowed to form a skin as a dry surface would impede the rising. It is most important to cover lightly or use a greased polythene bag at this stage or choose a warm and humid place.

Baking
Use a hot oven at first to kill the action of the yeast. This can be reduced later if necessary.

Common faults in bread	Causes
White pimples or spots on top of the loaf	Dough had a skin on it before being placed in the oven due to chilling or evaporation. A damp muslin or suitable covering for the dough will help to avoid this.
Coarse honeycomb texture	Too much liquid. Too little kneading.
A 'flying top' when the top breaks away from the rest of the loaf	The top crust baked hard before there is full expansion of dough due to under-proving or chilling – or dough too tight because not well worked.
Lack of volume, uneven texture	Under-proving and kneading or baking at too high a temperature.
Lack of volume, open texture and crumbly	Over-proving and weakening of gluten or baking at too low a temperature.
Smell of alcohol	Over-proving.

National Federation of Women's Institutes *Yeast Cookery*

Note for beginners

For richer doughs modifications of the method above for plain doughs are used and these are given in the individual recipes.

With buns and soft rolls, after the first rising, instructions often say 'knead lightly'. This means to knead only enough to shape the buns or rolls. If long kneading is given the dough must be allowed time to double its bulk again before baking; the usual procedure after 'light' kneading is to prove until the buns or rolls look light and puffy, about 20–30 minutes.

White bread dough
Four ½-kg (1-lb) loaves

Put the yeast, fresh, or dried plus sugar, in a pint jug or bowl and add to this 300 ml (½ pint) warm water just slightly hotter than blood heat. Stir and then leave about 10 minutes to become frothy (rather like beer).

Sieve flour and salt and rub in the fat if used. Add yeast liquid all at once together with the remaining warm water and oil if this is used to make a firm dough. A little more flour or water can be added at this stage to adjust the consistency but beware of making the mixture too tight (dry).

Knead the dough and put to rise to double the bulk. Knock back and divide the dough into four pieces.

Shaping
Tin loaf Flatten each piece and roll Swiss roll fashion to fit greased and floured ½-kg (1-lb) loaf tins. Place the crease underneath and push the ends well into the sides of the tin. Prove, and bake in a hot oven, 230°C (450°F), Gas 8, about ¾ hour.

When cooked it will sound hollow when tapped on the bottom.

Cob
Shape ¼ dough to a round ball and flatten slightly. Put on a floured baking sheet. Prove and bake.

National Federation of Women's Institutes *Yeast Cookery*

25 g (1 oz) fresh yeast or 15 g
  (½ oz) dried yeast plus 5 ml
  (1 teaspoon) sugar
900 ml (1½ pints) warm water

1½ kg (3 lb) strong plain flour
25 g (1 oz) cooking salt
25 g (1 oz) lard or 30 ml
  (2 tablespoons) corn oil

Note for beginners

Make half the recipe for ease in handling. For details of kneading and rising a dough, see page 214.

Wheatmeal dough
Quickly made

Put yeast, fresh, or dried plus sugar, into 300 ml (½ pint) of the

measured warm water. Leave 5–10 minutes to become frothy.
Sieve or mix the flour, salt and sugar and rub in the fat if used. Add
the rest of the warm water to the yeast liquid together with the oil if
preferred. Mix to a soft dough, leaving the basin clean and adding a
little more flour or water if necessary. Knead for 10 minutes on a
floured board.

Shape into a bap, cob, rolls, tin loaf or bake in earthenware
flower-pots. When shaped the dough is covered and put to rise.
Bake in the centre of a hot oven, 230°C (450°F), Gas 8, for about
40 minutes.

Note: For a soft crust brush with oil before proving, for a crisp
crust brush with salt and water and sprinkle with crushed wheat
before baking.

Flower-pot loaves The pot must be well greased before use. It is
advisable to grease and bake them empty several times.

Wheatmeal dough is strengthened by cooler rising and can be
refrigerated in the same way as white dough, see page 215.

Variations
Add an egg to enrich the dough.

Use honey, treacle or brown sugar in place of the white sugar.

Add oats, barley flakes or cereal bran (50–75 g – 2–3 oz) per ½ kg
(1 pound) of flour.

Using part of the dough, add a few caraway seeds, dried fruit and
nuts.

National Federation of Women's Institutes *Yeast Cookery*

40 g (1½ oz) fresh yeast or 20 g
  (¾ oz) dried yeast plus 5ml
  (1 teaspoon) sugar
900 ml (1½ pints) warm water
1½ kg (3 lb) flour, a mixture of
  brown and white in any
  proportions

25 g (1 oz) sugar
25 g (1 oz) salt
25 g (1 oz) lard or 30 ml
  (2 tablespoons) corn oil

Note for beginners

This mixture makes two 1-kg (2-lb) loaves.

For ease in handling make half the recipe. If this is made into two
small loaves they will take about 30 minutes to cook.

Wholemeal bread

Put 300 ml (½ pint) measured water into a jug. Add fresh yeast or dried yeast and sugar to the water and leave 5–10 minutes to become frothy.

Mix flour and salt in a bowl. Rub in the lard. Add the yeast liquid to the flour with the corn oil if used, with sufficient warm water to make a soft but firm dough which clings together and leaves the bowl clean.

Add a little more water or flour if necessary. Knead on a lightly floured board. Cover and leave to rise until it doubles in size. Divide dough into two pieces.

Knead each piece again. Shape into loaves, cobs or rolls. Cover and put to rise.

Bake in the middle of a hot oven, 230°C (450°F), Gas 8, for 30–40 minutes. The loaves will shrink from the sides of the tin when baked. Makes two 1-kg (2-lb) loaves.

National Federation of Women's Institutes *Yeast Cookery*

900 ml (1½ pints) warm water (45°C or 110°F)

50 g (2 oz) yeast or 30 ml (2 level tablespoons) dried yeast plus 10 ml (2 teaspoons) sugar

1½ kg (3 lb) wholemeal flour

30 ml (2 level tablespoons) salt

25 g (1 oz) lard or 30 ml (2 tablespoons) corn oil

Apricot and walnut bread

Mix flours, salt and sugar together in a bowl. Blend yeast in the water and add all at once to the dry ingredients. Mix to a clear, scone-like dough. Knead. Put bowl in greased polythene bag and leave in a warm place until dough doubles in volume.

Squeeze and work in all the other ingredients with one hand until the mixture is no longer streaky. Put into prepared 1-kg (2-lb) size tin (bottom lined and greased), and put inside polythene bag until the dough doubles in volume.

Put on the topping *before* baking.

Topping
Rub together the margarine, sugar and flour until it looks like coarse breadcrumbs. Sprinkle this over the dough, then sprinkle over crushed cornflakes.

Bake in centre of oven, 230°C (450F), Gas 8, for 30–40 minutes.
Cumberland

225 g (8 oz) plain brown flour
225 g (8 oz) plain white flour
10 ml (2 level teaspoons) sugar
10 ml (2 level teaspoons) salt
15 g (½ oz) fresh yeast or 10 ml
  (2 level teaspoons) dried yeast
300 ml (½ pint) water

100 g (4 oz) dried chopped apricots
50 g (2 oz) broken walnuts

Topping
25 g (1 oz) margarine
25 g (1 oz) sugar
40 g (1½ oz) flour
crushed cornflakes

Bara brith
Traditional Welsh recipe

Put the yeast or dried yeast and sugar into 150 ml (¼ pint) of the measured warm milk.

Sieve the flour in a warm basin, Rub in the fat. Add all dry ingredients. Make a well in the centre, add eggs and remaining warm milk to yeast liquid and use to mix to a soft dough. Knead. Cover and leave in a warm place to rise for 1½ hours or until twice its original size.

Knead lightly on a floured board. Divide into four and put into greased tins (½ kg or 1 lb). Put to prove in a warm place for about 20 minutes.

Bake at 180°C (350°F), Gas 4, for 1½–2 hours.

When cold, slice as for bread and butter, thinly, and butter well.

National Federation of Women's Institutes *Yeast Cookery*

40 g (1½ oz) yeast or 15 g (½ oz)
  dried yeast plus 5 ml (1 teaspoon)
  sugar
500 ml (1 pint) warm milk
1·3 kg (3 lb) flour
300 g (12 oz) lard or butter or
  mixed fats

300 g (12 oz) brown sugar
10 ml (2 level teaspoons) salt
400 g (1 lb) stoned raisins
800 g (2 lb) mixed dried fruit
100 g (4 oz) peel
5 ml (½ teaspoon) mixed spice
2–3 eggs

Bath buns

Rub the lard into the flour, cream the yeast, add the milk and the egg. Beat well to a dough. Put to rise to double the size.

Beat in the sugar, chopped peel and sultanas.

Form into small buns and leave to rise. Brush over with egg and sprinkle with crushed loaf sugar.

Bake at 240°C (475°F), Gas 9, for 10 minutes. Makes 12 buns.
Somerset

250 g (8 oz) flour	75 g (3 oz) caster sugar
75 g (3 oz) lard	40 g (1½ oz) chopped peel
15 g (½ oz) yeast	50 g (2 oz) sultanas
150 ml (¼ pint) milk	egg for brushing
1 egg	25 g (1 oz) loaf sugar

Bread sticks

Put the yeast or dried yeast and sugar into 150 ml (¼ pint) of the warmed milk and leave for 5 minutes. Sieve flour and salt into a warm bowl. Make a well in the flour and add the yeast liquid to the centre of the flour.

Stir a little flour in and leave to rise 20 minutes. Add remaining milk and melted butter, form into a dough and leave to rise for a further 10 minutes. Remove dough from bowl, roll into sticks the size and width of the little finger and about 20 cm (8 inches) long. Prove on prepared baking sheet 20 minutes. Brush with milk, sprinkle with rock salt, bake in a moderate oven, 180°C (350°F), Gas 4. May need crisping in a cooler oven for 20 minutes or left in the oven with the door door open and heat turned off. Store in tins for use. Makes 4 dozen sticks.

National Federation of Women's Institutes *Yeast Cookery*

15 g (½ oz) yeast or 10 ml (¼ oz) dried yeast plus	500 g (1 lb) flour
	10 ml (1 teaspoon) salt
2½ ml (½ teaspoon) sugar	25 g (1 oz) butter
300 ml (½ pint) warmed milk	rock salt

Chelsea buns

Sieve flour and salt. Put to warm. Rub in the margarine. Cream yeast and sugar. Warm milk, add beaten egg and sugar, add to the creamed yeast and place in a well in the centre of the flour. Mix to a light dough. Knead until smooth and free from creases. Allow to rise until double in bulk. Re-knead lightly and then roll out to a

square about 1 cm (½ inch) thick. Brush all over with melted
margarine. Spread with currants and dust thickly with the sugar.
Roll up like a Swiss roll. Cut into 3¾ cm (1½ inch) slices. Place
cut-side down on to a greased and warmed meat tin, 2½ cm (1 inch)
apart. Prove until touching. Bake in a hot oven, 220°C (425°F), Gas
7, for 10 minutes or until risen and lightly browned, then reduce the
heat to 190°C (375°F), Gas 5, for a further 10–20 minutes. Brush
while hot with hot glaze or alternatively, reserve a little of the beaten
egg, and brush with this *before* cooking. Makes 5–6 large buns.
Shropshire

225 g (8 oz) flour	*Filling*
5 ml (1 level teaspoon) salt	little melted margarine
25 g (1 oz) margarine	40 g (1½ oz) currants
15 g (½ oz) yeast plus 5 ml (1 level teaspoon) sugar	40 g (1½ oz) sugar
75 ml (⅛ pint) milk	*Glaze*
1 egg plus 25 g (1 oz) sugar	30 ml (1 tablespoon) sugar
	15 ml (1 tablespoon) water
	or
	beaten egg

Cornish splits

Cream the yeast and sugar together until they are liquid, then add
the milk; sieve the flour and salt into a basin. Melt the butter gently,
add it and the milk, etc, to the flour and mix all into a smooth
dough. Knead thoroughly. Put the basin in a warm place, to let the
dough rise for ¾ hour.

Then shape it in small round cakes and place them on a floured
baking tin. Bake in a quick oven, 230°C (450°F), Gas 8, for 15–20
minutes.

Split and butter them. Serve very hot. Or may be left until cold,
when split and butter them, or split and eat with cream, jam or
treacle.

Splits eaten with cream and treacle are known as 'thunder and
lightning'.
Cornwall

15 g (½ oz) yeast	500 g (1 lb) flour
15 g (½ oz) caster sugar	2½ ml (¼ teaspoon) salt
300 ml (½ pint) tepid milk	25 g (1 oz) butter

Cumberland tea cakes

Sieve flour and salt together. Rub in fat, add sugar and currants.
Disperse yeast in warm liquid. Add liquid to flour, etc, and knead to
a clear dough.

Put in a warm place to rise, until it doubles its volume. Scale into
75-g (3-oz) pieces. Mould round, place on greased sheet to prove.

Bake at 200–220°C (400–425°F), Gas 6–7, for 15 minutes. Cool
slightly before brushing with butter. This quantity makes 10 tea
cakes.

Cumberland

450 g (1 lb) plain flour
5 ml (1 teaspoon) salt
50 g (2 oz) lard
25 g (1 oz) margarine
25 g (1 oz) sugar

40 g (1½ oz) currants (optional)
25 g (1 oz) yeast
300 ml (½ pint) liquid, ½ milk
   ½ water, warm
melted butter for brushing

Devonshire splits

Grease and flour baking sheets. Sift flour and salt into a mixing
bowl. Warm the milk to blood heat. Cream the yeast with the sugar.
Melt the butter in the milk.

Pour all at once into the centre of the flour and mix to a soft dough.

Put into a floured bowl, cover with a damp cloth, and set to rise in
a warm place until double in bulk.

Turn out the dough and divide into equal portions (14–18).

Knead into small balls with the palm of the hand. Place on the
prepared baking tin. Prove for 10–15 minutes.

Brush with milk and place in a hot oven, 230°C (450°F), Gas 8, for
15–20 minutes.

When cooked, brush with a syrupy mixture to make them soft and
sticky.

When cold, split and fill with Devonshire cream and jam.

Note: Syrupy mixture consists of 100 g (4 oz) sugar, 75 ml (⅛ pint)
milk. Heat to 105°C (215°F).

Devon

500 g (1 lb) plain flour
5 ml (½ teaspoon) salt
300 ml (½ pint) skimmed milk
15 g (½ oz) yeast
10 ml (1 teaspoon) caster sugar

50 g (2 oz) butter
syrupy mixture for brushing (see page 223)
jam
Devonshire cream

Durham yule loaf
Traditional recipe

Rub butter and lard into the flour. Add the dry ingredients. Mix yeast with a little warm milk. Make a well in the centre and add yeast and beaten egg and the rest of the milk. Knead into soft dough, cover and allow to rise about 1 hour.

Turn on to a floured board, put into greased tins. Rise 15 minutes and bake in a moderate oven, 180°C (350°F), Gas 4, about 1 hour.

This quantity makes two 1-kg (2-lb) loaves. The recipe can be halved in which case use the whole egg.

Durham

800 g (1¾ lb) plain flour
50 g (2 oz) butter
50 g (2 oz) lard
175 g (6 oz) sugar
150 g (5 oz) currants
150 g (5 oz) sultanas

50 g (2 oz) lemon peel
2½ ml (½ teaspoon) nutmeg
20 g (¾ oz) yeast
300 ml (½ pint) warmed milk
1 egg

Guernsey biscuits
Type of tea cake

Mix most of milk and water with creamed yeast, sprinkle with flour, cover and leave until ready.

Mix dry ingredients, rub in fat and make well in centre. Pour in yeast and more milk and water if required. Knead well, cover with cloth, place in warm place and leave to rise for 1½ hours.

Turn on floured board, knead lightly and form into balls, flatten or roll into biscuit shapes. Stand on greased baking tray in warm place for 15–20 minutes. Bake for 20 minutes, 200°C (400°F), Gas 6.

This should make 24 biscuits.

Guernsey

300 ml (½ pint) milk and hot water
  (a little more may be necessary)
25 g (1 oz) yeast creamed with
  10 ml (2 teaspoons) sugar
900 g (2 lb) plain flour

good grating nutmeg
10 ml (2 teaspoons) salt
450 g (1 lb) margarine and small
  knob butter

Hot cross buns

Add the yeast or dried yeast and sugar to the warm milk and leave for
5 minutes to become frothy. Add melted butter and beaten egg.

Warm and sieve flour and salt, add sugar, fruit and spice.

Put yeast mixture into mixing bowl and add warmed dry
ingredients to make a soft dough and beat well until mixture leaves
the sides of the bowl and hands clean. Leave to rise in a warm place
covered with cloth or polythene. When doubled in size knead and
shape into 12–16 buns. Put on baking trays and leave to prove
15–20 minutes covered in a greased polythene bag to prevent a skin
forming.

Mark the tops with a soft pastry cross and bake in a hot oven,
200°C (400°F), Gas 6, for 20–25 minutes. Brush over with the glaze
while buns are still hot.

National Federation of Women's Institutes *Yeast Cookery*

25 g (1 oz) yeast or 15 g (½ oz) dried
  yeast plus 5 ml (1 teaspoon) sugar
250 ml (½ pint) milk (bare measure)
50 g (2 oz) butter
1 egg
450 g (1 lb) flour
10 ml (1 teaspoon) salt
25 g (1 oz) sugar

40 g (1½ oz) chopped peel
50 g (2 oz) sultanas
10 ml (1 teaspoon) mixed spice
soft pastry for cross

Glaze
25 g (1 oz) sugar dissolved in 15 ml
  (1 tablespoon) water

Lardy cake

Sift together flour and salt and leave in a warm place. Cream the
yeast with sugar, add the egg and warmed milk and mix with the
flour to make a soft dough.

Leave in a warm place and when the dough has doubled its bulk
roll out on to a floured board (about 1 cm or ½ inch thick). Divide
the creamed filling into two portions and spread one-half on to
two-thirds of the dough then fold into three as for flaky pastry and
roll out again. Spread on the remainder of the filling, refold and roll

out twice, finally shaping to fit a 20-cm (8-inch) cake tin. Allow to rise and bake in a hot oven, 200–220°C (400–425°F), Gas 6–7, for 30–35 minutes.

Northumberland and Durham

225 g (8 oz) flour
pinch of salt
15 g (½ oz) yeast
5 ml (1 teaspoon) sugar
1 egg
100 ml (¾ gill) milk

For the filling
50 g (2 oz) lard
50 g (2 oz) sugar
50 g (2 oz) currants

Malt bread

As this is a sweet bread a big rise is not needed. A soft plain flour is used in this recipe. This quantity makes 2 small loaves.

Add the yeast to the warm water. Stand 5–10 minutes to become frothy. Put the treacle, malt extract and margarine into a pan and warm them together. Allow to cool.

Sieve the flour and salt into a basin. Add the sultanas if used. Add the cooled malt mixture to the yeast liquid and then add both to the dry mix to form a soft dough.

Beat until the bowl becomes clean. Turn on to a lightly floured board and knead so that the dough becomes smooth and elastic.

Divide the dough into two pieces and then flatten them and roll each into a shape to fit the two ½-kg (1-lb) greased loaf tins. Put to rise inside loose fitting greased polythene bags. When risen bake in the centre of the oven at 200°C (400°F), Gas 6, for approximately 45 minutes.

The hot loaves can be brushed with honey or milk and sugar syrup.

National Federation of Women's Institutes *Yeast Cookery*

25 g (1 oz) fresh yeast or 15 ml
  (1 tablespoon) dried yeast plus
  5 ml (1 teaspoon) sugar
approximately 150 ml (¼ pint)
  warm water
50 g (2 tablespoons) black treacle
100 g (4 tablespoons or 4 oz) malt
  extract

25 g (1 oz) butter or margarine
450 g (1 lb) soft plain flour
2½ ml (½ level teaspoon) salt
50–100 g (2–4 oz) sultanas
  (optional)

To brush
honey or milk and sugar syrup

Pulled bread
Traditional recipe

Knead some white bread dough, place it in a greased loaf tin and let it prove just as when making bread. When sufficiently risen, bake it in a hot oven for about 20 minutes, just long enough to set the dough. Turn it out of the tin and with two forks separate it into irregularly shaped pieces suitable for serving. Place them on a baking sheet and bake them in a moderate oven until crisp and lightly brown.

Westmorland

Rich yeast dinner rolls

Sieve flour and salt, add sugar and mix. Rub in margarine. Disperse yeast in warm milk. Make a well in the centre of the mixture. Add egg and liquid. Beat and knead to a clear dough. Allow to rise in a warm place until double in volume.

Weigh out 30-g (1-oz) pieces. Mould and put on a greased baking sheet to prove.

Bake in a hot oven, 220°C (425°F), Gas 7, for 8 minutes or until brown and cooked.

Brush over tops with melted butter. This quantity makes 12 rolls.

Cumberland

225 g (8 oz) strong flour	15 g (½ oz) yeast
5 ml (½ teaspoon) salt	100 ml (3½–4 fl oz) milk
5 ml (½ teaspoon) sugar	1 egg
15 g (½ oz) margarine	melted butter for brushing

Saffron cake

Cut up saffron finely and place between greaseproof paper. Roll several times in order to bruise and infuse in 30 ml (2 tablespoons) of boiling water. Soak the saffron overnight. Strain and add the saffron water to the yeast liquid before mixing the dough.

Put the yeast or dried yeast and sugar in the lukewarm milk and water and leave for 5 minutes to become frothy. Add 100 g (1 cup) of the flour to the yeast liquid and mix together. Allow to sponge.

Rub the fats into the flour then add the salt, sugar, peel and fruit. Pour the yeast sponge and the saffron water into the rest of the

227

ingredients and mix to a soft dough. Knead. Prove for about 2 hours, or until the dough is light. Divide into three and knead lightly before putting in greased ½-kg (1-lb) tins. Put to rise in a warm place for 15–20 minutes inside greased polythene bags or cover them to prevent a skin forming.

Bake at 190°C (375°F), Gas 5, for 30 minutes, reducing heat to 180°C (350°F), Gas 4, for a further 30 minutes.

Cornwall

1 dram saffron (see note below)	175 g (6 oz) lard
25 g (1 oz) fresh yeast or 15 g	175 g (6 oz) margarine
(½ oz) dried yeast and 5 ml	5 ml (1 level teaspoon) salt
(1 teaspoon) sugar	175 g (6 oz) caster sugar
300 ml (½ pint) lukewarm milk	50 g (2 oz) lemon peel
and water	350–450 g (¾–1 lb) currants
900 g (2 lb) strong plain flour	

Note for beginners

Saffron is sold by chemists, usually in 1 dram amounts. If you just want to try one loaf the recipe can be divided by three. Rising is slow because the amount of yeast is fairly small and the mixture a rich one, so do not try to hurry the rising. Some recipes for saffron cake recommend only one rising, in the tin.

Sally Lunn

Put the yeast or dried yeast and sugar into the lukewarm milk and leave for 5 minutes. Sieve the flour and salt into a bowl. Melt the butter in a saucepan and add to the lukewarm milk, beat the egg and add this to the liquid mix. Make a well in the flour, add the liquid mix to form a dough with the hand. Beat thoroughly, leave to rise 30–40 minutes. Turn on to floured board, divide into two pieces, knead each till smooth and round, and place in greased round cake tin to 1 cm (¾ inch) from top, cover and set in a warm place for ½–¾ hour.

Bake in hot oven for 15 minutes, 220°C (425°F), Gas 7.

National Federation of Women's Institutes *Yeast Cookery*

15 g (½ oz) yeast or 10 ml (¼ oz)	350 g (12 oz) flour
dried yeast and 2½ ml	5 ml (½ teaspoon) salt
(½ teaspoon) sugar	25 g (1 oz) butter
200 ml (1½ gills) milk	1 egg

Note for beginners

The cake tins for the Sally Lunn should be about 15 cm (6 inch) and fairly shallow; small sandwich tins are suitable.

Scotch baps

Put the yeast, warm milk and water, 1 teaspoon flour and sugar into a jug and leave about 5 minutes to become frothy. Rub butter or margarine into the flour and add the salt. Make a well, add the egg to the yeast liquid and mix to a *slack dough* adding extra warm liquid if required. Allow to prove until doubled in size. Knead on a board till firm to handle.

Divide into small pieces about the size of a duck egg (oval shape). Cover and put to rise until double size.

Bake at the top of a hot oven, 200°C (400°F), Gas 6, 15–20 minutes approximately.

These should not be glazed but floury on top. Makes about 12 baps.

National Federation of Women's Institutes *Yeast Cookery*

15 g (½ oz or 1 level tablespoon) dried yeast plus 5 ml (1 teaspoon) sugar
or
25 g (1 oz) fresh yeast (if raised overnight use only half this amount)

250 ml (approx ½ pint) milk and water mixed and warm
450 g (1 lb) strong plain flour
50 g (2 oz) butter or margarine
10 ml (2 teaspoons) salt
1 egg

Swedish tea ring

Sieve flour and salt into a warm bowl. Rub in margarine, add sugar. Dissolve yeast in a little tepid milk and add to beaten egg. Add to flour and mix to a soft dough. Knead. Leave to rise in warm place.

Divide mixture into two. Roll out to strips 38 cm (15 inches) long and 10 cm (4 inches) wide. Lay roll of almond paste along middle. Roll up and shape into ring. Rise on greased tray approximately 15 minutes.

Bake at 220°C (425°F), Gas 7, for 15 minutes approximately. When cool, ice with glacé icing and decorate with cherries, angelica and flaked almonds.

Durham

225 g (8 oz) plain flour
2½ ml (¼ teaspoon) salt
50 g (2 oz) margarine
25 g (1 oz) sugar
15 g (½ oz) fresh yeast
60 ml (4 tablespoons) milk
2 small eggs

Almond paste
25 g (1 oz) ground almonds

25 g (1 oz) caster sugar
little beaten egg

Glacé icing
100 g (4 oz) icing sugar
a little water

Decoration
cherries, angelica, flaked almonds

Yorkshire tea cakes

Add the yeast or dried yeast and sugar to the warmed milk and
water and leave for 5 minutes to become frothy. Sieve flour and salt
into a warmed basin. Rub in the lard and add the sugar.

Mix to a light dough using the yeast liquid. Knead well until the
mixture is no longer sticky. Cover and leave to rise in a warm place
until doubled in size.

Knead once more, divide into five portions making each into a
round cake 1 cm (½ inch) thick. Place on warmed greased tray –
enclose in a greased polythene bag or cover and prove until twice
their original size.

Bake in a hot oven, 240°C (475°F), Gas 9, approximately
12 minutes. When ready brush over tops with butter or lard.

National Federation of Women's Institutes *Yeast Cookery*

Alternative:
Add 25 g (1 oz) currants with the sugar. Shape the mixture into five
cubes and flatten and roll to 1 cm (½ inch) thick.
Yorkshire

15 g (½ oz) yeast or 10 ml (2
  teaspoons) dried yeast plus
  2½ ml (½ teaspoon) sugar
300 ml (½ pint) warm milk and
  water

500 g (1 lb) flour
1 level teaspoon salt
25 g (1 oz) lard
25 g (1 oz) sugar

17 Home-made Confectionery

Apricotines

Sieve apricots with very little juice. Add sugar and lemon juice.
Boil, stirring frequently, until the mixture is very thick and sets
when dropped on a plate, about 20–30 minutes.

Pour at once into greaseproof sweet cases and sprinkle with
granulated sugar. Keep in airtight box. Makes 24 sweets.
Cumberland

tin of apricots (454 g or 1 lb)
approximately ⅛ of juice from tin
of apricots
175 g (6 oz) granulated sugar

10 ml (2 teaspoons) lemon juice or
1 ml (¼ teaspoon) tartaric acid
granulated sugar to sprinkle on
top

Brown nougat

Blanch, shred, chop and brown almonds, and keep them warm. Melt
sugar (sieved if necessary) with lemon juice over gentle heat. Heat
until golden brown.

Stir in almonds quickly and pour at once into a greased tin, about
15 cm (6 inches) square. Mark in squares before it sets.

Cut when cold, and wrap in waxed paper or coat with chocolate.
Cumberland

50 g (2 oz) shelled almonds
50 g (2 oz) icing sugar

10 ml (2 teaspoons) lemon juice
chocolate (optional)

Butterscotch

Put ingredients in a thick saucepan and boil slowly until a nice golden colour, and a little sets hard when dropped into a cup of cold water – about 15–20 minutes.

Pour quickly into a buttered shallow tin (about 15 cm or 6 inches square), and leave to set. Break up and store in an airtight jar.
Lincolnshire

200 g (7 tablespoons) sugar
15 ml (1 tablespoon) vinegar
15 ml (1 tablespoon) water

50 g (2 tablespoons) golden syrup
100 g (4 oz) butter

Coffee fudge

Put the sugar, milk and water into a heavy-bottomed pan, heat very slowly until the sugar has dissolved. Add the butter and coffee. Bring to the boil and boil gently up to 170–200°C (328–400°F). Stir all the time or it will burn. Remove from the heat, add the nuts if used, and beat with a wooden spoon until thick and creamy.

You can use electric beaters if you do not add the nuts (the beaters knock them into crumbs). When it shows signs of setting pour into an oiled Swiss roll tin. When cool, mark into squares. When cold, cut. Makes about 1 kg (2 lb).
Hampshire

700 g (1½ lb) caster sugar
300 ml (½ pint) evaporated milk
300 ml (½ pint) water
100 g (4 oz) butter

15 ml (1 tablespoon) instant coffee
dissolved in 15 ml (1 tablespoon)
water
50 g (2 oz) chopped walnuts can
be added

Coffee truffles

Mix everything very well together in a basin using a wooden spoon. Form into small balls with the hands. Roll some in sieved cocoa,

some in chocolate vermicelli, some in nibbed almonds. A little rum improves them, naturally, if the occasion of both making and eating is suitable. Put in paper sweet cases. Makes 2 dozen or more.
Hampshire

100 g (4 oz) melted chocolate
15 ml (1 tablespoon) instant coffee
  dissolved in the chocolate as it
  melts
2 egg yolks
175 g (6 oz) icing sugar
50 g (2 oz) butter

rum (optional)

For coating
sieved cocoa
chocolate vermicelli
almond nibs

Marshmallows

Soak the gelatine in half the water (use bowl or large basin). Boil the remainder of the water and sugar together for 4 minutes, this forms a syrup. Pour syrup over soaked gelatine. Add salt and vanilla essence. Whisk until the mixture becomes the thickness of cream and has turned white.

Pour half the mixture on to a dish which has been greased with margarine and dusted with cornflour. To this first dish add the walnuts and cherries.

Colour the remainder of the mixture with a little pink colouring and pour into a second dish. Leave to set. Turn out on to a board. Dust with a mixture of equal quantities of sifted icing sugar and cornflour. Cut into shapes and pack into boxes.
Cumberland

15 g (½ oz) gelatine
150 ml (¼ pint) water
225 g (8 oz) caster sugar
good pinch of salt
5 ml (1 teaspoon) vanilla essence
30 ml (1 tablespoon) chopped
  walnuts

30 ml (1 tablespoon) chopped
  cherries
pink colouring
icing sugar and cornflour for
  dusting

Marzipan
Uncooked

Whisk egg white and sifted icing sugar together, add essence and lemon juice. Stir in ground almonds. Store in polythene bag. Use for moulding marzipan sweets.

Stuffed dates

Choose good quality dessert dates. Remove stones and fill cavity
with marzipan. Put in paper cases.

Lincolnshire

1 egg white
225 g (8 oz) icing sugar
2½ ml (½ teaspoon) almond essence

5 ml (1 teaspoon) lemon juice
225 g (8 oz) ground almonds

Old-fashioned cinder toffee

Heat the sugar and syrup slowly in a saucepan over a low heat until
mixture 'toffees'. Smooth out the bicarbonate of soda on a saucer
and add to the mixture when it is still boiling, whipping vigorously
with a spoon. It will 'froth' up and should then be placed in a greased
loaf tin and left to cool. While cooling keep it out of any draught.
Break into pieces when cold.

Cumberland

50 g (2 tablespoons) sugar
25 g (1 tablespoon) golden syrup

5 ml (1 teaspoon) bicarbonate of
 soda

Peanut toffee

Boil all together, stirring well when the mixture starts to thicken,
until a little sets hard in cold water. Pour into a greased tin about
15 cm (6 inches) square, and mark in squares before it sets.

Yorkshire

50 g (2 oz) peanut butter
50 g (2 oz) golden syrup
100 g (4 oz) sugar

15 ml (1 tablespoon) water
2½ ml (½ teaspoon) vanilla essence

Peppermint creams

Whisk egg whites, add icing sugar (do not put essence or colouring
directly on to egg whites). Beat well and then knead until smooth.
Roll out and cut into shapes, dust with caster sugar if a rough
surface is preferred or coat with chocolate.

Yorkshire

2 egg whites
450 g (1 lb) icing sugar
10 ml (2 teaspoons) peppermint
  flavouring

green colouring if desired
caster sugar or chocolate coating

Plum pudding candies

Pass the prepared fruits through a food mincer. Add the nuts finely chopped. Blend all thoroughly. Form into balls and roll in caster sugar.
Yorkshire

50 g (2 oz) stoned raisins
50 g (2 oz) stoned dates
50 g (2 oz) figs
50 g (2 oz) glacé cherries

6 tinned apricot halves, well
  drained
50 g (2 oz) finely chopped nuts
caster sugar

Rum truffles

Melt sugar, syrup, margarine, cocoa and jam in a pan. Slowly bring mixture to the boil, then leave to cool.

Meanwhile, sieve the sponge cake. Mix cake crumbs into the mixture; flavour with rum or rum essence. Divide the mixture into small pieces, coat each with vermicelli, roll into balls with the palm of the hand. Put into small sweet paper cases.
Durham

50 g (2 oz) sugar
15 ml (1 tablespoon) syrup
50 g (2 oz) margarine
15 ml (1 level tablespoon) cocoa
15 ml (1 level tablespoon) apricot
  or pineapple jam

150–170 g (6 oz) stale sponge cake
  or biscuits
few drops rum or rum essence
chocolate vermicelli or cocoa for
  coating
small paper cases

Russian caramel

Put all ingredients in pan together. Bring to boil and boil until stiff, stirring all the time, about 5 minutes. Pour into greased tin, about 15 cm (6 inches) square. When cold cut into shapes and put into sweet paper cases.
Durham

50 g (2 oz) margarine
150 ml (small tin) condensed milk
25 g (1 dessertspoon) sugar

5 ml (1 teaspoon) vanilla essence
25 g (1 tablespoon) treacle

Salted nuts

Any nuts can be used for this, and they are so much cheaper to do yourself than to buy.

Blanch them, by taking their skins off. Then fry them in butter with a little oil added, for a minute or two. Drain them on kitchen paper and toss in salt while hot. Sprinkle the salt on greaseproof paper and shake the nuts up and down in it.

For a different flavour add a little cayenne or paprika to the salt.
Hampshire

any nuts
butter and oil

salt
cayenne or paprika (optional)

Treacle toffee

Place all ingredients except cream of tartar in pan and dissolve. Add cream of tartar when it boils. Boil till it sets hard when dropped in cold water (about 15–20 minutes). Pour into buttered tins (two, about Swiss roll size). When cold break up and keep airtight in tin.
Cheshire

100 g (4 oz) butter
225 g (8 oz) treacle
450 g (1 lb) pale soft brown sugar

90 ml ($\frac{1}{2}$ teacup) cold water
5 ml (1 teaspoon) cream of tartar

Truffles

Bring cream to boil and pour on to chocolate. Beat until it begins to set. Add flavouring and leave to cool. Then turn on to slab and roll into lengths. Cut into even-sized pieces, form into balls and roll in cocoa. Very delicious. Makes 3–4 dozen balls.
Herefordshire

125 ml ($\frac{1}{4}$ pint) cream
400 g (1 lb) melted chcolate

flavouring to taste
cocoa

Turkish delight

Place water, sugar, acid, orange rind and gelatine in a saucepan, stir over gentle heat until dissolved. Bring to boiling point and boil for 20 minutes. Do not stir after it boils. Remove from heat and allow to cool 10 minutes. Pour half into a lightly buttered tin. Colour remainder pink and pour into another tin. Leave at least 24 hours. Cut into squares, and roll in a mixture of equal quantities of icing sugar and cornflour. Store in airtight tins with plenty of icing sugar between.

Westmorland

250 ml (1 pint) hot water
400 g (1 lb) granulated sugar
1 saltspoon citric acid

¼ teaspoon grated rind of 1 large
  or 2 small oranges
40 g (1½ oz) powdered gelatine
pink colouring

Unboiled coconut ice

Mix the coconut, milk and sugar and cream of tartar together and work to a stiff paste. Cut the paste in half. Colour one half pink, with considerable discretion. Roll each half separately to an oblong. Put on top of each other, having brushed the bottom half with egg white. Trim neatly and leave to set overnight.

Hampshire

100 g (4 oz) desiccated coconut
50 ml (2 tablespoons) sweetened
  condensed milk
75–100 g (3–4 oz) caster sugar

pinch of cream of tartar
little beaten egg white
red colouring

Unboiled fondant

Sieve icing sugar and add cream of tartar. Add cream and sufficient egg white to make a pliable consistency. Knead well together. Cut into 4 pieces.

Flavour:
1st   piece with 6 drops peppermint essence.
2nd piece with raspberry essence.
3rd piece with strawberry essence and a little pink colouring.
4th piece with lemon essence and a little green colouring.

Mould or cut to shape with sweet cutters.
Cumberland

200 g (8 oz) icing sugar	white of egg
1 ml (¼ teaspoon) cream of tartar	flavouring and colouring
10 ml (1 dessertspoon) cream	

Uncooked chocolate orange nut fudge

Melt chocolate and butter in a bowl over hot water. Add evaporated milk, grated orange rind and nuts and mix well. Work in the sifted sugar until mixture is quite stiff. Turn into a Swiss roll tin approximately 19 × 29 cm (7½ × 11½ inches). Leave to set. Cut into squares.
Yorkshire

100 g (4 oz) plain chocolate	grated rind of one orange
50 g (2 oz) butter	100 g (4 oz) nuts, chopped
60 ml (4 tablespoons) evaporated milk	450 g (1 lb) icing sugar

White nougat

Line a tin approximately 15 cm (6 inches) square with rice paper. Cut piece for top.

Put sugar, honey, egg white, glucose into a pan. Whisk over gentle heat until thick and white. It should form a firm ball when dropped into cold water. Remove from heat. Add almonds (warmed), cherries and pistachios if used. Mix well.

Turn on to board with thick layer of icing sugar and press into shape of tin. Put in tin. Cover with rice paper. Press and put weight on top.

When cold, cut into size required and wrap.
Cumberland

75 g (3 oz) icing sugar	25 g (1 oz) cherries
50 g (2 oz) honey	5 g (¼ oz) pistachios (optional)
1 egg white	sieved icing sugar
2½ ml (½ teaspoon) glucose	rice paper
50 g (2 oz) almonds (dried and warmed)	

18 Beverages

Apple ale
A delicious drink

Wash the apples and grate them, complete with skins, on a suet grater. Add the pulp to the water, and the cores too, to improve flavour.

Stir the apple water every day for a week and then strain.

Add sugar, ginger (well bruised), cinnamon and cloves, stir until the sugar is dissolved, and leave until the following day.

Then strain through a clean tea cloth, pour into bottles, cork lightly and leave for a week, when it will be ready for drinking.
Devon

To make 4½ l (a gallon) use: 25 g (1 oz) root ginger
4½ l (1 gallon) cold water   2½ ml (½ level teaspoon) cinnamon
1 kg (2 lb apples) (any kind)   2½ ml (½ level teaspoon) cloves
700 g (1½ lb) sugar

Apple toddy

Wipe the apples and cut up roughly without peeling. Place the
pieces in a casserole with the water, put on the lid and simmer
slowly until the apples are thoroughly softened. Press through a
sieve to pulp the apples, add the honey and bicarbonate of soda and
sip slowly while hot.

This is a children's drink and the bicarbonate of soda is added to
make the drink fizz which probably makes it more interesting for
young folk. Serves 4 or more.

National Federation of Women's Institutes *Home Made Wines,
Syrups and Cordials*

2 large apples   2½ ml (½ teaspoon) bicarbonate of
600 ml (1 pint) water   soda
15 ml (1 tablespoon) honey

Blackcurrant shake

Mix the milk and flavouring in a jug. Add the brickette and beat
with a rotary whisk, till frothy. Pour into a tall glass and serve with a
straw.
Cumberland

150 ml (¼ pint) milk   1 brickette vanilla ice-cream
30 ml (2 tablespoons) blackcurrant   40 g or 1½ oz
  syrup or cordial

Cider cup

Dissolve sugar in the water. Add thinly peeled lemon rind. Bring to
the boil. Strain into a jug. Chill. Add cider. Strain in lemon juice.
Stir in sherry or rum. When required add soda water, apple, and a
sprig or two of mint or borage. Makes about 1½ l (2¾ pints).

Note: If able to buy sparkling cider, use instead of still cider and
double the remaining ingredients.
Somerset

240

200 g (8 oz) loaf sugar
300 ml (½ pint) water
1 lemon
600 ml (1 pint) chilled cider

½ glass sherry or rum (45 ml)
600 ml (1 pint) soda water
3 or 4 slices red-cheeked apple
sprigs of mint or borage

Cider fruit cup

Put all ingredients together in a large bowl, add cider and lemonade just before the cup is to be served. Ice if liked.

Makes about 4 l (7½ pints).

Gloucestershire

1 tin pineapple juice (500 ml)
300 ml (½ pint) pear, apple, cherry
   or apricot juice
600 ml (1 pint) concentrated

orange squash
2¼ l (4 pints) cider
300 ml (1 pint) fizzy lemonade

Cider toddy

Heat the cider, bruised ginger and a twist of lemon peel in an aluminium, stainless steel or enamelled saucepan until bubbles just begin to rise in the liquid. Quickly remove from the heat, stir in the honey and strain into a warmed glass. This is excellent for drinking just before bedtime. Drinking it in bed and taking two aspirins is said to prevent a cold. Even if this is a false hope it certainly induces sleep.

National Federation of Women's Institutes *Home Made Wines, Syrups and Cordials*

1 glass dry cider (250 ml)
10 g (¼ oz) root ginger (or 1 small
   piece)

lemon peel
10 ml (1 dessertspoon) honey

Fruitade

Put fruit into preserving pan, allowing 1¼ l (1 quart) water to every 450 g (pound) of fruit. Heat them up and strain through a jelly bag.

Add juice of 1 lemon and 100 g (¼ lb) sugar to every 1¼ l (1 quart) of juice. Stir till sugar is dissolved. Delicious served with a piece of ice in the glass.

Gloucestershire

blackcurrants, redcurrants,
   raspberries, etc

lemon juice
sugar

Ginger beer

Peel lemons, cut fruit into slices. Place in a bowl with the sugar, cream of tartar and ginger, cover with the boiling water. When lukewarm, add the yeast (well creamed). Leave in a warm place overnight, strain through muslin, then bottle in screw-topped bottles.

The ginger beer is now ready for drinking, but will keep for several weeks.

Gloucestershire

2 lemons
700 g (1½ lb) granulated sugar
15 g (½ oz) cream of tartar

25 g (1 oz) bruised root ginger
6½ l (6 quarts) boiling water
15 g (½ oz) yeast

Ginger drink

Put all the ingredients except the sugar in a large pan and bring to the boil. Add the sugar, stir till it is dissolved, then boil for 15 minutes. Strain and bottle when cold.

Dilute with water to taste. A refreshing drink.

Makes about 1¼ l (2 pints) undiluted.

Westmorland

25 g (1 oz) root ginger
1¼ l (1 quart) water
5 ml (½ teaspoon) tartaric acid

1 or 2 chillies
450 g (1 lb) loaf sugar

Grapefruit cordial

Wash fruit and peel rind thinly. Cut fruit into small pieces, removing white and pips. Cut up rind and pour over all the boiling water. Add sugar and tartaric acid.

Allow to stand overnight and strain. Dilute to taste.

Makes about 1½ l (just under 3 pints) undiluted.

Cumberland

2 grapefruit
1 orange
900 ml (1½ pints) boiling water

700 g (1½ lb) sugar
25 g (1 oz) tartaric acid

Honey coffee

Combine and drink while hot.
West Kent

200 ml (1 breakfast cup) hot milk 10 ml (1 dessertspoon) honey
5 ml coffee essence (1 teaspoon
  or more to taste)

Hot lemon toddy

Put the lemon juice, glycerine and honey in a warmed tumbler and
fill up with boiling water. Serve with a thin twist of lemon peel
floating on the surface.

National Federation of Women's Institutes *Home Made Wines,*
Syrups and Cordials

1 lemon   10 ml (1 dessertspoon) honey
5 ml (1 teaspoon) glycerine   boiling water

Iced coffee

Extra strong freshly made coffee is essential for this. You cannot,
incidentally, make good coffee unless you buy top quality beans or
ground coffee in the first place.
   Make the coffee, strain it and let it get cold and put it in the
refrigerator. Do not put ice cubes into it. Keep it in the refrigerator
until you want it, and serve it with chilled whipped cream. You may
add a little milk to the chilling coffee but do not try to chill coffee
with cream in it. Hand bar syrup with it if sweetening is wanted.

Bar syrup

Melt ½ kg (1 lb) caster sugar very gently over a low heat with a
teacup of water (150 ml) until all the sugar has completely vanished.
It will keep indefinitely stored in a bottle.
Hampshire

Lemonade

Squeeze and grate lemons, add all together and pour on boiling
water. Stir well and bottle when cold. Dilute to taste.

This quantity makes 1¼ l (2¼ pints) of undiluted lemonade.
Durham

2 lemons   25 g (1 oz) citric acid
700 g (1½ lb) sugar   900 ml (1½ pints) boiling water

Lemonade or orangeade

Remove the rind thinly from the lemon or oranges and squeeze out
the juice. Place the rind, juice and sugar in a jug and pour on the
boiling water. Cover till cold. Strain and serve in a glass.
    Makes about 400 ml (just under ¾ pint).
Cheshire

1 lemon or 2 oranges   300 ml (½ pint) boiling water
4 lumps sugar

Mint lemonade

Peel the lemons finely and pound the rind with the flesh, mint
leaves and sugar. Add water, stir well and leave for 1 hour. Strain
through fine muslin, serve with bits of lemon peel and a sprig of
mint in each glass. Makes about 650 ml (just over 1 pint).
Cumberland

handful of fresh mint leaves   600 ml (1 pint) water
150 g (5 tablespoons) sugar   lemon peel and mint to garnish
3 lemons

Orange squash

Cut away the outside of the orange peel thinly then extract the
juice. Place peelings in the liquidizer with enough of the water to
fill the goblet. Switch to top speed for 30 seconds. Pour into saucepan
with the rest of the water.
    Bring to the boil, add sugar, citric acid and orange juice. Lower
the heat, stirring until sugar is dissolved. Pour through a strainer
and bottle in hot sterilized bottles. Dilute with water or soda water.
Colour as required.
    Makes 3 l (5¼ pints).
Cumberland

3 oranges

$2\frac{1}{4}$ l (4 pints) water

$1\frac{1}{2}$ kg (3 lb) sugar

40 g ($1\frac{1}{2}$ oz) citric acid

orange food colour

water or soda water for diluting

Pineapple fizz

Pour boiling water over sugar and boil for 5 minutes. Add lemon juice and pineapple, leave until cold.

Strain and add the soda water. Children just love this.

Makes about 2 l ($3\frac{1}{2}$ pints).

Cumberland

600 ml (1 pint) boiling water

350 g (12 oz) sugar

2 lemons

a tin of pineapple juice 540 ml or (19 fl oz) (or crushed pineapple)

3 bottles soda water (284–340 ml or 10–12 fl oz size)

Pussyfoot

Put the pieces of fruit in a tumbler, add the grenadine and leave for a few minutes. Measure in the orange and lemon squash and add soda water to taste. Serve after chilling. This makes a drink for one person. It is even more pleasant if made in a 600-ml (1-pint) tumbler, a dessertspoonful of gin added before filling the tumbler with soda water.

National Federation of Women's Institutes *Home Made Wines, Syrups and Cordials*

1 small piece orange

1 small piece lemon

4 drops grenadine syrup

25 ml ($1\frac{1}{2}$ tablespoons) orange squash

25 ml ($1\frac{1}{2}$ tablespoons) lemon squash

soda water

10 ml (1 dessertspoon) gin (optional)

Rhubarb cordial

Gently simmer the chopped rhubarb, sugar, water, cloves and bruised ginger in a saucepan until the rhubarb is soft, replacing any water that boils away. Strain well and serve from a warmed glass jug decorated with a few mint leaves.

National Federation of Women's Institutes *Home Made Wines, Syrups and Cordials*

1 kg (2 lb) rhubarb
100 g (4 oz) white sugar
2 cloves

6 g (¼ oz) root ginger (2 medium-sized pieces)
1¼ l (1 quart) water

Summer punch

Squeeze juice from fruit. Dissolve sugar in a little water. When cold add to fruit juice. Add slices of fruit.

Add soda water just before serving. Makes about 1½ l (2½ pints).
Cumberland

4 oranges
1 grapefruit
3 lemons

100 g (4 oz) sugar
1¼ l (1 quart) soda water
slices of fresh fruit

The Cardinal

Melt the barley sugar in the hot water and combine with the other ingredients. Warm up and infuse for a while. Strain before serving. Makes 1¾ l (3 pints).
Hampshire

100 g (4 oz) barley sugar (quite essential)
600 ml (1 pint) hot water
1¼ l (1 quart) cheap red wine
a good powdering of freshly grated nutmeg

5–7 cm (2–3 inches) of cinnamon stick
3 slices tangerine, de-pipped
a few cracked cardamom seeds
a blade or two of mace

Three fruit punch

Dissolve the sugar in hot water. When cool add to the juices of fruits and chill.

A few slices of orange and several cherries frozen in the cubes improves the appearance of this punch. Makes 900 ml (1½ pints).
Cumberland

200 g (7 oz) granulated sugar
300 ml (½ pint) hot water
2 lemons

2 oranges
2 grapefruit

Treacle posset 1

Heat the milk until near boiling point, then add the treacle and lemon juice. Boil slowly until the curds separate, strain and serve hot as a remedy for a cold.

600 ml (1 pint) milk   1 lemon
30 ml (2 tablespoons) treacle

Treacle posset 2

Heat the milk and dissolve the treacle in it, serve hot.

National Federation of Women's Institutes *Home Made Wines, Syrups and Cordials*

For each person use:
5 ml (1 teaspoon) black treacle   1 glass milk

White wine cup

Put the wine, fruit and syrup into a 1-kg (2-lb) Kilner jar, shake, chill. Add the soda water and brandy, shake and serve in a glass bowl or jug or glasses with the decoration floating on top. Sufficient for 6–8 small glasses.

Sugar and water syrup
Dissolve the sugar in the water, add the glucose and boil to 105°C (220°F). Cool slightly, pour into a hot jar and tie down with paper. Store in a cool place. Use cold for the wine cup.
Cambridgeshire

400 ml (13½ fl oz) dry white wine
a little fruit in season or from a can
a little sugar and water syrup or syrup from can to taste
200 ml (6¾ fl oz) soda water
40 ml (¾ fl oz) brandy (optional)
a little decoration to float on top of the fruit cup, e.g. borage flowers, eau-de-cologne mint leaves, thinly sliced cucumber or lemon

Sugar and water syrup
450 g (1 lb) granulated sugar
300 ml (1 pint) water
5 ml (1 teaspoon) liquid glucose (if syrup to be stored for some time add glucose)

Yard of flannel

Serve this hot or cold. If hot be careful not to cook the eggs. Heat the other ingredients first, remove from the stove and add the rum and then the beaten eggs, still beating as you go. Enough for 12–16 glasses.

Hampshire

1¼ l (1 quart) of barley wine
5–10 ml (1 teaspoon) powdered
  ginger

100 g (4 oz) 'pieces' brown sugar
150 ml (¼ pint) rum
4 eggs very well beaten

19 Preserves

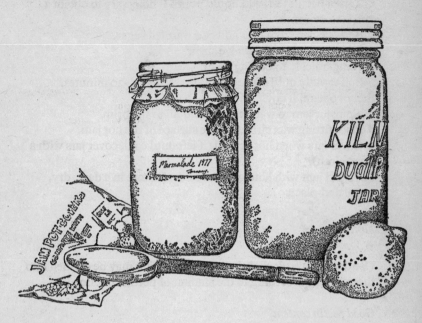

The material for jams and chutneys has come from two National Federation of Women's Institutes publications, *Preservation* and *Unusual Preserves*. That on crystallizing comes from a Yorkshire publication, *Crystallization of Fruit and Flowers*.

Information on drying herbs will be found in Chapter 8, 'Herbs and Flavourings'.

Metric conversions are given with all the recipes. The figures have been adjusted to give the same proportions of fruit, sugar and other ingredients as in the original recipes; but these have not been re-tested using the metric weights and measures.

Jam making
General method

1 Simmer fruit (adding water and extra acid when necessary) until the skins are tender and the volume has decreased by one-third when water has been added. The time will vary from a few minutes for a small quantity of, say, raspberries to 30–45 minutes for a large quantity of, say, blackcurrants.

2 Take a pectin test, add liquid pectin if necessary to obtain a satisfactory result.

3 Remove pan from heat and add warmed sugar.

4 Stir thoroughly to dissolve sugar.

5 Bring quickly to boiling point.

6 Boil rapidly until setting point is reached, 5–20 minutes. Remove scum if any.

7 Transfer jam to warmed jars, and fill to the brim.

8 Place fitting wax circles on the surface of the hot jam.

9 Cover jars when hot or cold (if left until cold, cover jars with a clean cloth).

10 Label jam with kind of jam and date. Store in a dark, dry, ventilated place.

Notes

Fruit

Use dry fresh fruit slightly under-ripe. Fruit may be divided into three groups according to the amount of pectin contained.

Good pectin content

Black- and redcurrants, cooking apples, gooseberries, damsons, some plums, quince.

Medium pectin content

Early blackberries, greengages, loganberries, fresh apricots.

Poor pectin content

Strawberries, pears, rhubarb, cherries, medlars, late blackberries, elderberries, tomatoes, marrows.

Acid

Acid is added to fruit before it is cooked, to help extract pectin, to improve colour, and to prevent crystallization. It must be added to fruits with a poor acid content, and to any vegetable jams. The quantity of acid to be added is as follows:

To 2 kg (4 lb) of fruit –
30 ml (2 tablespoons) lemon juice (1 average lemon) OR

2½ ml (½ level teaspoon) citric or tartaric acid OR
150 ml (¼ pint) redcurrant or gooseberry juice.

Pectin test
The setting property of jam is dependent on its pectin content. To
test for this:
1 Take 1 teaspoon of juice from pan, and place in a glass. Cool.
2 Add 3 teaspoons of methylated spirits.
3 Shake gently together.
  If plenty of pectin is present, a clear jelly-like clot is formed.
  If a medium amount of pectin is present, several small clots will be
present.
  If a poor amount of pectin is present, no real clot will be formed,
and if after further cooking no clot is formed, additional pectin
should be added. The quantity to be added is 50–100 ml per 500 g
of fruit (2–4 liquid ounces per pound of fruit).

Pectin may be made as follows:
1 Simmer unpeeled sliced apples, redcurrants, or gooseberries in an
equal volume of water.
2 Cook for 25 minutes, mashing down.
3 Strain through scalded jelly bag.
4 Use immediately OR
5 Sterilize in small vacuum jars at boiling point for 5 minutes.

Note: Sterilized juice, when opened, loses its setting properties
quickly. Use before 24 hours have elapsed.

Sugar
Lump, granulated or preserving may be used. It must be
thoroughly dissolved before the jam or jelly is brought to the boil.

Setting point
A keeping jam should have 60 per cent added sugar content, ie.
three parts sugar to five parts jam.
  To determine whether this point has been reached, either of the
following tests may be used, temperature or weight test.

Temperature test
1 Stir jam.
2 Dip sugar thermometer in hot water.

3 Submerge bulb fully in jam.
4 When it registers 105°C (220°F or 221°F), jam is cooked.

Weight test
1 Note weight of pan and spoon BEFORE preserving has begun.
2 When jam weighs 5 kg (10 lb) for every 2.5 kg (6 lb) sugar used, jam is at setting point.
3 To find final weight, multiply the quantity of sugar used by 10, divide by 6.
Example: 1.5 kg sugar = 1.5 × 10 ÷ 6 = 2.5 kg jam
(3 lb = 3 × 10 ÷ 6 = 5 lb).

Flake test
The set of the jam can be determined by the following test:
1 Dip clean wooden spoon in boiling jam.
2 Allow the cooling jam to drop from spoon.
3 If drops run together and form a flake or 'curtain' it is sufficiently cooked.

Note: For jam with whole fruit, i.e. strawberry, leave to cool in pan for 10 minutes. Stir gently and fill jars, this prevents the fruit rising.

Recipes

Apple and pineapple jam

Peel, core and cut up apples (tying peel and cores in muslin bag and hanging them in pan). Place apples, pineapple juice and lemon juice in pan and cook until tender. Remove bag of peel after squeezing out juice. Add sugar and pineapple and boil rapidly until setting point is reached – approximately 10 minutes. Finish.

3 kg (6 lb) cooking apples
1¼ l (2 pints) tinned pineapple juice, including that from 1 tin pineapple pieces

2 lemons (juice)
3 kg (6 lb) sugar

Apple ginger

Make a thick syrup of the sugar and water by boiling them together. Pare, core and cut apples into thin pieces and boil in the syrup until transparent. Then add the ginger, boil for another 5 minutes, bottle and seal.

Useful either as a preserve or for tart fillings.

2 kg (4 lb) granulated sugar   2 kg (4 lb) apples
1¾ l (3 pints) water   50 g (2 oz) ground ginger

Dried apricot jam

Wash the apricots, cut up small and soak in the water for 24 hours. Then make the jam by the general method. Yield 5 kg (10 lb) jam.

1 kg (2 lb) apricots   3 kg (6 lb) sugar
3½ l (6 pints) water

Fresh apricot jam

Fruit must be just ripe for best results. Make by the general method, removing stones. Yield 5 kg (10 lb) jam.

3 kg (6 lb) fresh apricots   600 ml (1 pint) water
3 kg (6 lb) sugar

Blackcurrant jam

Use the general method. Yield 5 kg (10 lb) jam.

2 kg (4 lb) blackcurrants   3 kg (6 lb) sugar
1¾ l (3 pints) water

Gage plum

Use the general method. Yield 5 kg (10 lb) jam.

3 kg (6 lb) gages   3 kg (6 lb) sugar
600 ml (1 pint) water

Glencar jam

Cut up figs very finely, also rhubarb and peel; put all together with sugar and let it stand for 24 hours; then boil till it sets.

500 g (1 lb) dried figs
2 kg (4 lb) rhubarb
175 g (6 oz) candied lemon peel or

rind and juice of 1 lemon
2 kg (4 lb) sugar

High dumpsie dearie jam

Cook the fruit separately, in a little water, till soft and tender, then add warmed sugar to the proportion of 500 g to 600 ml (1 lb to 1 pint), together with the grated lemon rind and ginger. When the sugar is dissolved, heat and bring to boiling point. Test for set at the end of 10 minutes' boiling. Finish in usual way.

equal quantities of apples, pears and plums
500 g (1 lb) sugar to 600 ml (1 pint) cooked fruit

lemon rind and root ginger for flavouring

Mulberry jam

Simmer the mulberries in their own juice until they are tender; simmer the peeled, cored and cut apples separately, until they are tender. Add to the mulberries and stir. Add sugar, bring to the boil, test for set. Finish in the usual way.

1½ kg (3 lb) ripe mulberries
500 g (1 lb) apples

1¾ kg (3½ lb) sugar

Pear, apple and quince jam

Peel and core the fruits and cut into pieces. Retain peel and cores and tie them in a muslin bag with the lemon rind. Simmer fruit in water (adding the muslin bag and its contents) until completely tender. Remove muslin bag and squeeze out the juice. Add the warmed sugar and allow it to dissolve, then add the lemon juice and boil rapidly until set. Finish.

1 kg (2 lb) cooking apples
1 kg (2 lb) cooking pears
750 g (1½ lb) quinces

rind and juice of 1 lemon
1¼ l (2 pints) water
3 kg (6 lb) sugar

Raspberry jam

Use the general method. Yield 5 kg (10 lb) jam.

3 kg (6 lb) raspberries　　　　　　　3 kg (6 lb) sugar

Rhubarb and orange jam

Peel oranges, remove as much of the white pith as possible, divide them and take out the pips, slice the pulp into a preserving pan; add the rind of half the oranges cut into thin slices, simmer with the lemon juice.

  Peel the rhubarb, cut it into thin pieces, and add to orange pulp. Add warmed sugar, allow it to dissolve, then bring to boiling point; test after 10 minutes. Finish.

6 oranges　　　　　　　　　　　$1\frac{1}{4}$ l (1 quart) finely cut rhubarb
juice of 2 lemons　　　　　　　$1\frac{1}{2}$ kg (3 lb) loaf sugar

Rhubarb and rose-petal jam

To each 500 g (1 lb) prepared rhubarb add the juice of 1 lemon and 500 g (1 lb) sugar. Cover the cut up rhubarb with the sugar and lemon juice and leave to stand overnight.

  Chop up two handfuls of scented rose-petals, red if possible, to each 500 g (1 lb) of fruit, and cook all together until set. This is a delicious jam and a lovely colour.

  If preferred, 50 g (2 oz) angelica, fresh or crystallized, can be used in place of rose-petals.

rhubarb　　　　　　　　　　　sugar
lemon juice　　　　　　　　　　scented rose-petals, red if possible

Strawberry jam

Use the general method. Yield 5 kg (10 lb) jam.

$3\frac{1}{2}$ kg (7 lb) hulled strawberries　　juice of 4 lemons
3 kg (6 lb) sugar

Green tomato jam

Shred the orange as for marmalade (short shreds) and cook in AS
LITTLE WATER AS POSSIBLE until tender. Cut up the tomatoes and add
to the cooked orange rind; simmer for about ¾ hour. Add sugar,
dissolve, and boil fast for 20 minutes, or until it sets. Finish in usual
way.

rind of 1 sweet orange   750 g (1½ lb) sugar
1 kg (2 lb) green tomatoes

Ripe whortleberry jam

Wash fruit in cold water, drain thoroughly. Put in preserving pan.
Crush with wooden spoon, add lemon juice, simmer until fruit is
soft and thick. Add warmed sugar, dissolve, bring to boil. Boil until
setting point is reached. Pot and cover.

1 kg (2 lb) whortleberries   750 g (1½ lb) sugar
juice of 1 lemon

Chutneys
Equipment

Only enamel-lined, monel metal, stainless steel or aluminium pans
should be used. Avoid anything that may give a metallic flavour.

Use nylon or hair sieves, stainless steel knives, wooden spoons.
Clean, dry, warm jars or bottles must be used. Covers must be
vinegar resistant, i.e. a ceresin disc under a metal top; unless cover is
plastic-coated.

General method

1 Chop or mince the fruits and vegetables.
2 Cook in a closed pan with a very small amount of water (a pressure
cooker is recommended).
3 Combine the cooked mixtures with spices and half the required
amount of vinegar, cook for 45 minutes (approximately).
4 Dissolve the sugar in the remaining vinegar, add to that in the
pan and simmer the whole amount, very slowly, until the required

256

consistency is reached, i.e. when a wooden spoon is drawn through the mixture it leaves a clean path and no trace of free (unabsorbed) liquid.

5 Fill dry hot jars to the brim.

Cover with vinegar-resistant lids and store in cool dark place.

Note: Chutney needs to mature. Store jars at least 6 months.

Apple chutney

Use the general method. Yield about 2¾ kg (5½ lb) chutney.

1¾ kg (3½ lb) apples	2½–5 ml (½ teaspoon) cayenne
250 g (8 oz) sultanas	pepper
100 g (4 oz) crystallized ginger	2½–5 ml (½ teaspoon) salt
25 g (1 oz) garlic	2½–5 ml (½ teaspoon) ground
600 ml (1 pint) vinegar	coriander
2½–5 ml (½ teaspoon) mixed spice	750 g (1½ lb) sugar

Apricot chutney   Hot

Soak apricots for 48 hours.

Chop or mince raisins, onions and apricots and cook in 300 ml (½ pint) of water in which the apricots were soaked, for about 30 minutes. Add half the vinegar, simmer till tender, then leave to get cold.

Next day, add the rest of the ingredients except mustard (spices should be put in a muslin bag) and the rest of the vinegar, and simmer for 2 hours. Remove the muslin bag, add the mustard, simmer for a further 10 minutes, and pot. It is necessary to stir frequently when the chutney is nearly cooked as it becomes thick.

250 g (8 oz) dried apricots	15 ml (1 tablespoon) salt
500 g (1 lb) stoned and chopped	10 ml (1 dessertspoon) cayenne
raisins	50 g (2 oz) ground ginger
500 g (1 lb) onions	25 g (1 oz) coriander seed
1¼ l (2 pints) vinegar	30 ml (2 tablespoons) made
500 g (1 lb) sugar	mustard

Banana chutney   Hot

Chop onions finely, mince ginger and dates, slice bananas. Place in saucepan with salt and bag of spices. Cover all with vinegar. Boil for

5 minutes – take spice bag out. Add treacle and cook in the oven – or over an even heat until a brown colour.

This is a specially good recipe.

1 kg (2 lb) large onions
250 g (8 oz) crystallized ginger
500 g (1 lb) dates
16 ripe bananas

15 ml (1 tablespoon) salt
25 g (1 oz) pickling spice in bag
vinegar
500 g (1 lb) black treacle

Date and apple chutney
Mild and sweet

Use the general method.
Note: This chutney is quickly made.

1 kg (2 lb) dates
1 kg (2 lb) apples
500 g (1 lb) onions
5–10 ml (1 teaspoon) ground ginger
5–10 ml (1 teaspoon) mustard

5–10 ml (1 teaspoon) salt
1–2½ ml (¼ teaspoon) cayenne pepper
600 ml (1 pint) vinegar
250 g (8 oz) brown sugar

Gooseberry chutney

Use the general method. Yield 2 kg (4 lb) chutney.

1½ kg (3 lb) gooseberries
250 g (8 oz) eschalots or onions
175 g (6 oz) stoned raisins
600 ml (1 pint) vinegar
15 g (½ oz) mixed spice
15 g (½ oz) crushed mustard seed or mustard

25 g (1 oz) salt
2½ ml (⅛ teaspoon) cayenne pepper
15 g (½ oz) paprika pepper
275 g (10 oz) sugar

Orange chutney

Peel and mince onions and cook in a little water; peel and core the apples; mince orange peel and flesh (having removed pith), apples, chillies and dried fruit. Put ingredients, except sugar, in a pan with one-third of the vinegar, and simmer till thick. Add a second one-third of the vinegar, and simmer till thick. Add the rest of the vinegar, and the warmed sugar, and simmer till thick; pot and cover.

500 g (1 lb) onions
1½ kg (3 lb) apples
1½ kg (3 lb) sweet oranges
minced chillies, the number
  depending on taste – about one
  dozen would make a moderately
  hot one

500 g (1 lb) sultanas or raisins
10–20 ml (2 teaspoons) ground
  ginger
20–40 ml (2 dessertspoons) salt
2¼ l (4 pints) vinegar
1 kg (2 lb) sugar

Red and green pepper chutney

Prepare vegetables, discarding seeds of peppers. Mince or chop finely all fruit and vegetables. Put in pan with spices (those that are whole in a piece of muslin) and one-third of the vinegar, and simmer till thick. Add a second one-third of the vinegar, and simmer till thick. Add the rest of the vinegar, and the warmed sugar, and simmer till thick; pot and cover.

500 g (1 lb) red and green peppers,
  mixed
1 kg (2 lb) green tomatoes
1 kg (2 lb) sour apples
750 g (1½ lb) onions
25 g (1 oz) salt

40 g (1½ oz) mixed (more or less as
  liked) chillies, cloves, allspice,
  root ginger, mustard seed,
  peppercorns
900 ml (1½ pints) vinegar
500 g (1 lb) sugar

Prune chutney
All-the-year-round chutney

Soak prunes for 48 hours; remove stones.
  Put prunes and onions through mincer. Put one-third of the vinegar and all other ingredients except sugar into a pan (spices in muslin bag) and simmer till thick. Add a second one-third of the vinegar, and simmer till thick. Add the rest of the vinegar, and the warmed sugar, and simmer till thick; pot and cover.

1 kg (2 lb) prunes
500 g (1 lb) onions
600 ml (1 pint) vinegar
50 g (2 oz) salt
5–10 ml (1 teaspoon) ground ginger

5 ml (1 teaspoon) cayenne pepper
50 g (2 oz) mustard seed
25 g (1 oz) mixed pickling spice
500 g (1 lb) sugar

Rhubarb chutney

Use the general method. Yield about 1½ kg (3 lb) chutney.

1¼ kg (2½ lb) rhubarb
250 g (8 oz) onions
15 g (½ oz) ground ginger
5 g (¼ oz) salt

15 g (½ oz) curry powder, best
quality
450 ml (¾ pint) vinegar
500 g (1 lb) sugar

Green tomato chutney

Use the general method. Yield about 1¾ kg (3½ lb) chutney.

1 kg (2 lb) green tomatoes
500 g (1 lb) apples
250 g (8 oz) shallots
500 g (1 lb) raisins or sultanas
25 g (1 oz) garlic
2½ ml (½ teaspoon) salt

2½ ml (½ teaspoon) cayenne
2½–5 ml (½ teaspoon) cardamom
(ground)
2½–5 ml (½ teaspoon) ginger
450 ml (¾ pint) vinegar
350 g (12 oz) brown sugar

Ripe tomato and marrow chutney

Use the general method. Yield 1¾ kg (3½ lb) chutney.

Note: This chutney is quickly made.

2 kg (4 lb) tomatoes, blanched
500 g (1 lb) marrow, peeled
250 g (8 oz) onions
15 g (½ oz) salt
pinch of cayenne
2½–5 ml (½ teaspoon) paprika

1–2 ml (¼ teaspoon) ground
cinammon
1–2 ml (¼ teaspoon) ground allspice
1–2 ml (¼ teaspoon) ground mace
300 ml (½ pint) vinegar
350 g (12 oz) white sugar

Sloe chutney

Put the sloes in a casserole in the oven till they are soft. Rub through a sieve and add the other ingredients (spices in a muslin bag). Boil gently for ½ hour. Put in small jars and cover to avoid evaporation.
Improves with keeping.

1 kg (2 lb) sloes
500 g (1 lb) brown sugar
250 g (8 oz) stoned raisins

1 stick of cinnamon
10 ml (1 teaspoon) cloves
300 ml (½ pint) vinegar

Three fruit chutney

Prepare marrow, sprinkle with salt and leave overnight.

Pour off liquid, steam and mash with a fork. Cook apples, pears and onion in as little water as possible till soft, then mash with a fork. Put one-third of vinegar and all ingredients except sugar into a pan, and simmer till thick. Add a second one-third of the vinegar and simmer till thick. Add the rest of the vinegar and the warmed sugar, and simmer till thick; pot and cover.

250 g (8 oz) marrow
250 g (8 oz) cooking apples
250 g (8 oz) cooking pears
25 g (1 oz) chopped onions
300 ml ($\frac{1}{2}$ pint) vinegar
5 ml ($\frac{1}{2}$ teaspoon) flour

5 ml ($\frac{1}{2}$ teaspoon) dry mustard
5 g ($\frac{1}{4}$ oz) cayenne pepper
5 g ($\frac{1}{4}$ oz) turmeric
5 g ($\frac{1}{4}$ oz) ground ginger
100–150 g (4–6 oz) white sugar

Crystallization of Fruit and Flowers

Candied fruits

The most suitable fruits are those which have a pronounced flavour, as delicate flavours are frequently masked by the large quantity of sugar absorbed. Pineapples, apricots, peaches and pears which are among the most successful are, for reasons of cost in this country, generally prepared from canned fruits. Among the fresh fruits suitable are fleshy plums, greengages and apricots; angelica, orange and lemon peel may also be used.

From canned fruits
The can of fruit should be opened and the syrup drained and measured. For every 500 g (pound) of drained fruit the syrup must be made up to 300 ml ($\frac{1}{2}$ pint), with water. Usually there is sufficient juice.

Now follow the processing table below:

Sugar syrup – sufficient for 500 g (1 lb) of fruit
To each 300 ml ($\frac{1}{2}$ pint) of syrup drained from the fruit, add 250 g

($\frac{1}{2}$ lb) of sugar, or preferably 125 g ($\frac{1}{4}$ lb) sugar and 125 g ($\frac{1}{4}$ lb) glucose. Dissolve sugar slowly in fruit syrup, add glucose and bring to boil.

For 500 g (1 lb) drained fruit
Day 1 Make the syrup as above and whilst boiling pour over the fruit. See that the fruit is immersed – leave until the next day.
Day 2 Drain off the syrup, add 50 g (2 oz) sugar to the syrup, bring to the boil and pour over the fruit – leave until next day.
Day 3 Repeat the process as on day 2.
Day 4 Repeat the process again.
Day 5 Drain off the syrup from the fruit and this time add 75 g (3 oz) sugar and when dissolved, add the fruit and simmer for 3–4 minutes. Leave 2 days.
Day 7 Repeat the process as on day 5. Leave 4 days. If the syrup is still thin, repeat the process of day 5 yet again, until the thickness of run honey.
Day 11 (*or later*) After leaving 4 days, drain off the syrup and place fruit on a cake rack over a plate to catch the syrup and dry off, by placing in a cool oven, 50°C (120°F), with the oven door slightly open until dry. Drying can be intermittent and can be done also in an airing cupboard, or in the sun during the summer. The fruit is sufficiently dry when the surface is no longer sticky.

From fresh fruit
Fresh fruit should be firm and sufficiently ripe so that the flavour is good. Small crab apples, apricots and fleshy plums should be punctured in numerous places with a silver fork. After preparing the fruit it should be placed in sufficient boiling water to cover it and cooked until tender. For 500 g (1 lb) of drained fruit, measure 300 ml ($\frac{1}{2}$ pint) of the liquid in which the fruit has been cooked. Usually it is easier to work with halved plums. Care must be taken not to lose the shape of the fruit.

For 500 g (1 lb) drained, cooked fresh fruit
Day 1 Add either 175 g (6 oz) sugar or 50 g (2 oz) sugar and 125 g (4 oz) glucose to the fruit juice.

Continue as for canned fruit, but repeat the process for 3 more days, then add the 75 g (3 oz) sugar as on the 5th day and continue adding 50 g (2 oz) sugar from there.

Crystallized finish

Take pieces of candied fruit and dip each one quickly into boiling water. Drain off any excess moisture, then roll each piece in some fine granulated sugar.

Glacé finish

To give a glacé finish to the candied fruit, fresh syrup should be made consisting of 500 g (1 lb) of sugar dissolved in 150 ml (¼ pint) of water. The fruit should be dipped in boiling water for 20 seconds and drained. A small quantity of syrup should be poured into a hot cup and the pieces of fruit quickly dipped into it with a fork and placed on a wire tray. As soon as the syrup is cloudy a fresh portion of hot syrup should be taken. The glacéd fruit should then be dried, but the temperature should not be more than 50°C (120°F).

Candied angelica

The stalks should be picked in April when they are young and tender and the colour bright. The stalks should be placed in a basin and a boiling brine, 5 g (¼ oz) salt to 2¼ l (2 quarts) water, poured over them. They should be soaked for 10 minutes, rinsed in cold water, then placed in a pan of fresh boiling water and boiled for 5–7 minutes. They should then be drained and scraped to remove the outer skin. The angelica should then be candied as directed previously for fruit.

Candied peel 1

Orange, lemon or grapefruit peel requires cooking for about 1 hour, changing the water three times (grapefruit peel needs several changes of water). It is then drained and can be candied as directed previously for fruit.

Candied peel 2

Put the peel into a saucepan with sufficient water to cover it. Simmer gently for about 2 hours until the peel is quite tender, replenishing water as necessary. Add the sugar, 50 g (2 oz) to each orange or lemon peel, stir until this has dissolved and bring to the boil. Simmer for 20 minutes with saucepan lid on. Put on one side to cool without a lid on the pan. Next day reboil the syrup and simmer for a few minutes. On the third day simmer gently until the peel has absorbed nearly all the syrup. Drain the peel and dry. Any remaining syrup can be poured into the hollow of the peel before drying.

Candied peel 3
Crystallized orange peel

Use only oranges with thick round skins (Jaffa types). Wash well and peel in quarters, removing any white skin from the pith. Soak in a brine solution, 175 g (6 oz) salt to 600 ml (1 pint) water, until ready to use. In this way one can collect orange skins as the oranges are eaten, over about 14 days.

Rinse well, then put peel in saucepan with sufficient water to cover, bring to the boil, drain, repeat this three times, the last time allowing the peel to cook until tender (test with the head of a pin). Weigh drained peel and use equal weight sugar to fruit. Dissolve sugar in water in saucepan, approximately 300 ml (½ pint) water to 250 g (½ lb) sugar. Boil for 2 minutes.

Add peel to syrup, boil gently for 20 minutes with saucepan lid on pan. Leave now 2–4 days. Simmer again 20 minutes without lid. Leave again 2–3 days, and now simmer until only a quarter of the syrup is left when you *boil hard*, shaking the pan from time to time to prevent peel burning.

When most of the syrup is cooked away, lift out peel gently, dip in boiling water, place on waxed paper on cooling rack and allow to dry. Dip in sugar and put in jar but *do not seal*.

Marrons glacés

Snip the tops of the chestnuts, put a few at a time in boiling water and scald for about 2½ minutes. Peel them carefully while hot, removing all the brown inner skin. Put the peeled chestnuts into cold water in a large pan and bring gradually to simmering point and simmer very gently until the nuts are tender but not broken. Make a syrup from 500 g (1 lb) sugar, the glucose and about 350 ml (12 fl oz) of water in a pan large enough to hold the chestnuts. Bring the syrup to the boil, add the drained chestnuts, and bring the syrup back to boiling point. Remove from the heat, but leave if possible in a warm place. Next day, reboil the syrup with the chestnuts in the pan without the lid and leave covered overnight.

Repeat this on the third day with the addition of 6–7 drops of vanilla essence added before heating the syrup. Lift the chestnuts out carefully and drain on a wire rack.

For the glacé finish follow the directions given previously. If the chestnuts are to be kept for any length of time, they should be wrapped in aluminium foil to prevent them from hardening.

Packing
The fruit should be packed in cardboard or wooden boxes, waxed paper being used as a lining to separate the layers. If desired it may be stored in jam jars or fruit bottles by tying papers or cloth over the top. The container must not be sealed or airtight as the fruit may ferment or become mouldy under these conditions.

1 kg (2 lb) sweet chestnuts	vanilla essence
500 g (1 lb) granulated sugar	500 g (1 lb) additional sugar for
500 g (1 lb) glucose or dextrose	glacé finish
water	

Crystallized flowers

Crystallized flowers have become very popular as decorations for cakes, party sweets, etc. The method is simple and with care the flowers will last for months, keeping a fresh natural colour.

Method
Place 5 ml (1 teaspoonful) of gum arabic (crystals *not* powder) in a small screw-top bottle, cover with 15 ml (1 tablespoon) of rose or orange water. Leave for 2 or 3 days to dissolve into a sticky glue, shaking the bottle occasionally.

Using a small soft brush, cover the petals, calyx and as much stem as is needed of the flower with the gum arabic solution. Big loose flowers are best taken apart, when each petal is dealt with separately and the flowers made up again when wanted. The painting MUST be done very thoroughly, as bare spots shrivel and will not keep.

Dredge lightly two or three times with caster sugar until each flower is well covered, and dry off in a warm place on muslin or sugared greaseproof paper. Difficult flat blooms can be placed on the edge of a shelf, held down by something over their stems. Twenty-four hours in the linen cupboard is usually long enough for the flowers to become stiff and dry.

Store in the DARK, preferably in a cardboard box.
The following crystallize very satisfactorily: primroses, violets, pansies, forget-me-nots, mimosa, cowslips, plum and apple blossom, rose leaves, sweet peas, lilies of the valley and mint leaves, etc. A little vegetable colouring in the gum arabic solution will give the flowers a more cheerful appearance, but care should be taken not to use too much, when the result is most unnatural.

Never crystallize poppies, buttercups, nightshade, foxgloves, laburnum or lupins.

Edible frosting

Using the same gum arabic solution, brush on a warm plate and dry off in a cool oven.

The solution dries and chips off as frost for cake decorations.

20 Home Freezing

This chapter has been compiled from books published by
Denbighshire, Leicestershire, West Kent and Yorkshire.

The true value of a home freezer is:
1 To provide variety of food at all seasons.
2 To facilitate buying at low prices, e.g. special offers, bulk buying,
seasonal prices.
3 To eliminate waste.
4 To serve as a labour-saving appliance.
5 To preserve home produce at peak condition.
6 To facilitate entertaining.

One could go on listing points of value – the scope is limited only by
the capacity of the appliance and the requirements, ideas and ability
of the owner.

When choosing a home freezer, initial cost, accommodation, time,
available produce and general usage are all points that must be
considered. A well-stocked freezer need not only contain meat,
poultry and vegetables, but also snacks readily prepared, fully
prepared meals for holiday times, picnic meals and a week's stock
of bread, cakes and scones.

It is worth while to calculate how often various foods are likely to
be served over a period of a month. Where there is a garden or farm
it may be possible to calculate how much produce can be expected
for preservation for winter use or, on the other hand, how much is
required.

All manufacturers will supply specific directions for the care and
maintenance of their freezers.

Very little supplementary equipment other than the packaging
materials is required.

Equipment for packing and labelling

Correct packaging need not be costly but it is absolutely essential for good results. All food must be sealed in moisture- and vapour-proof wrappings or containers to prevent evaporation and consequent 'freezer burn' or drying out. Materials that are brittle at low temperatures are not suitable for wrapping. Polythene and moisture- and vapour-proof cellulose tissue bags are inexpensive and suitable materials. These can be sealed with a warm iron or, more conveniently, by twisting the open end of the bag, doubling it over in a swan's neck and securing firmly with fine string, plastic-covered bell wire or specially made seals. Aluminium foil is suitable and can be double-folded to give a seal. With all thin packaging materials there is danger of puncturing, and an overwrap of brown paper or stockinet (mutton cloth) is advisable.

Plastic and waxed containers are more expensive. If the lids are a good fit, no further seal will be required, but a special frost-resisting tape is available for looser fitting lids. Glass preserving jars can be used but are fragile at low temperatures and poor conductors of cold.

Even-shaped packets pack more compactly than odd ones; cubes much more tightly than tubs. If rigid containers are in short supply, the packaged food can be frozen in a suitable container and removed when frozen to the required shape. This will leave the container free for shaping further packages.

Greaseproof, waxed and brown papers are not suitable.

Most frozen food wrappings and containers can be re-used if carefully washed and dried after use.

Much time can be wasted unless packages are marked. Tie-on labels should be used and chinagraph (wax) or lead pencil is better than ink, which tends to smudge. Full details of the contents of each package will be most helpful when required for use. Coloured pencil can be used to indicate contents at a glance, e.g. green for peas, red for strawberries.

It is usually possible to buy wire mesh baskets to fit into the freezer and these are most convenient for keeping foods of the same kind together. A cheaper alternative is to use net bags.

A stock chart hung near the freezer will be invaluable if kept up-to-date.

The quantity to freeze at one time

The quantity of food frozen at one time should be limited as it is essential that the food freezes as quickly as possible. Some freezers have a separate compartment for freezing new additions which can then be transferred to general storage. Air spaces should be allowed between packets of food which should be packed in contact with a refrigerated surface.

Not more than 10 per cent of the cubic capacity of a freezer should be frozen at once.

Storage life

Most fresh products will store for 12 months. It should not be necessary to keep them for longer as fresh supplies will then be ready for freezing. Pork, cured meats, sausages and cooked bakery products should be eaten preferably within 6 months and uncooked bakery products within 3 months.

Accidental thawing and power cuts

Should a power failure occur, *do not open the freezer*. The food in it will keep perfectly for 12–72 hours – the fuller the freezer the longer it will take to thaw.

Check that the switch has not been inadvertently turned off before telephoning for help; avoid this by the use of sticky tape over the switch.

It is wise to have emergency plans in case anything goes wrong. Local shopkeepers or friends' freezers may have spare space for your food, or you may find a local supplier of dry ice which should protect the food for 2 or 3 days.

Provided ice is still present, partially thawed food can be frozen again – except shellfish, rissoles and similar foods. If doubtful it is better to cook the food and re-freeze when cooked.

Useful general notes

1 See food is always cooled to at least room temperature before putting into the freezer. If possible, chill foods before putting them in the freezer.
2 Allow air space between packs for rapid freezing. When food is frozen it can be moved and stacked closely.
3 For successful results the freezer should run at $-10°C$ ($0°F$).
4 Pack food in family meal quantities.
5 Don't keep food in the freezer any longer than necessary and certainly no longer than the recommended storage period.
6 Food does not improve in freezer storage.

7 Handle food quickly to cut down deterioration. Deal with small quantities at a time.

8 Observe the basic rules of hygiene.

9 Limit additions of foods to the freezer to the quantities advised by the manufacturer of the freezer.

10 Freeze quickly, thaw slowly.

Freezing fresh foods
Meat

Meat should be hung as required before freezing and frozen in joints of up to 2 kg (4 lb). Large pieces of meat take a long time to freeze and are difficult to utilize. Surplus fat should be removed, bones trimmed and the joint shaped so there are no awkward edges. Overwrap any bones protruding with greaseproof. Several chops or steaks can be packed together with a double fold of greaseproof paper between each one. This makes it possible to open the pack and take out as many chops or steaks as required. Boned meat stores economically and stock from the bones freezes well. Liver can be wrapped in small parcels before putting into bags or muslin.

Cured meat is not usually frozen as it keeps satisfactorily at normal temperatures. If it is desired to freeze it, it should be matured before putting into the freezer.

Sausages can be frozen but care must be taken to cut down salt and spices in the recipe; keep only 2–4 weeks.

When freezing made-up dishes avoid spices and onion and reduce the salt content.

Poultry and game

Game should be hung before freezing and all poultry and game should be prepared for cooking before freezing. Stuffing should not be put into the carcass and giblets should be wrapped so that they do not mark the bird. Chicken livers make a good separate pack for savouries if not required with the giblets. When shank bones or feet are likely to protrude, they should be wrapped in greaseproof paper and tied close to the body before the bird is packed. An overwrap of mutton cloth is useful. Whole carcasses are bulky and halved or jointed birds are recommended if they are to be finally used in that form.

Rabbits and hares are better jointed and each joint wrapped separately then packed together, but take care to avoid air pockets.

Fish

Fish should be frozen as soon as possible after being caught. It should be very well washed after gutting. Cut again into usable pieces or steaks or fillets, packing a number of steaks or fillets together with greaseproof paper between each piece. Dip white fish in a salt solution – 100 g (4 oz) salt per 1¼ l (1 quart) of water, to improve texture.

The head and fins are removed from small fish which are packed whole.

Boil lobsters and crabs before freezing.

Fish has a comparatively short freezer life and should be used within 6 months.

Fruit

Most fruits freeze well. Fresh, good quality fruit should be picked over and, if necessary, rinsed in small quantities of ice-cold water.

Dessert fruit is usually frozen with dry sugar, 100–150 g (4–6 oz) per 450 g (1 lb), or syrup, 225–450 g (½–1 lb) sugar per 600 ml (1 pint) water.

Pears and peaches are subject to discoloration and should be kept under water containing 15 g (½ oz) salt and 15 g (½ oz) citric acid per 1¼ l (1 quart) during preparation; a rigid container is preferred for storage and the syrup should cover the fruit. A crumpled up piece of greaseproof paper under the lid will keep the fruit submerged and allow the necessary head space.

Good cooking apples can be sliced, dipped in fast boiling water for 2–3 minutes, cooled in very cold water and packed unsweetened.

Purées, sweetened with 1 part sugar to 3–4 parts purée, freeze excellently. When cooled down, put into moisture/vapour-proof bags and shape in oblongs or pack into trays to freeze. Remove from box or trays when frozen as packages store in much less room.

Soft fruits can be frozen in 1–1½ kg (2–3 lb) batches for jam- and jelly-making later. This saves work in the busy summer months and gives bright-coloured and fresh flavoured jam as required throughout the year.

Recommended soft fruits

Blackberries	Cultivated or wild, if large, juicy and ripe.
Cherries	Black varieties.

Loganberries	Red ripe.
Raspberries	Early red, Lloyd George, Malling Promise, Norfolk Giant.
Strawberries	Cambridge Prizewinner, Cambridge Vigour, Royal Sovereign, if sliced.
Whortleberries	Wild or cultivated blueberries.

Vegetables

Good quality summer vegetables freeze excellently. Leafy salad plants are not suitable for freezing; celery loses its crispness. Tomatoes can be frozen but the final product is no better than if canned or bottled. It is a waste of freezer space to store vegetables that keep well otherwise.

To control spoilage and off-flavours, vegetables require to be scalded. This important process is carried out as follows: The vegetables are prepared in the usual way. A large saucepan containing at least $2\frac{1}{4}$ l (4 pints) of boiling water will be required and also a quantity of cold water containing ice – a supply of ice can be easily obtained if cake tins half-filled with cold water are placed in the freezer 2–3 hours before required. About 225 g ($\frac{1}{2}$ lb) of the prepared vegetable is placed in a straight-sided mesh basket or a net or butter muslin bag and plunged into the fast boiling water. The coldness of the vegetables will take the water off the boil and it

Vegetable	Preparation	Scalding time (minutes)
Asparagus	Grade for size, cut into 15-cm (6-inch) lengths	2 (thin) 4 (thick)
Broad beans	Pod	3
French beans	Wash, string if necessary	2–3
Runner beans	Wash, string and slice	2–3
Corn on the cob	Use when just mature, remove silk and husk, wrap cobs individually	4–6
Peas	Use in prime condition, pod	1–2
Spinach	Wash carefully, remove stems, blanch in 75-g (3-oz) batches	$2\frac{1}{2}$

is essential that the source of heat be sufficient to reboil the water within 1 minute. The scalding time is reckoned from the moment of reboiling, according to the times following. As soon as the scalding time is completed, the basket or bag is drained and transferred to the ice-cold water. When the vegetables are cold they are ready for packing and freezing. The scalding and cooling water can be used for subsequent batches provided the quantity of boiling water remains sufficient and the cooling water is kept cold with added ice.

Corn on the cob should be thawed before cooking, but other vegetables are placed frozen in a small quantity of boiling water. Cooking time is about half as long as with fresh vegetables. Corn on the cob should be cooked in unsalted water and seasoned when tender.

Recommended vegetables

Asparagus

Beans

Broad	All varieties when young.
Dwarf	Divil Fin Precoce, Granada, Perpetual, Tender Green, The Prince, The Victory.
Runner	Cockham Dene Improved, Kelvedon Wonder, Scarlet Emperor, White Monarch.
Broccoli	Green Sprouting (Calabrese), Purple Sprouting, White Sprouting.
Brussels sprouts	Small firm sprouts preferred. Cambridge varieties, Noisette, Sanda.
Carrots	Shorthorn varieties with good orange colour, young, Amsterdam Forcing, Early Nantes, Perfect Gem.
Cauliflower	Divide into sprigs. Majestic.
Peas	Early June, Kelvedon Wonder, Lincoln, Newburgh Gem, Onward, Perfected Freeze, Peter Pan, Phenomenon, Thomas Laxton.
Spinach	Giant Savoy Leaf, Goliath, New Zealand, Perpetual, Prickly New Giant, Zenith XXX.
Sweet corn	Canada Cross, Earliking, Golden Bantam, John Innes.
Mushrooms	Very fresh. Do not blanch.

Herbs

See Chapter 8, 'Herbs and Flavourings'.

Dairy produce

Butter
Butter freezes well if closely wrapped, but tends to become rancid as all fat does.

Cheese
Mature cheese, closely wrapped in foil, freezes well but must be thoroughly thawed before use. There is a tendency for the texture to become rather crumbly. Grated cheese is a useful standby.

Cream
Will freeze quite well but tends to become granular and needs beating very hard on thawing to reduce to smoothness.

Eggs
They should not be frozen in the shell, but if broken and packed in containers add 1 teaspoon of sugar or $\frac{1}{2}$ teaspoon of salt per egg. Egg whites freeze very easily, better than egg yolks. Hardboiled eggs are not successful as the whites become rubbery.

Milk
This is inclined to separate unless homogenized milk is used.

Freezing ready-cooked foods

A wide range of pies (meat or fruit), cakes and breads can be wrapped and frozen either raw or cooked. Many savoury dishes freeze well.

When packed meals have to be prepared regularly, it is a great convenience for the housewife to pack sandwiches, pasties, etc, in daily packs and freeze them until required.

Many complicated sauces can usefully be made in bulk and frozen in small containers, but seasonings and flavourings tend to intensify when frozen so under-season to start with and adjust after thawing.

Goods for short-term freezing, say for use in two weeks, can be stored well wrapped in wax paper. Goods to be stored for any longer period should be packaged as for fresh produce.

Index